'93

JK
1
6

COLORADO MC
LRC---WE
Glenwood Spri

D0338023

Watergate and the American Political Process

DISCARDED

COLORADO MOUNTAIN COLLEGE
LRC---WEST CAMPUS
Glenwood Springs, Colo 81601

Watergate
and the
American
Political Process

EDITED BY

Ronald E. Pynn

PRAEGER PUBLISHERS
New York

Published in the United States of America in 1975
by Praeger Publishers, Inc.
111 Fourth Avenue, New York, N.Y. 10003

© 1975 by Praeger Publishers, Inc.

All rights reserved

Library of Congress Cataloging in Publication Data

Pynn, Ronald, comp.
  Watergate and the American political process.

  CONTENTS: Commager, H. S. The shame of the Republic.—Wildavsky,
A. Government and the people.—Bickel, A. M. Watergate and the legal
order. [etc.]
  1. United States—Politics and government—1945- —Addresses, essays,
lectures. 2. Watergate Affair, 1972- —Addresses, essays, lectures. I. Title.
JK271.P96   320.9'73'0924   74-20604
ISBN 0-275-33600-X
ISBN 0-275-85220-2 pbk.

Printed in the United States of America

Contents

Introduction

On August 9, 1974, Richard M. Nixon, thirty-seventh President of the United States, resigned from office. The dramatic culmination came two years after the break-in at the Democratic National Headquarters and one week after the House Judiciary Committee had voted three articles of impeachment against the President. In releasing the subpoenaed June 23, 1972, Presidential conversation that revealed his involvement in the Watergate cover-up, Nixon said, in part, "Those arguing my case, as well as those passing judgment on the case, did so with information that was incomplete and in some respects erroneous." At this dramatic moment the nation seemed to find an answer to Senator Howard Baker's question "What did the President know and when did he know it?"

Watergate has come to represent two related—yet distinctively separate—phenomena. From the creation of the "plumbers" unit in the summer of 1971, through the break-in at the Democratic National Headquarters in 1972, to the denial of Congressional subpoenas for White House tapes of Presidential conversations in 1974, Watergate represents the unraveling of the abuses of power in the Nixon Administration. Including campaign dirty tricks, surreptitious entry, perjury, obstruction of justice, and conspiracy, the events of Watergate had the nation waiting for the answer to Senator Baker's question.

On another level, something fundamentally more far-reaching than specific events and personal guilt has been occurring within the American political system. Watergate stands as the capstone for events and trends—not all fully appreciated even at this time—that have been working to alter the American Constitution, as well as the institutions and conduct of politics in American society. Far beyond the acts of a group "whose zeal exceeded their judgment," the series of events known as Watergate has raised issues involving every sector of American politics. From the big money of special interest groups seeking to peddle influence to the conduct of impeachment investigations by the Congress of the United States,

Watergate has affected the Presidency, Congress, the bureaucracy, political parties, campaigns and elections, and public opinion.

Watergate is a course in American politics itself. Although the resignation and pardon of Richard M. Nixon may have had an immediate cathartic effect, the focus of this book is on the repercussions of Watergate in the American political process. What Watergate has revealed about our government is the theme of this book. Through Watergate, we can come to understand better the functioning of American politics. But, as several of the authors suggest, Watergate demonstrates that those institutions and processes are undergoing profound change. This too is a part of the lesson of Watergate.

In recent years, the United States moved through a period of great unrest with regard to policy both at home and abroad. The longest and most unpopular war in America's history took much of the country's energy and resources. Disenchantment with the two political parties surfaced in the streets of Chicago in 1968 and was heightened by an incumbent President's erecting a re-election organization separate from his party in 1972. Population and social problems too were enmeshed in a complex web of public demands, governmental responses, and sprawling bureaucracy. It seems that more was expected of government and less was being delivered.

Shortly before the election of 1972, President Richard Nixon stood beside the Great Wall of China enjoying the greatest personal triumph of his career. His popularity with the American people was at a high of 61 per cent as registered by the Gallup Poll. America was on the verge of the new era of which Theodore White graphically writes in *The Making of the President—1972*. Richard Nixon wanted to preside over that transition. Yet, at the very time when the President was toasting with the Chinese in Peking, G. Gordon Liddy was preparing in the offices of the Committee to Re-elect the President the final version of a proposal for illegal intelligence-gathering—including the break-in at the Democratic National Headquarters. This is the greatest incongruity. The re-election of the President was virtually ensured. The nomination of George McGovern with the Eagleton affair, the prospects for peace in Vietnam, and the mood of the American public suggested that the election of 1972 would provide a mandate for Nixon.

Nixon moved in to take control. The chronology of events of Watergate serves to illustrate the extent to which the Nixon Administration moved toward its mandate. The chronology also serves to point how far an incumbent President could go.

The two strains coalesced. The 1972 election was, as Samuel Lubell wrote, America's first total election. "The main event was how, to win reelection, Nixon transformed the presidency, organizing it for political over-kill and upsetting the Constitutional balance with Congress and the electorate." * Here personal skulduggery and the forces of change combined to shake the Constitutional structure of the rule of law in the United States.

The effort to manipulate the election was a deliberate attempt to secure a mandate for Richard Nixon, to bestow upon the Presidency a virtually plebiscitary right to rule. Funds appropriated by Congress were not spent; Presidential aides were not permitted to testify before Congress; the first Watergate special prosecutor was fired; Congressional subpoenas were not honored. The consolidation of power into what Arthur Schlesinger, Jr., has labeled the "imperial presidency" was an attempt to alter the Constitutional balance of power.

This collection of readings is not a chronology of events but a discussion of the ramifications of Watergate in the American political process. The power of the Presidency and the misuse of that power, with its serious Constitutional issues of executive privilege and impeachment, are critical for a nation nearing its bicentennial. But, just as no branch of government operates in a vacuum, so too Watergate affected all of the branches of government, the electorate, and America's role in world affairs. Ultimately Watergate raises the question of the nation's ability to see itself accurately and to keep its government responsive to a democratic society. Henry Steele Commager has remarked, "We are confronted with the spectacle of our corruption, a corruption not only moral and social but psychological and intellectual, confronted with a threat not only to the Constitutional and political system, but to Constitutional and political thought." †

* Samuel Lubell, *The Future While It Happened* (New York: W. W. Norton, 1973), p. 31.
† Henry Steele Commager, "The Shame of the Republic," *New York Review of Books,* 20 (July 19, 1973), p. 14.

Watergate and the American Political Process

1. Watergate in a Democratic Society

The patterns of conflict and consensus that weave the United States together illustrate how a nation lives together and governs itself. In this section, authors Commager and Wildavsky examine the beliefs and values of the American community that were highlighted by Watergate. Ultimately the issues of Watergate turn back to the nation. Watergate challenges the community to conduct its politics in a democratic manner. Aaron Wildavsky writes, "The system is being asked to make good on its most ancient and deeply held beliefs." Watergate is a crisis of confidence.

Most Americans believe the United States is governed by democratic principles. The personal beliefs shared by most Americans support the political freedoms, such as equal opportunity, fair treatment, and free expression, guaranteed by the Bill of Rights. This faith underlies a political system organized by a Constitutional mechanism setting forth representative and limited government. The events of Watergate have shaken these assumptions. The incredible Huston Plan proposed surreptitious entry, wiretapping, mail surveillance, CIA coverage of students living abroad, and a new Inter-agency Group on Internal Security. The Internal Revenue Service was asked to harass political enemies. Daniel Ellsberg's psychiatrist's office was broken into. Senator Sam Ervin noted that a "Gestapo mentality" was dominating the White House.

Henry Steele Commager looks at two explanations of this mentality. The first suggests that Watergate represents a breakdown of the Constitution. The document drawn in 1787 for 4 million people is ill equipped to meet the needs of 200 million people living in a technologically complex urban setting. The seventeenth- and eighteenth-century beliefs in separation of powers, limited executive authority, and political freedom are dangerously out of date. However, a second explanation intrigues Commager more. Here Watergate is seen as a reflection of American society, even of the American

3

character. We are, in fact, getting the government we want, Commager says.

Politics in a plural society like that of the United States stresses conflict resolution—the peaceful moderation of social pressures via regularized constitutional processes. In times of tension, America's liberal Constitutional ethos has acted as a stimulus for change and also as a brake on radicalism. How is Watergate different? Aaron Wildavsky sees Watergate as one consequence of the mid-1960's expansion of government programs and federal spending. In those years, demands for social action and the political activation of large segments of the community threatened peaceful moderation.

In the areas of housing, welfare, employment, and participation came demands from new and broad segments of the population. From other groups came criticism of higher taxes, welfare rolls, unemployment, and dysfunction in the system. For Wildavsky it was a particular feature of the period that there was a proliferation of incompatible demands on government. The net result: To many Americans, government appeared to be delegitimated. Increasingly under attack, government fought back, and Watergate, Wildavsky suggests, was one response to its attackers.

Watergate makes an unlikely scandal. Historians have noted the curious fifty-year cycle of corruption in the White House. There was Teapot Dome during the Harding Administration; before that, there had been the 1873 Gold Conspiracy during the Grant Administration. What makes Watergate different is—unlike the earlier scandals, where personal enrichment was the motive—we have come face to face with ourselves and our comfortable assumptions about how the American political process works.

The Shame of the Republic [*]

HENRY STEELE COMMAGER

I

Watergate and all those attendant usurpations, subversions, and corruptions for which the word has become both a symbol and a short cut, is neither a "deplorable incident"—to use Mr. Nixon's revealing phrase—nor a historical sport. It is a major crisis, constitutional, political, and moral, one that challenges our governmental system. Public attention is, and will long remain, focused on what happened, but already the interest of publicists and scholars is shifting to the more troublesome question of why it happened. That is really the subject of these three books—all of them written before the Watergate scandal broke, but all in a sense anticipating the psychological and moral problems that Watergate has raised.

The roots of our current malaise go back to the paranoia about communism—first Soviet, then Chinese—that obsessed Americans after 1947. So deep and pervasive was this paranoia that—like the Southern commitment to slavery before the Civil War and to white supremacy after the war—in time it came to dominate our lives and our thoughts, to color our views of politics, economy, education, science, and morality. As in the worlds of Kafka and Orwell, it justified adopting the tactics of the enemy in order to defeat him—just what the Nixon Administration has been doing for the past four years, just what that half-baked "Jeffersonian liberal" Mr. Thomas Huston achieved when he sold Mr. Nixon a vast scheme of repres-

[*] A review article on David Wise, *The Politics of Lying: Government Deception, Secrecy, and Power;* J. William Fulbright, *The Crippled Giant: American Foreign Policy and Its Domestic Consequences;* and Charles Goodell, *Political Prisoners in America*—all published by Random House, New York, in 1973.

Reprinted with permission from *The New York Review of Books.* Copyright © 1973 Nyrev, Inc. Henry Steele Commager is Professor Emeritus and Simpson Lecturer in History, Amherst College. He is the author of numerous works on American civilization, among them *The Growth of the American Republic, The Heritage of America,* and *The American Mind.*

sion in order to avert repression. In both the McCarthy and Watergate eras it has justified undermining the Constitution and the Bill of Rights in order, presumably, to save them.

Inevitably Watergate (perhaps we should find a different name, like Nixonism) conjures up and reflects McCarthyism. But something new has been added; indeed much has been added that makes it more dangerous, more corrupt, and more subversive than that earlier foray against sanity and decency. For war has been added— a ten-years' war which benumbed the American conscience and blunted the American political intelligence.

The cold war itself was largely a product of deductive and *a priori* reasoning, and therefore a self-delusion, and so, too, in added measure, was the ten-year war against Vietnam. The doctrinaire state of mind lends itself eagerly to paranoia, for real dangers are nothing compared to those our imagination can conjure up. It was almost inevitable that the psychology which imagined the domino theory and envisioned a million Chinese landing (after a good healthy swim) on the shores of California should see in every student demonstration, every sit-down at an airport or a napalm factory, every revelation of government chicanery or of overruns in naval contracts a threat to the survival of the republic. For if the threat of communism is so importunate as to justify the longest war in which we have ever been engaged, the satanic arsenal of weapons used against friends and enemies indiscriminately, the use of napalm, the My Lai and other massacres, the violations of international law and of the laws of war, the destruction of a whole nation, then surely it justifies such minor peccadilloes as wiretapping, or the use of provocative agents, or breaking into safes, or the corruption of elections, or Watergate.

Basic to an understanding of the usurpations, duplicities, and irresponsibilities of the Nixon era is paranoia, which has a life of its own, and which still lingers on—even after the "end" of the war and the rapprochement with China—polluting the moral and intellectual atmosphere of the country. Certainly there is little evidence that Mr. Nixon or his underlings think the new relationship with the Soviet Union and China justifies the mitigation of their own paranoia about "national security," or their conviction that any attack upon official policy is itself a potential threat to security. How else explain the vindictiveness of the prosecution of Daniel Ellsberg and the readiness to subvert justice in that prosecution; how else explain the political skulduggery that persisted long after the 1972 election, the persistent use of the FBI and the CIA for political purposes, the readiness to employ provocative agents, the contumacious boast at the POW dinner that reliance on secrecy, even useless secrecy, would go on and on; how else explain the determination to bomb Cambodia back to the Stone Age?

Successive presidents have tried to wash their hands of personal responsibility for the lawlessness and corruption so pervasive in our government in the last decade or so. But whoever planned and launched the Bay of Pigs; whoever engineered the Tonkin Bay fraud, deceived the nation about the danger of communism in Santo Domingo, directed the secret war in Laos, authorized the use of napalm and of free-fire zones, acquiesced in the torture and murder of prisoners; whoever concocted Watergate, rifled the safes, installed the bugging devices, planted the agents, accepted and paid bribes, doctored the polls and the cables—for all these ultimate responsibility lodges in the White House. It is the president who sets the moral tone, who selects the assistants he wishes to work with him—above all the attorneys general—and it is the president who profits from such successes as the chicaneries of his associates and subordinates may produce. It is the president therefore who must be assigned responsibility not only for failures—as with the Bay of Pigs—or for violations of international law—as with Santo Domingo—but for debasing the political standards and polluting the moral atmosphere of the nation.

II

But it is insufficient, it is almost trivial, to assign full responsibility for our current sickness to particular presidents. After all it is the American people who elected them—in the case of Mr. Nixon by the largest majority in our history. Two competing explanations, or at least illuminations, require consideration. One is that we are confronted not merely with personal offenses and particular failures, but with a major breakdown in our constitutional and political mechanisms. The second is that our government and politics, with all their knaveries, vulgarities, and dishonesties, more or less reflect American society, and even the American character, and that we are, in fact, getting the kind of government that we want. The fault, in short, is in ourselves.

The first of these explanations lends itself more readily to analysis than the second. Put most simply it argues that a Constitution designed for the modest needs of a society of four million people, whose business was mostly farming, and whose political needs were adequately served by local and state governments, and based on the principle that government, like dress, was the badge of lost innocence and that wherever possible the authority of government should be limited rather than enlarged, is no longer adequate to the importunate needs of a nation of 200 million, for effective controls over the economy and technology, for the operation of traditional democracy, or for the requirements of world power and of modern war. Thus those famous constitutional principles established in England and America in the seventeenth and eighteenth centuries—separation and balance of powers, limitations on government inscribed in bills of rights, restrictions on executive authority, especially in the realm of making war, legislative control of the purse, due process of law and the impartial rule of law—are dangerously put out of date.

Equally out of date, so President Nixon proclaims by his conduct if not by his words, are those assumptions about the relations of men to government so fundamental that they were either taken for granted or left to the rhetoric of preambles and bills of rights rather than put into the body of the Constitution. Thus, with respect to the assumption that public servants are precisely that, the Virginia Bill of Rights puts it that "all power is vested in and derived from the people; that magistrates are their trustees and servants, and at all times amenable to them." "Amenable" is not the word that pops into our minds when we contemplate Mr. Nixon, nor does he think of himself and of the Praetorian Guard with which he surrounds himself as servants. He regards the American people as essentially children; he treats their elected representatives with contempt; he says, in effect, that the people have no inherent right of privacy, no inherent right to differ or dissent on great issues of policy, no inherent right even to a free, open, and honest ballot.

No less important, in the eyes of the Founding Fathers, was the assumption of candor and openness in government—the assumption, that is, that the people have a right to know. This was the reason for those provisions in almost every constitution for freedom of the press; this was the logic behind Jefferson's famous statement that given a choice between a government without newspapers and newspapers without a government, he would choose the latter; this was the philosophy that animated that passion for education ex-

pressed by most of the constitution makers: that without enlightenment about politics, and information about government, democracy
simply would not work.

It is sometimes argued that the Constitution itself was drawn up
in secret session. So it was. It was also debated in twelve state conventions during a period of a year, and by almost everyone who had
participated in its making. Not only in the *Federalist Papers* but
in scores of books and pamphlets every line and word of the document was subjected to the most searching scrutiny. No other political
document of our history was more thoroughly—or more publicly—
analyzed and explored. And on the whole since Washington, presidents have faithfully continued this early tradition, though there are
exceptions. The oft-cited case of Washington's "refusal" to make
available to Congress the papers bearing on the Jay Treaty is of
course not an exception. Washington gave the Senate everything it
asked for, and the House everything that bore on its constitutional
authority to make appropriations. Just as Nixon's is the first administration in our history to attempt prior censorship of the press
—the *New York Times* and *Washington Post*—and the first systematically to withhold from the Congress information it requires to
fulfill its constitutional obligations, so it is the first to adopt wiretapping as an almost official political instrument, and to condone
that habitual politics of lying which is the subject of David Wise's
enthralling and sobering book.

All of this—so runs the argument—is rooted nevertheless not in
the inadequacy or corruption of the men who happen to be in
office at any moment, but in the inadequacy and corruption of the
anachronistic mechanisms with which we are saddled when we
undertake to deal with the complex problems of modern economy,
technology, and war.

This brings us back to the central question: can we run a
Leviathan state with an eighteenth-century Constitution?

Perhaps the obvious answer is also the right one: so far we have.
Needless to say the Constitution is not merely the original document of 1787; it is also the score and more of amendments, some of
them fundamental. It is the gloss of four hundred volumes of Supreme Court opinions. It is that organic growth presided over by
President and Congress and not unacceptable to the Court. That
growth has been extensive, even prodigious. In the case of the Civil
War amendments, it has been revolutionary. But both the organic

growth and the revolutions were constitutional. So too were such political revolutions as produced, over the years, judicial review, the transformation of the federal system, and the evolution of the welfare state.

Is the crisis of the present so imperative that it requires an unconstitutional revolution—requires, that is, abandoning the separation of powers, discarding limitations on the executive authority, weakening legislative control of the purse, subverting the traditional rule of law, and covering with a fog of secrecy the operations of government? Clearly Mr. Nixon and a good many of his followers think that it is—and now we are back with the phobia about communism and paranoia about national security.

Each generation tends to think—it is of course one of the many forms of vanity—that the crisis which it happens to confront is the gravest in history. Nothing that we face today compares in gravity with the crisis of the Civil War—when it seemed that the nation might be rent asunder and slavery prosper—or the crisis of the great depressions of the 1890s and the 1930s. All three of these were attended by political and constitutional revolution—the Civil War crisis by a very disorderly revolution, but constitutional nevertheless. It might well be questioned whether we even face a crisis today other than the crises we have masochistically brought upon ourselves—the crisis of the cold war, the crisis of our paranoia about China, the crisis of the reckless betrayal of our fiduciary obligation to posterity through the destruction of natural resources, the crisis of confidence in republican government brought about by unconstitutional war and unconstitutional domestic policies, the crisis of morals. It is of course all familiar enough: you create a real crisis by moving convulsively against an imaginary one.

There is indeed no reason to suppose that the problems which confront us cannot be solved by regular political and constitutional means. While it is no doubt true that this administration would be unable to function as it has functioned over the past four years if it were required to observe the strict limits of the Constitution, the conclusion is not that we should therefore acquiesce in the relaxation of constitutional restrictions but that the administration should abide by them. For in every instance of administrative challenge to the Constitution and the Bill of Rights, it was the challenge that proved disastrous, not the constitutional limitation.

Would we be worse off if Nixon had confined himself to the constitutional limitations of his office? Would we be worse off if he had been unable to wage war in Laos, invade and bomb Cambodia, mine Haiphong Harbor; spread a pall of secrecy over not only military, but domestic operations that had any connection with "national security"; establish censorship in many areas of governmental operations; use the CIA not only to subvert foreign governments but in domestic politics, and violate the constitutional obligations to "make a regular Statement of all . . . Expenditures of all public Money" with respect to the five or six billion dollars which the CIA annually spends; destroy domestic programs that the Congress had voted by impounding appropriations; authorize wiretaps on foreign embassies, congressmen, the National Security Council, newsmen, and others; invoke executive privilege, and spread the mantle of executive immunity over his henchmen, use *agents provocateurs* to smoke out "antiwar radicals," and subvert the processes of justice by turning the Justice Department into a political agency? What Mr. Nixon complains of being unable to do under a strict interpretation of the Constitution is precisely what those who wrote the Constitution intended he should not do and should be unable to do.

Yet we cannot ignore the fact that one part of the Constitution has always given us trouble, and that is precisely the provision for the executive and for executive power. In no other area has the Constitution had to be so patched up—four amendments no less, all dealing with the executive branch—this compared to one dealing with the judiciary (and that speedily nullified), and one—popular election of senators—dealing with the legislative. Not surprising; after all the office was new and, with the possible exception of some American states, unprecedented; after all, everyone took for granted that Washington would be the first president, and there he sat, presiding over the Convention, the very symbol of rectitude; after all there were as yet no national parties to take charge of elections and even of administrations.

The framers were confronted by an almost insoluble dilemma: fear that power always corrupts and awareness that the man who presided over their deliberations and would be the first president was incorruptible; conviction that the executive power, especially in the area of making war, was highly dangerous, and awareness that Washington had already demonstrated that with a man of honor there was no danger. Nor could they devise any method which would ensure a Washington—or an Adams, a Jefferson, a Madison —in the presidential chair.

They took refuge therefore in studied ambiguity, and ambiguity has presided over the executive power from that day to this. Consider, for example, the problem of the executive power in foreign relations. It is, said Woodrow Wilson a century or so later, "very absolute"; clearly Mr. Nixon thinks so too. But it rests on very uncertain constitutional authority, for that document says merely that the President shall be commander-in-chief (which does not necessarily concern the conduct of foreign relations), that he shall, with the advice and consent of the Senate, appoint ambassadors and make treaties, and that he shall receive ambassadors. That is the whole of it, and what a superstructure has been reared on that foundation!

The dilemma persists. To allow the president to take us into war, as he did on two recent occasions, is to invite disaster; to tie his hands in emergencies is also to invite disaster. Experience, to be sure, has so far justified only the first, not the second, of these dangers. Perhaps such a bill as the Javits-Stennis War Powers Act may at least mitigate the problem, but it is improbable that any legislation can deal adequately with the many-sided façade of executive powers as well as with complex problems of tenure, removal, impeachment, succession, and so forth. Perhaps in this respect the only ultimate reassurance can come in a courageous and revitalized Congress, a truly independent judiciary, and that eternal vigilance which the Founding Fathers took for granted.

III

Watergate then cannot be explained merely as the consequence of incompetence or knavery of men in high office: these terms can be applied to the Grant and Harding administrations as well, when not only the republic but the presidency survived and flourished. Nor can the American people so easily shift responsibility onto Mr. Nixon. After all he had not led a precisely private life, and 42 million Americans who should or could have been familiar with his public career after 1946 voted for him. Surely we must conclude that they got not only what they deserved but what they wanted, and that in a democracy the people have a right to get what they want as long as they do so according to law.

Nor can Watergate be explained as the result of intolerable stresses and strains on our constitutional and political mechanisms; these have held up under far greater strains during the Depression and the Great War, and indeed it is not the Constitution and laws that have failed us, but persistent resort to lawlessness.

A third possible explanation is that implied in different ways by Senators Fulbright and Goodell, and by Mr. Wise, namely that responsibility for our crisis is rooted in changes in the American character, the American mind, American habits or traits—use what term you will—over the past quarter century, changes reflected in Mr. Nixon and his associates and in the current style of American politics.

Much here is in the realm of conjecture, for to fix national traits is like fixing quicksilver, and to go on from there to trace cause and effect is almost to indulge in mysticism. Yet, at some moments of history anyway, national styles do seem to be reflected in politics: the style of the Old South, for example, in the politics of slavery; the style of Bismarck's Germany in the war and diplomacy of the last half of the nineteenth century—how different from the almost music-box Germany of early romanticism; the style of the Japan that launched the great Pacific war. Styles change, and have in the South, in Germany, and in Japan. If Jefferson is a representative figure of the American Enlightenment, faithfully reflecting its virtues, its optimisms, its faiths, its limitations, so perhaps Mr. Nixon is a representative figure of contemporary America, reflecting its arrogance, its violence, its passion for manipulation, its commercialism, but not reflecting its generosity or idealism or intellectual ferment.

Consider first something very large, the shift in the concept of America's role in history, and of the American "mission." To Jefferson's generation that role was clear—to provide a model and a moral example to the peoples of the world. The American empire was, in the almost hackneyed phrase of the Founding Fathers, an Empire of Reason. Mr. Nixon too believes in an American mission. That mission is to be achieved, however, not by reason but by power—force at home to whip recalcitrants into line, force abroad to whip lesser breeds into line—force in little things like breaking into safes, force in big things like building the greatest arsenal in the history of the world.

The corruption of the Jeffersonian view of mission emerges wherever we look: for moral mission, the military; for a unique vision of self-government, hostility throughout the globe to the forces of popular insurgency; for a welcome to radicals and dissenters who had fled the tyranny of the Old World, a refusal to grant visas to those whose ideas might be thought radical by the Daughters of the American Revolution; for faith in the wisdom of the people, a conviction that the people are children whose judgment is not to be trusted; for what Jefferson called "the illimitable freedom of the human mind," a deep distrust of freedom as something inescapably tarnished by subversion; for passion for peace and disarmament, an exaltation of the military and a readiness to rely on it without mercy or compassion.

Our search for peace is rooted in the assumption that we are—far more than other great nations—selfless, idealistic, and peace loving. If this is indeed so, then it follows logically that the wars we fight must be an expression of those qualities. When we develop the most elaborate weapons system in the world, it is for peace; when we maintain two thousand military establishments overseas, it is for peace; when we authorize the CIA to operate secretly in sixty countries and subvert those governments we do not approve of, it is for peace. We changed the government of Guatemala for peace, we invaded Cuba for peace, we landed marines in Santo Domingo for peace, we support the Generals in Brazil and the Colonels in Greece and the colonialists in Portugal for peace; we came to the aid of Diem and Thieu for peace. Now that the war in Vietnam is over, we are bombing Cambodia every day as a kind of peace mission. What is most frightening about all this is that from Mr. Nixon on down the American people can swallow this wonderland logic without gagging.

Nowhere is our changing sense of history more pronounced than in the changing attitude of most Americans toward posterity. The generation whose bicentennial achievements we are about to celebrate was deeply and pervasively posterity-minded: the conviction that everything must be done for the benefit of future generations animated almost every one of the Founding Fathers. That attitude profoundly influenced the American concept of history, too—that though Old World nations were the prisoners of history, America was not, that though in the Old World history is retrospective, in America it was prospective. Both these attitudes pretty well faded out in the past half century or so and now they are but a memory: who now believes that America is the model for the world, or that the new nations of India and Africa look to us for moral and spiritual guidance?

We early got into the habit of taking the future for granted. As President Wilson said in his first inaugural address, "We were very heedless, and in a hurry to be great." The passion to be great joined with the passion to be rich, in justifying exploitation of those resources which should be the property of posterity, with almost unparalleled ruthlessness. What we sometimes overlook is that it is not only the material heritage we lay waste with our exploitations, our strip mining, and our pollution, it is the political and the moral heritage as well. How little thought our government, our Corps of Engineers, our great corporations, our road builders and "developers" give to posterity; but how little thought, too, those who are prepared to sacrifice the Constitution, the Bill of Rights, the principle of due process of law, the ideal of even justice, the respect for the integrity of the ballot box, the dignity and privacy of the individual human being, give for posterity.

The growing habit of taking refuge in such terms as "national commitments," "national security," "obligations of power," "peace with honor," along with that jargon which burgeoned so luxuriantly during the Vietnam war—the "free-fire zones," the "protective aerial reaction," the "surgical strikes," and "incontinent ordnance"—all this bespeaks a steady drift away from the world of realism to the world of self-delusion, from the inductive, the functional, the pragmatic in American thought to an indulgence in the abstract, the deductive, and the doctrinaire.

The rationalization of the cold war, and of the Vietnam war, was rooted in this kind of abstraction. We conjured up a world conspiracy, a monolithic communism, a domino theory—what did we not conjure up?—without feeling any need to provide supporting evidence for our fears. President Nixon reduced the whole thing to a kind of obscene absurdity when he announced that the most powerful nation in the world would be a "helpless, crippled giant" if it could not invade Cambodia! It is the implications of that concept, the cost of that kind of thinking, that Senator Fulbright has explored with his customary lucidity, cogency, and judiciousness, but with passion too. "This kind of thinking," he writes, "robs a nation's policy makers of objectivity and drives them to irresponsible behavior. The perpetuation of the Vietnam war is the most terrible and fateful manifestation of the determination to prove that we are 'Number One.'" And he adds that Assistant Secretary of Defense McNaughton's conclusion that "to avoid a humiliating United States defeat" accounted for some 70 percent of the logic of our war in Southeast Asia, "suggests a nation in thrall." We sometimes forget that thrall means slavery.

The two other books under review reveal how we transferred this same psychology—and tactics—from the foreign to the domestic arena. In the realm of the law—the Dennis case is the most notorious example—we conjured up "conspiracy," searched out not dangerous acts but dangerous "tendencies," and created crimes almost as remote from reality as that of "imagining the death of the King." We took refuge in public manifestations of patriotism like compulsory flag salutes, loyalty oaths, and the antics of the state and congressional un-American activities committees whose business was to provide such activities if they could not discover them, and who did.

Senator Goodell's account of the politicizing of our justice—or resort to wiretapping, the use of provocative agents, the misuse of the grand jury, the readiness to prosecute as a kind of political punishment even when evidence of a crime was lacking—and sometimes to provide the evidence itself—all this is chilling but convincing. He was himself, he recalls, a victim of harassment: "When I was in the Senate, speaking out against administration policies, I learned that my official telephone was tapped and that Military Intelligence agents were following me around the country, building a dossier on my public remarks." He learned more about these techniques when he was counsel for Ellsberg in the Pentagon Papers case—the only criminal prosecution, he reminds us, in more than 4,000 instances of the violation of government regulations concerning classified materials; his book was written before the revelations of breaking into the office files of Ellsberg's psychiatrist.

Perhaps even more sobering are two statements which he quotes from men who occupied positions of great power. The first is from William Rehnquist, now sitting on the Supreme Court, who, when assistant attorney-general, told the Senate Subcommittee on Constitutional Rights that the Constitution "empowers the President to prevent violation of law by maintaining surveillance of those who *in his opinion, might* violate it" (italics mine). As no one over five can safely be excluded from this category we shall all have to engage in surveillance over each other. The quotation comes from the now happily retired Attorney General Kleindienst, who, in 1971, assured us that it would be unnecessary to suspend the Constitution in order to cope with political unrest because:

There is enough play at the joints of our criminal law—enough flexibility—so that if we really felt that we had to pick up the leaders of a violent uprising we could. We would find some things to charge them with, and we would be able to hold them that way for a while.

Mr. Nixon and his attorney-general have indulged in the same kind of thinking, and used the same weapons; if the current *cri de coeur* is no longer simple communism or international conspiracy but "protecting the national interest," the animus is the same, and the logic. The current phrase is potentially even more dangerous than its predecessors; it is broad enough, as Mr. Wise's book shows, to embrace supporting Pakistan against India, asking for prior censorship on the Pentagon Papers, resorting to wholesale wiretaps, authorizing mass arrests without warrants, the corruption of the election process, secret agreements that imply, if they do not require, military commitments with Spain and Portugal—the list could go on and on, and in Mr. Wise's horrifying book it does. But as Governor Reagan has sagely observed, those guilty of misdeeds are not criminals for they meant well. So, no doubt, did Benedict Arnold.

With growth, complexity, and technological impersonality has come, almost inevitably, a weakening of individualism and of that "contrary-minded" quality which used to be so pronounced in the American character. This has meant a readiness to "follow" the president on the ground that he must know best, to accept official handouts at face value, and to resent criticism of the government as something faintly unpatriotic. It has meant, too, a ready acquiescence in regimentation, manipulation, and secrecy.

This attitude is not of course confined to military matters; it is more ostentatious in the readiness to accept the erosion of individual personality and the invasion of privacy in the world dominated by the computer. We are, statistically, far better educated than we were a century ago, but our education takes the form of thinking for ourselves rather less than it did a century ago. Whether because television has shortened our attention span, or the war benumbed our capacity for moral response, we do not appear seriously shocked by My Lai or wiretaps, or even by Watergate until it appeared to be connected with the White House. Many Americans see nothing wrong in political threats against newspapers and television networks; indeed there is a kind of curious counteremotion that the newspapers are being unfair to the president.

We look with indifference, too, at the growth of what would once have been regarded as royal attributes in our rulers—the numerous luxurious residences they require, the special jet planes, the fleets of limousines, the vast entourage which accompanies them wherever they go. How odd to remember that when Thomas Jefferson walked back to his boarding house after giving his inaugural address, he could not find a seat available for him at the dinner table, or that a quarter century later President John Quincy Adams should have the same experience on a ship sailing from Baltimore to New York.

Now government policies and tests screen out strong-minded individualists. It is improbable that any one of our greatest diplomats —Albert Gallatin, John Quincy Adams, Charles Francis Adams— could even get into the Foreign Service today. The world of business, finance, the military, even the world of the great universities, testifies to the same preference for the impersonal chairman of a board rather than a powerful but abrasive personality who will set his stamp on an institution; perhaps it is only in the films, sports, art, music, and literature that Americans still have a cult of individualism.

One of the most pronounced shifts in the American character appears to be a function of this decline in individualism. I mean the growth of a habit of mind that responds uncritically to manipulation. Advertising and "public relations" are the most familiar symbols—and instruments—of manipulation. No previous administration has been so "public relations" minded or has relied so heavily on the manipulation of the public as Nixon's. Everything, so Mr. Nixon and his "team" seem to believe, can be manipulated: elections, justice, the economy, science, great issues of war and peace, the Constitution and the courts; it all depends on the "game plan," on your control of the media, and on your cunning.

Mr. Nixon thought that the Democratic party nomination could be manipulated—and perhaps he was right; that the election could be manipulated—and perhaps it was. Newspapers were not to be won over by sound policies and sound arguments but by petty pressures like excluding reporters from social functions, and by powerful measures like denying them access to information. Congress is to be won over not by arguments but by force or cunning; the courts by playing games with appointments—remember the Nixon caper of the six possible nominees to the Supreme Court. Justice is to be achieved by using provocative agents or rifling files; public opinion polls are made by flooding the White House with phony telegrams; history by doctoring cables; the economy is directed by Alice in Wonderland statistics that never mean what they seem to mean. The president himself is to win the support of the people not through the force of his personality but by some "image" that is created for him.

Wars can be manipulated, too, both for our side and for the enemy—thus the monthly assurance that the war was really over, thus the lies about the Vietnam invasion in 1964 and about Tonkin Gulf; thus the glowing picture of thousands of Asians from Korea to Australia fighting on our side, almost all of whom turned out to be mercenaries (we didn't use to like mercenaries, but that has changed!); thus the famous body counts which made clear that there were really no North Vietnamese males left to fight.

Supreme Court decisions, such as those on wiretapping and busing, can be manipulated to mean something different from what they seem to mean. The Constitution itself can be manipulated to prove the opposite of what the Founding Fathers had written. None of this would work if the American people had not been corrupted for more than a generation by the kind of advertising which floods all media day and night, and whose essential principle is manipulation and seduction. A society trained to accept the preposterous claims, the deceptions, and the vulgarities of American advertising can perhaps be manipulated into accepting anything.

An administration which relies so largely on images and packaging and manipulation has neither respect nor capacity for larger ideas or views. In the end it may not be corruption but intellectual aridity that is the distinguishing feature of this administration.

IV

These reflections raise more questions than they answer. We are confronted with the spectacle of our corruption, a corruption not only moral and social but psychological and intellectual, confronted with a threat not only to the constitutional and political system, but to constitutional and political thought. Where is the center of gravity? Is it in the White House; is it in the Praetorian Guard that has infested the White House; is it in the apparatus of secrecy we associate not only with the FBI and the CIA and with the Pentagon, but with the whole of the administration? Or is there perhaps no center of gravity at all, no center of corruption even; do we have the sociological equivalent of Hannah Arendt's "banality of evil"?

Those guilty of what is moral treason to the Constitution, and of subverting the political system, are not evil conspirators, consciously bent upon destroying the America we have known. They are, at the top, the proud products of the American system of Private Enterprise, the very vindication of the American success story; those down the line are for the most part clean-limbed, clear-eyed, upstanding young men, the kind who figure in all our most stylish advertisements, the kind who are commonly voted "most likely to succeed" by their admiring classmates. These are not the makers and shakers of O'Shaughnessy's poem; they are the squares and the jocks of the postcollege generation. What kind of society is it that produces—and cherishes—men of these intellectual and moral standards? If our own conduct was scrupulous, if our own standards were honorable, would we really have permitted the Mitchells and Magruders and Deans and Haldemans and Kleindiensts to have imposed their moral standards upon us? Are we sure we have not imposed our moral standards upon them?

Our indignation and our outrage are both a bit shame-faced. After all there is nothing new about the illegalities and immoralities of the Vietnam war, but we still tolerate the Cambodian war. After all there is nothing new about the iniquities of the CIA; that has been going on now for almost twenty years with scarcely a murmur of protest. After all there is nothing new about the warnings of secrecy in government—that goes back 180 years to the principles of the Founding Fathers. After all there is nothing new about the danger of the arrogance of power and the impropriety of using men and societies for our advantage; that goes back to Kant's great categorical imperative. After all there is nothing new about the moral that power corrupts—you can read that in Plutarch, if you ever bother to read Plutarch—or about warnings against imposing your will on weaker peoples—you can read that in Thucydides, if you bother to read Thucydides.

The Founding Fathers did read Plutarch and Thucydides. They knew that power tended to corrupt, and set up a system of checks and balances which they thought would protect the Commonwealth against that corruption. This administration has tried to paralyze those checks and balances—and who has protested? Who but a handful of journalists, senators, and scholars?

The Founding Fathers knew instinctively what Montesquieu

proclaimed in his *Spirit of the Laws,* that virtue is the animating principle of a republic. And to the Commonwealth they served— almost always at great personal sacrifice—they paid the tribute of virtue. But this administration, which gibbers about "peace with honor," does not exalt virtue, and does not practice it.

But do we?

Government and the People

AARON WILDAVSKY

We shall never learn what needs to be learned about the American political system until we understand not only what the system does to the people, but what the people do to the system. Political institutions are no different from other organizations: to the great question of organizational life—who will bear the costs of change? —the answer, in the public as in the private sphere, is, "someone else, not me." The universal tendency to make life easy for ourselves and to impose difficulties on others applies equally to politicians, and when they find their lives intolerable no one should be surprised that they react by seeking to lay their burdens on the shoulders of others.

Especially during the past decade, almost our whole attention as citizens has been devoted to the ways in which politicians have failed to serve the people. Few have asked how politicians manage to live in the world, because it is assumed that they are doing fine and that the problem is to make them behave decently toward us —almost as if politicians lived somehow apart from American life. Yet it would be strange indeed if our politicians were a special breed, uninfluenced by their milieu, springing full-born like Minerva from the head of Jove in a world they never made, but on which they work their mythical powers.

Politicians are like other animals; indeed their behavior, like our own, can often be analogized to that observed in lower forms of life. Laboratory experiments show that rats who are consistently given contradictory commands become neurotic, if not psychotic. The same phenomenon is readily visible among politicians. Give them incompatible commands, insist that they fulfill contradictory impulses at the same time, and they too will show the classical symptoms—withdrawal, self-mutilation, random activity, and other

Reprinted from *Commentary*, by permission; copyright © 1973 by the American Jewish Committee. Aaron Wildavsky is Dean of the Graduate School of Public Policy at the University of California at Berkeley and the author of *The Revolt Against the Masses and Other Essays on Politics and Public Policy*.

forms of bizarre behavior unrelated to the ostensible task at hand. An occasional deviant is even known to lash out at his experimenters, or at least at the apparatus in which he is enmeshed, though he remains quite incapable of understanding why he worked so hard to accomplish so little, or why life is so bitter when it should be so sweet.

We are all, in fact, doing better and feeling worse.* Every standard of well-being, from housing to health, shows that every sector of the population, however defined, including all racial, religious, and ethnic groupings, has improved its lot in past decades. Even the twin problems of crime and drugs, areas in which we are vividly conscious of recent deterioration, have been considerably reduced in severity, so far as we are able to judge, since the turn of the century. When heroin was legal there were proportionately more addicts in the population; when the nation was younger and poorer there were more criminals, or at least a correspondingly greater degree of crime. Why, then, do so many feel so bad—and why do they continue to feel so bad when, of the two causes reflexively invoked to explain this feeling, the first, the Vietnam war, has come to an end while the second, racial inequity, has clearly and visibly diminished? I cannot pursue this subject in all its ramifications here. Instead I wish to add another element to the puzzle—the manufacture of incompatible policy demands that impose burdens on government which no government can meet.

The fact that the public demands on government in the various areas of policy are contradictory, in the sense that pursuing one policy inevitably means prohibiting the enactment of another, does not mean that an evil genius has been at work programming the political system for a nervous breakdown. Coordination need not require a coordinator; it can be tacit and informal as well as overt. Men coordinate their activities through adherence to a common body of assumptions or through the sharing of a common world view. Quite the same kinds of contradictions can be created by various people in different places making vocal demands that turn our to be mutually opposed. The lack of central direction, in fact, is an advantage because it adds to the general confusion: politicians

* See my essays, "The Empty-head Blues: Black Rebellion and White Reaction," *Public Interest*, No. 11, Spring 1968; "The Revolt Against the Masses," *The Revolt Against the Masses and Other Essays on Politics and Public Policy* (Basic Books, 1971); "The Search for the Oppressed," *Freedom at Issue*, No. 16, November-December 1972.

are given a hard time but they do not know on whom to vent their own frustration. For our purposes it is not necessary to know whether demands on government are made by those who wish to see it fail, and therefore delight in giving it tasks it cannot manage, or who wish to see it succeed, and take pleasure in asking it to perform feats hitherto unaccomplished. Whether it stems from those who love government too little or from those who love it too much, the results of this pressure are the same: government is asked to perform wonders, but the attainment of one wonder often automatically precludes the possibility of attaining another, or many others.

The incompatibility of policy demands is a manifestation of a more general withdrawal of sovereignty from government in America. The rights of government and of politicians are being systematically whittled down. Public officials and professional politicians can no longer organize their political parties as they please, or hold meetings in closed sessions, or keep their papers secret, or successfully sue others for slandering them—even when they can show the allegations to be false—or make the smallest decisions without being hauled into court to convince judge and attorney they have followed standards of due process, considered every conceivable alternative, consulted all who might possibly be injured, or otherwise abandoned virtually every sense of what it used to mean to rule by enforcing binding regulations. We demand more of government but we trust it less. Angered and annoyed by evident failures, our reaction is not to reduce our expectations of what government can accomplish but to decrease its ability to meet them. That is how a society becomes ungovernable.

The legislation proposed by Lyndon Johnson and enacted during the first eighteen months of his Presidency wiped out the New Deal and destroyed both the historical coalition and the universe of common assumptions on the basis of which American citizens and political activists alike had long understood what was happening in the national life. By enacting every piece of social legislation it could lay its hands on, Congress obliterated all the old issues; where once a citizen knew on which side of a given question he stood, now all was confusion.

The passage of the Great Society legislation, in addition, had a devastating effect on many sectors of the federal bureaucracy. The second worst thing that can happen to anybody is to strive for a

COLORADO MOUNTAIN COLLEGE
LRC---WEST CAMPUS

lifetime and fail to get what he wants. The first worst thing is to strive and to get and to discover that it is not good. Think of people who spent, say, twenty years in the Department of Health, Education, and Welfare and its predecessors, trying desperately to secure huge federal appropriations for education. In the mid-1960's they got them; they still have them, but they have discovered that the ground has shifted and that the clientele whose interests they thought they were serving is not the clientele the new policies are aimed at. So they fail and they are bewildered.

In the past, the clients of the New Deal had been the temporarily depressed but relatively stable lower and middle classes, people who were on the whole willing and able to work but who had been restrained by the economic situation; if a hand were extended to them or if the economic picture brightened, things improved for them right away. It hardly mattered one way or the other what government did or did not do in their behalf. Now, however, government policy was being designed to deal not with such people but with the *severely* deprived, those who actually needed not merely an opportunity but continuing, long-term assistance. No previous government had ever attempted to do for this sector of the population—those whom Marx had called the lumpenproletariat— what the American government set out to do. Yet nobody knew *how* to go about it, either. In the field of education, for example, no one had the faintest clue as to what amount of "input" would produce the desired result, and so vast amounts of money and even vaster amounts of enthusiasm were poured into various programs that ultimately ended in failure and bewilderment (as it turns out, we have learned that variations in expenditures of almost four to one make absolutely no difference—or only slight difference—in student performance, and that other variables, known and unknown, must be taken into account).

Far from giving up in the face of such complex ignorance, the tendency instead was to place the emphasis on those variables that did seem controllable. This led to the concept of community action. If no solutions were available and no one had the foggiest notion of how to do anything, it *was* possible to increase the demand for solutions, to create pressure from below that would effect the release of ever increasing amounts of federal money. But the fact that government was trying to deal with a different clientele and that no one knew how to do it meant that an awful lot of money was invested without accomplishing very much. The escalation of demands together with the lack of knowledge of solutions meant a multiplication of programs, each under- or overfinanced, each justified by the notion that it was somehow an experiment that would prove something.

There is perhaps nothing new in all this, but the political consequences have not been seen as clearly as they might be. Welfare today has become a political albatross. In the past, those who paid for welfare may not have liked it while those who received it, if they did not love it, at least found it preferable to the alternative. Government got credit from those who received the money and demerits from those who had to pay. Since the poor were more numerous than the wealthy, a political trade-off was effected and things seemed to work out. Today the taxpayers curse and the welfare recipients tell government where to get off. The welfare system gets credit nowhere.

People who are involved in revolutions are usually the last to recognize what has been happening all around them. While the War on Poverty was being waged, those fighting the battles understandably lacked the time, energy, or discernment to see anything like the full implications of their actions. Like good soldiers everywhere, they went from skirmish to skirmish, leaving the grand strategy to generals who, as every classic account of warfare tells us, understood less than anyone else. First, as noted, the generals radiated a sense of hope: wonderful things could be done. On this basis many new programs were launched and even more were proposed, to capitalize on the new potential for eliminating poverty. Second, also as noted, they generated a sense of despair: hardly anything seemed to be working. Out of this was born a new determination to overcome obstacles—in the form of new programs. Third, whether one had hoped or despaired, it became almost a reflex action to call on government to justify the hope or overcome the despair. One consistent trend in this concatenation was the proliferation of demands on government from all quarters. Another trend, seldom noticed, was the incompatibility of the demands.

This particular characteristic of the public-policy debate of the 1960's is still very much with us, and it can be seen at work in areas as diverse as welfare and election reform. Thus the same people who demand that government increase the levels of support and the numbers of people on welfare are just as likely to assert in the next breath that welfare is a total failure, that it costs too much, and that it should be scrapped. Similarly, the demand that the political parties be "democratized" and made more representative is often linked to the demand that the costs of elections be reduced so that the rich will not control the democratic process. As Nelson Polsby has pointed out, it is impossible to do both: democratization in practice means more primaries, more conventions, more meetings—in other words, increased costs.

Or consider employment. There have basically been two objectives in this area of policy: employ the hard-core and create jobs at reasonable costs. It is very expensive to train the hard-core; that is why they are hard-core. It is also very discouraging, because many will not get jobs and many others will not keep them. But in addition, if a government agency has actually been able to show that it created a number of jobs that people filled and stayed in for a while at some kind of reasonable cost (by reasonable cost I mean that it has cost less than it would have just to give them the money), it has then been criticized for dealing with people who were too employable. This is known as "creaming," getting jobs for the best of the worst, so that anyone who has actually found a job was, *ipso facto,* as Groucho Marx might have said, not the right kind of person to have tried to employ in the first place.

Consider housing, where the demand has been to give preference to the worst-off and provide a better environment. That has led to such monstrosities as the Pruitt Igoe project in St. Louis, finally dynamited in order to reduce the incidence of social evil. Or consider the environment. It is tempting to condemn both pollution and high prices, but there is an intimate connection between the two. Today we expect our government to provide pure air and use less energy: it cannot do both at the same time.

How about community action? We demand widespread participation and we want fast action on the problems of the poor. Participation, however, requires built-in delays; the more committees, the more levels, the more people, the more time lost. It may not really be time wasted if greater participation results, but few remember the original impetus when frustration sets in.

The mischiefs unwittingly created by placing the phrase "maximum feasible participation" in legislation have been amply documented so far as government agencies are concerned. The documentation, however, is incomplete. Efforts to implement the spirit of the phrase have also wreaked havoc with the minority communities themselves. The idea was to facilitate the emergence

of indigenous leadership, but, as Judith May has persuasively demonstrated,* the paradoxical result has been to delegitimate virtually
everyone in black communities who could claim to be a leader
because there is always some criterion he does not meet. If poor,
he may not live exactly in the right neighborhood. If professional,
he may not be poor enough. And so forth. Thus the only people
who fit the prescription are those who are poor and are in no danger
of getting rich, who have lived in the neighborhood for a long time
and who cannot get out, and who often care so little they seldom
attend meetings of the numerous poverty programs. Such people,
it has turned out, have precisely the characteristics—lack of motivation, lack of experience, lack of ability—that do not commend them
to their neighbors.

The essential perversity of the policy milieu is its ability to frustrate nearly everyone at the same time. Few programs, for instance,
are more noble in intent than those calling for the provision of
extra resources and services to the educationally deprived. Since
there is not enough money to go around to all who might be considered poor, amendments have been passed at the federal and state
level requiring that the most severely deprived be given substantial
additional increments so that the massing of resources will have
some palpable effect on them. It is difficult to argue with this sensible point of view, but the political impact on the near poor, who
are too well off to receive aid but poor enough to need it, has been
severe. They are more easily helped because they have a bit more
with which to begin. As they observe extra resources going to the
very poor, who are most in need but least likely to be helped, they
cannot help but wonder why they, who need less help but can use
it more, are being left out. Their dissatisfaction with government
is bound to rise as they watch the competition to gather up the
funds for which they cannot qualify. And so is government dissatisfaction with itself bound to rise, for officials are asked to aid
the least able and to sacrifice the more able.

The political ramifications are potentially disastrous: rising dis-
content on the part of both those who pay the costs and those who
get the benefits. The have-littles are plunged into conflict with the
have-nots (the working and lower-middle classes with the poor)
because compensatory mechanisms fail to help the one, and do not

* Judith V. May, *The Struggle for Authority: Four Poverty Programs in
Oakland* (doctoral dissertation in progress, University of California, Berkeley).

stretch far enough to reach the other. Observing dissatisfaction on the part of those receiving extra resources, the people who pay are likely to call it ingratitude. Part of the secret of winning, as any football coach knows, lies in arranging an appropriate schedule. Governmental performance depends not only on the ability to solve problems but on selecting problems government knows how to solve.

What are the consequences of constructing and defining issues so as to pose incompatible demands on decision-makers? Both the kinds of policies that we get from government and the kinds of attention paid to the various realms of policy are affected. Within the executive branch a greater emphasis will naturally come to be placed on foreign than on domestic policy because the foreign realm seems less forbidding to Presidents and even given a random occurrence of events it seems likely that some good can be achieved —for which, moreover, credit may accrue to the President. In domestic policy, on the other hand, Presidents have come to see little for which they will be applauded, and much for which they will be condemned for even attempting.

When a government does not expect that anything it does will garner credit it tends to push for form over substance. This comes out in the various "funny money" policies we have become accustomed to recently. An official thinks he has money for model housing—but is that not the money he should have spent three years ago and did not? Is it the money that was allocated for something else; that he thought he had but never received; that he once spent but was returned? Or is there actually a dollar or two of real money? It becomes increasingly difficult to know.

There are also substantive consequences of having incompatible demands made on government. One is a growing stress by analysts on an incomes policy as opposed to a services policy for the poor. Why should government continue to administer a welfare system that everyone hates when one of the few things that can really be done well in Washington is programming a computer to write checks? If guarded with exceptional closeness such a machine will actually write the checks it is supposed to write and people will actually receive them. In this way government does away with the middle men, the agitators for welfare rights. It may spend more money, but it will reduce the size of the bureaucracy and may actually make it possible for people to realize that the help they are getting has come from the government. Another policy consequence is revenue sharing, a bone thrown to cities and towns with a warning attached that if the bone should taste bad or if indigestion should ensue they have no one to blame but themselves. Cities are now beginning to understand that they are getting a little money and a lot of trouble. Increasingly *they* become the center of demand and lack the capacity to respond.

Making incompatible demands on government is bound to have an impact on the federal system. When there is no way to garner credit, when everything attempted is clearly slated to fail, an effort will be made by government to rid itself of the source of anxiety —namely, its responsibility for policy. Any time the federal government can trade trouble for money, it will. Miniature revenue-sharing proposals in the fields of health and welfare are now being seriously considered. The consequences, of course, need not all be bad: people with demands to make will find it more worthwhile to approach the cities and states because these will have more to give. But in a federal system in which each level deliberately seeks to pass its worst problems on to the next, in which blaming the other party has become a national pastime, it will become harder than it is already to know who is responsible for not solving our latest set of insoluble problems.

Fairly construed, the government's record on social policy during the last decade has been one of vigorous effort and some noteworthy if nevertheless defective accomplishments. Food stamps do feed the hungry (as well as the hippies), and public housing is better than its alternatives. Steps have been taken in numerous areas to meet the needs of those who had previously been neglected. The men who have contended with these confusing times deserve compassion rather than contempt, and even a measure of applause. Yet it is only now, when programs are threatened with reductions, that a chorus of concern arises—and this, from quarters that had previously denounced the nation's social programs as too little, too late, misguided, or even positively harmful. It is in any event certain that these programs will die unless those who benefit from them (or who identify with the beneficiaries) come forward with vocal support. The critics of social policy have overplayed their hand; they wanted more and better, instead they are getting less and worse. The Nixon administration eventually came to the conclusion that since no visible credit was forthcoming from the presumptively natural supporters of social programs, it might as well gain whatever benefits it could from the conservatives who opposed them. Like any other institution that wishes to remain solvent, governmental bodies must re-establish their credit when their policies begin to earn a deficit of political support.

"Government," Alfred Marshall wrote, "is the most precious of human possessions; and no care can be too great to be spent on enabling it to do its work in the best way: a chief condition to that end is that it should not be set to work for which it is not specially qualified, under the conditions of time and place." Once government is given not just one or two things it cannot do, but a whole host, the effects will be felt throughout the political system. Voters, for instance, have begun to lose their sense of identification with the major political parties, because they, like the government, cannot deliver on their promises. The nature of political campaigns has also changed. In 1972, instead of defending their record, the leaders of government concentrated on the alleged horrors about to be perpetrated by the opposition—or that had been perpetrated by their own party's past. "Elect me," promised Richard Nixon in effect, "and I will save you from that fellow who created a $33 billion deficit. Elect me, and I will protect you from my Justice Department's former position on busing. Elect me, and I will save you from quotas imposed by my Department of Health, Education, and Welfare." The President was running against himself, monopolizing the advantages of incumbency while at the same time pretending he had never been in office. No doubt future challengers will learn the wisdom of being vague, lest their promises, rather than the government's performance, become the focal point of the campaign.

If parties cannot make good on the promises of their candidates for office, what can they make good on? Party structure, for one thing; they can promise to organize themselves in a given way, if only because this is something over which they can exercise control. Thus parties, like politicians, move more strongly into the realm of the expressive and the symbolic rather than of substantive policy. The Democratic party can arrange itself in order to contain certain proportions of this or that ethnic group or gender. It can conduct endless meetings, primaries, conventions, all the while gradually shifting the definition of a party from an instrument seeking to govern the nation to an instrument seeking to govern itself. What parties contribute to the nation, then, is not so much candidates attached to a policy as procedures that meet certain visible but internal norms.

Politicians, too, are shifting emphasis from substantive policy to

personal political style. They talk of basic changes in the political
process, but move into action only when this consists of a form of
opposition. They offer adherence to proclaimed moral principle,
where they cannot fail, instead of offering innovation in policy,
where they cannot succeed. They are often "against" what is happening but see themselves under no obligation to suggest viable
alternatives. A sign of the political times is the growing proportion
of Presidential candidates who come from the United States Senate,
for that is the office which combines the longest term and the
highest national visibility with the least responsibility. When people
are angry they may picket mayors and shout down governors, but
they rarely advance on the Senate or its occupants. The Senate is
the place where a man can say his piece while others worry about
the responsibilities of office.

Not only the Senate but the House as well, Congress as a whole,
is involved in the dilemma of acting responsibly at a time when
substantive achievements are hard to come by. The quandary in
which Congressmen find themselves is illustrated in the controversy
over impoundment. It is all too easy to blame the conflict entirely
on the President; he had ample discretionary powers under the
Anti-Deficiency Act of 1951, but he chose instead to throw down
the gauntlet by saying that he might refuse to spend money in
appropriations bills even after they were passed over his veto. That
bit of arrogance deserves what it got. But underneath the surface
clash of personalities lies a deepseated unwillingness in Congress to
accept responsibility for raising the revenues required to support its
own spending desires. It is easier to vote for this or that while laying the burden of reduced expenditures, or of finding new revenues,
at the door of the President. The growing practice of Presidential
impoundment may be part of a tacit agreement that Congress will
get credit for voting the funds while the President takes Congress
off the hook by refusing to spend. By allowing impoundment to go
on for as long as it did and to cover so extensive a range of policies,
Congress demonstrated its apparent willingness to see spending cut
if only the blame could be placed elsewhere.

Of all our institutions, the Presidency has been the one most
deeply affected by government's inability to get credit for domestic
policy, because it is the single most visible source of authority and
hence the most obvious target of demands. Even the Watergate
affair, about which it is plausible to argue that the mentality that

produced it is of a singular kind attributable only to President
Nixon and his close associates, may be seen to have connections with
the fate of the Presidency as an institution in recent years. This is
hardly to deny, much less to excuse, the element of personal pathol-
ogy, or criminality, involved, but even so extreme a series of events
as those surrounding the Watergate affair may be clarified by reference to the general issue of the impact of public policy on the
Presidency in the past decade.

The climate of opinion that made Watergate and its cover-up
possible is part of (and will contribute further to) the delegitima-
tion of government that I alluded to earlier. Although it is convenient now to forget this, from the middle 1960's onward, national
leaders of government have been subject to a crescendo of attack
and even personal abuse. They have been shouted down, mobbed,
and vilified in public. It was not possible for men like President
Lyndon Johnson and Vice President Hubert Humphrey to speak
where they wished in safety, or to travel where they wished without
fear. Not merely their conduct as individuals, but the political system of which they were a part, has been condemned as vicious,
immoral, and depraved. This, after all, was the justification offered
for the stealing of government documents—that the government
from which they were taken had no right to be doing what it was
doing, that it was not legitimate. The rationale offered by Daniel
Ellsberg for taking and publishing government documents was the
same as that offered by the Watergate conspirators—national interest, a higher law than that applying to ordinary citizens.

Watergate emerged, in my opinion, out of an environment in
which people who identified with government sought to delegitimate
the opposition just as they believed the opposition had sought to
delegitimate government. Presumably no one, in their view, had a
right to beat President Nixon in 1972, so they sought to get Senator
Muskie out of the race.* They broke into Watergate ostensibly to
find evidence that the Democrats were being financed by Cuban
(Communist) money, as if to say that their own illegality was
permissible because the Democrats were not then a legitimate American political party. The blame, to be sure, is not the same. Ellsberg
was not entrusted with the care of government, and the Watergate

---

* I pass over the intriguing question of what lesson the Democratic party
might learn when its worst enemies conspire to nominate the candidate it
was bent on selecting itself.

conspirators were. But they cohere in the same syndrome; the one is a reaction to the other, each party rationalizing its exceptional behavior on the grounds of its enemy's illegitimacy.

Watergate is a curious scandal by American standards, in that it is not concerned with money; nor is it, like a British scandal, concerned with sex. By contrast, it resembles a French scandal, one in which small groups of conspirators make and execute their clandestine plans in the service of ideologies held by no more than 1 or 2 per cent of the population. Watergate may thus represent another step in the "Frenchification" of American political life begun in the mid-1960's, a mode of politics in which apparently inexplicable behavior is found to derive from attachment to ideologies of which the vast bulk of the citizenry knows little and cares less. We may have to accustom ourselves to men on the Left out to save us from Fascism and men on the Right from Communism, men who point to one another's activities as justification for illegal acts.

The French analogy gains strength in light of the entire pattern of President Nixon's conduct before Watergate. Seemingly disparate occurrences fall into place once we understand that Nixon had adopted a plebiscitary view of the Presidency, a view that has echoes in the American past but none in the contemporary Western world except in the Presidency of Charles de Gaulle and his successor in France. From this perspective the position of Nixon's Attorney General on executive privilege, with its suggestion that the Presidency exists wholly apart from other institutions, becomes more explicable. So does Nixon's march on the media. For if the Presidency is not part of a separation of powers with Congress, but of a unity of power with the people, then its survival is critically dependent on direct access to them. His victory at the polls in 1972 seems to have inspired in him the conviction that as the embodiment of the national will he should brook no opposition from Congress. If he said "no" on spending and the legislature said "yes," so much the worse for *it*. Even the Republican party could not share in his triumph—it neither ran his campaign nor got any of its leaders appointed to high positions—lest it become another unwanted intermediary between the President and the people; Vice President Agnew and the Republican National Committee owe their spotless reputations on Watergate (apart from their undoubted integrity) to having been kept out of (or away from) the Presidential branch of government. It was his plebiscitary view of the Presidency that led

Nixon to attempt to run a foreign and defense policy without the Senate, a budget policy without the House, and a domestic-security policy without the courts.*

I have momentarily digressed on the subject of Watergate only to suggest that there was more than personal idiosyncrasy at work here, and that there is reason to look upon Nixon's Presidency as the continuation and exemplification of a number of long-term trends in the political system as a whole. In like fashion, the organization of the executive office under Nixon continues an ever-growing trend toward bureaucratization, a reaction in turn to the perceived failure of the Presidential office to influence public policy in ways that will redound to its credit. And just as President Kennedy's and President Johnson's associates sought to lay the blame for bad public policy on the regular bureaucracy, so Nixon's men were following precedent when they sought to debureaucratize the bureaucracy while themselves becoming more bureaucratic. For bureaucratization is a way of seeking shelter from a stormy world.

The Presidential office has, as everybody can now see, become a bureaucracy in the same sense that Max Weber meant by the term: it has grown greatly in size and it is characterized by specialization, division of labor, chain of command, and hierarchy. At the same time it criticizes, castigates, and blames the regular federal bureaucracy and attempts to circumvent it and intervene directly in the political process at lower and lower levels. From the perhaps three secretaries that Franklin Roosevelt inherited, the executive bureaucracy has risen to several thousand. There are (or recently were) two specialized organizations for dealing with the media, one to handle daily press relations and the other concerned with various promotional ventures. There is a specialized bureaucracy for dealing with foreign policy, begun when John F. Kennedy appointed McGeorge Bundy to the White House; Henry Kissinger's shop now boasts a staff of about one hundred. There is a domestic council to deal with policy at home, started by Richard Nixon. And there is also the Congressional liaison machinery instituted by President Eisenhower. Since 1965 the growth of the executive office of the President has been geometric. The largest increases of all occurred

* Nixon did not have these views when he came into office. It was his experience in office that led him to such desperate expedients. No doubt each man comes bringing his own desperation with him. But Nixon was already President. To go so far after four years in office he must have been more frustrated than anyone knew.

in Nixon's first term, but he was merely accelerating a trend, not initiating it.

Because President Nixon, especially at the start of his second term, apparently set out to alienate every national elite—the press, Congress, the Republican National Committee—the fact that he had long been attacking his own federal bureaucracy has escaped notice. Such incidents abound, however. At ceremonies establishing the special Action Office for Drug Abuse Control, for example: "the President told an audience of 150 legislators and officials that 'heads would roll' if 'petty bureaucrats' obstruct the efforts of the office's director, Dr. Jerome H. Jaffe. . . . The President said that above all the law he just signed put into the hands of Dr. Jaffe full authority to 'knock heads together' and prevent 'empire building' by any one of the many agencies concerned" (*New York Times,* March 22, 1972). President Nixon also "informed a group of Western editors in Portland that he had told Secretary Morton 'we should take a look at the whole bureaucracy with regard to the handling of Indian affairs and shake it up good.' The President blamed the bureaucracy for Indian problems, saying that 'the bureaucracy feeds on itself, defends itself, and fights for the status quo. And does very little, in my opinion, for progress in the field' " (*New York Times,* September 29, 1971).

Here too, Nixon was not so much initiating as continuing a trend. Much the same hostility to the bureaucracy had been manifested by his immediate predecessors. Accounts of staff men under Johnson and Kennedy frequently reveal a sense of indignation, if not outrage, at the very idea of the separation of powers; federalism is an anathema to agents of the executive branch. Who are all those people out there thwarting us? they ask all but explicitly. Who do they think they are in the Congress and the state capitals? Strongest of all is the condemnation of the bureaucracy. The White House staff has great ideas, marvelous impulses, beautiful feelings, and these are suppressed, oppressed, crushed by the bureaucratic mind.

Why is it that the President on the one hand seeks to bureaucratize his own office, while on the other hand he holds the bureaucracy to blame for all his ills? In the end we return to our beginnings. Presidents have been impelled to attempt stabilization of their own office and destabilization of the regular bureaucracy because of radical changes in public policy demands. The structure of domestic political issues is now such that no government, and hence no President, can get the credit for what is done. Like all the other actors in this drama the President and his men head for cover in the White House stockade and shoot at others more vulnerable than themselves.

It would appear amazing, in retrospect, that we thought about the Presidency as if it were uncaused, as if the things that affected and afflicted us as citizens had no impact on the men who occupy public office. How long did we expect attacks on the man and the institution to go on before there was a response? Nixon's counterattack, it now appears, may have threatened our liberties. Did the growing popularity of the idea that illegality was permissible for a good cause have no impact on the men surrounding the President? Did this political peril have nothing to do with the demands we make on our Presidents but only with their designs on us? John F. Kennedy struggled mightily with a sense of failure before he was assassinated. Lyndon B. Johnson was forced to deny himself the chance for re-election. Now Richard Nixon fights for a chance to serve out his term. One or two more experiences like these and someone may think it is more than coincidence.

It might be argued that my portrait of the Presidential office in particular, and of politicians in general, treats public officials as if they were the innocent victims of social pressures rather than active participants in the political process capable of shaping it to their own ends. Politicians, moreover, have faced conflicting demands in the past, and might reasonably be expected to face them successfully in the future. Problems arising from incompatible goals are what leaders are there to help solve. A purpose of leadership, after all, is to clarify what can and cannot be done, to set priorities, and to gain some agreement on a schedule of accomplishment. Is this too much to ask of a politician who wants to make a career out of leadership?

It is not. My thesis, however, is that the problems being allocated to government are not just a random sample of those ordinarily associated with governing, some of which, at least, are eminently soluble, given hard work and good judgment, but that government is increasingly getting a skewed distribution of problems that are insoluble precisely because people demand of government what government cannot do. What remains to be explained is how politicians have become strapped to this particular wheel and why they are so maladroit in getting off it.

Politicians are Americans and they, too, are caught up in American optimism. Just as the Vietnam war was a symptom of the optimistic belief in the boundless possibilities of American intervention abroad, so, too, the War on Poverty was a symptom of an optimistic belief in the boundless possibilities of government intervention at home. By the time public officials began to realize they could not do everything all at once, or even some things at all, they had become committed to a broad new range of social programs. And they did not call a halt to these indecisive engagements because they were liberals, that is, Americans.

America lacks an intellectually respectable conservative tradition. It has always, as Louis Hartz has sought to show, had a liberal tradition. For present purposes this means that equality, no matter how abused or disused, has always been the prevailing American norm; the long tradition of hypocrisy on the issue is itself eloquent testimony to its power. The new social and political programs, whether designed for increased participation in decision-making or a greater share in the good things of life, came into the world bearing the banner of the liberal concept of equality. It was hard to oppose, or even think clearly about opposing, these programs without appearing to be against equality or in favor of inequality. Individual politicians might have doubts, a few deviants might voice them, but there was too much guilt engendered by the rhetoric of equality to make collective action possible.

After the deed comes the rationalization. John Rawls's distinguished book on equality, *A Theory of Justice,* though long in the making, appears now as a gloss on the domestic programs of the 1960's. Its guiding principle is that no inequality is justified unless it helps those who are worst off. Armed with this communitarian thrust to liberal principle, one can defend any sort of policy which proclaims its purpose as that of aiding the worst off but which does not bother to balance smaller benefits to some against larger benefits to others. A few pundits aside, there is not now, if there ever was, a social stratum able to support a conservative ethic against the forces in favor of pushing public policy over the egalitarian precipice. Under the Nixon administration, instead of a social response we got a pitiful outbreak (or break-in) like Watergate.

The American politician, like the American political system, has been attacked at the most vulnerable point. The system is being asked to make good on its most ancient and deeply held beliefs, and it hovers between an inability to abandon its faith and an inability to make its faith manifest to the believers. This is the American crisis of confidence, evident in professors who do not profess, scentists who call for alternative approaches to science that smack of witchcraft, and politicians who condemn politics.

The expectations created by the body politic (or by a small but influential part of it), the rewards and punishments it administers, go far to shape the successes and failures of public officials. Anyone who writes or speaks or thinks seriously about public policy has a special obligation to consider what his contribution, even when placed in the context of many others, implies for the ability of government to perform adequately. Otherwise, private vices will become public vices as well (to reverse Mandeville), and government, seeing that the game is rigged, will respond once again by secretly attempting to change the rules.

2. Civil Liberties and the First Amendment Freedoms

So fundamental is the Bill of Rights that any effort to subvert individual freedom affronts America's sense of justice. Already troubled by the "wiretap mentality" dominating the White House in 1971, the nation was rocked when it learned of the "White House horrors," as former Attorney-General John Mitchell so piquantly described the events of Watergate. Through the summer of 1973, as the Senate Watergate Committee held publicly televised hearings, the nation learned of campaign dirty tricks, break-ins—both at the Watergate and in Daniel Ellsberg's psychiatrist's office—White House cover-ups, and the existence of taped Presidential conversations.

The pattern of secrecy, political use of the bureaucracy, and obstruction of justice in the Nixon Administration challenge political freedom and the Constitutional rule of law. For many Americans, safeguarding and broadening of political freedom are the essence of democratic government. Learning of the abuse to civil liberties lent credence to the long-standing charge from the Left that the Nixon Administration was a closed corporation, undemocratic and unsympathetic to civil liberties. The revelations of the "enemies list," the Huston Plan, and the Ellsberg break-in served to confirm suspicions. Hans Morgenthau has gone so far as to compare the Nixon Administration to fascism, noting that in both cases a "dual state" was being created wherein duplicated agencies perform functions statutory agencies are legally prohibited from performing.

Lawlessness, however, is not new or limited to the Nixon Administration, as Alexander Bickel is quick to point out. In fact the civil-rights demonstrations and anti–Vietnam war protests challenged the rule of law. That decade and a half produced a moral firestorm, a prologue to Watergate, which Bickel sees as the latest in a series of assaults on the law. Much as the civil dissidents of the 1950's and 1960's defended their protest actions by citing moral imperatives, so too the brash young men coming to Washington to serve Richard Nixon felt a higher purpose. The legal and social order, Bickel argues, was under moral attack from all sides.

The abuses of power largely were defended in the name of national security, the doctrine of separation of powers, and executive privilege. In this vein Nixon conducted secret bombings of Cambodia, placed wiretaps on the telephones of executive assistants, refused compliance with Congressional subpoenas, and argued against supplying information to Congress and the courts. In his article, Thomas I. Emerson sets out to examine the role of secrecy in a democratic society; as a proposition, Professor Emerson thinks governmental secrecy illegitimate in a democratic society, on both philosophical and political grounds. And yet, the Constitution is unclear regarding secrecy, and Emerson himself can point out areas of possible exception to disclosure of information.

An individual's personal freedom must be balanced by the needs of government to operate in an orderly, peaceful way. Watergate goes to the heart of this question. Can a government function in the face of moral imperatives, as Bickel argues? Just how much discretion will national security and executive prerogative sustain? The management of information by government requires responsibility. The pursuit of responsibility does not justify the subordination of truth. Indeed truth and responsibility are necessarily partners in legitimate government. "Fundamental to our way of life is the belief that when information which properly belongs to the public is systematically withheld by those in power, the people soon become ignorant of their own affairs, distrustful of those who manage them, and—eventually—incapable of determining their own destinies." (Richard M. Nixon, 1972.)

Watergate and the Legal Order

ALEXANDER M. BICKEL

Months ago, when the scandals of the Nixon administration were fewer and relatively simpler, there was some self-serving talk of a commonalty of error among the Watergate perpetrators, as the arresting officers might have called them, and the radical Left of the 1960's. Too much zeal, that had been the sin of his people, the President himself suggested in one of his Watergate speeches in the spring; it was a sin and inexcusable, but also venial. Like the zealots of the Left, these people had put their cause above the law. They had been led into their error by the toleration that much liberal opinion had shown for the zealotry of the Left, for draft-dodgers and demonstrators of all sorts. The lesson to be drawn was that the law is sacred, rising above all causes, and no violation of it is excusable, none. A rededication to law and order on all sides, by all factions, was called for. The President indeed had been long calling for it. Watergate, we were left to infer, was actually a vindication of the President's long-held position, and a reproach to that large body of liberal opinion which had tolerated lawlessness, and ended by infecting even the righteous with it.

The point was most vividly if plaintively called to attention by Jeb Stuart Magruder. (We lawyers kept cringing as lawyer after lawyer turned up. But there was enough to cringe at for everybody. Why does Magruder have to be called Jeb Stuart, my colleague C. Vann Woodward has asked?) Magruder noted that he had been taught ethics at Williams College by William Sloane Coffin, Jr. The symbolic expression of the theme!

This was all a vulgar attempt to exonerate the dishonorable, a prelude to plea-bargaining. And the symbol chosen for the theme was a bad fit. When William Sloane Coffin, Jr., taught Jeb Stuart

Reprinted from *Commentary,* by permission; copyright © 1974 by the American Jewish Committee. Alexander M. Bickel, who died late in 1974, was Chancellor Kent Professor of Law and Legal History at Yale University and the author of many works on the American constitutional system, including *The Supreme Court and the Idea of Progress* and *Politics and the Warren Court.*

Magruder ethics, he wasn't William Sloane Coffin, Jr. That was in the 1950's, before Yale, and before there was any "Movement." It was when Benjamin Spock was still Dr. Spock, and before Coffin was Coffin.

And yet, to use the idiom of the Watergate actors, there is a point of contact, and it is of some interest, even though quite without taking account of it, sufficient explanations for much that has happened and for many of the actors may no doubt be found, or found unnecessary.

I don't know how many of Mr. Nixon's men can be credited, if that is the word, with self-righteous moral or ideological motivation. But perhaps for some of them moral or ideological imperatives clashed with the legal order more or less as they did for the radical Left in the 1960's. There is a well-known passage in E. M. Forster's essay "What I Believe" where he says that if he had to "choose between betraying my country and betraying my friend," he hoped "I should have the guts to betray my country." This was written in 1939, and Forster had witnessed the attempt by both the Nazi and Soviet dictatorships to impose a total commitment and obligation to the state, itself embodying an ideology, which was to override all other commitments and relationships. The world was full of wretched stories of children informing against parents, wives against husbands and possibly also vice versa, friends against friends, all glorying in it. Against this, Forster was in revulsion. He says just before the passage I quoted that he believes in personal relations, which in the age of faith, of the clash of creed against creed, in which he was sorry to find himself, were regarded as "bourgeois luxuries" to be got rid of so as to make room for dedication to "some movement or cause." He says he hates the idea of causes, and then goes into the passage declaring his choice of friend over country.

But the passage has most often been taken out of historical context. Country has been read literally as meaning any organized society and its legal order, which perhaps is what Forster meant; and friend has been read to refer not only to the personal loyalties Forster had in mind but also, very much against his sense, to ideologies and causes—precisely what he hated. And so in Forster's dictum, as received if not altogether as intended, we can find a connection between some at least of Mr. Nixon's men and part at least of the radical Left. Ideological imperatives and personal loyalty prevailed over the norms and commands of the legal order. They kept faith with their friends, and had the guts to betray their country.

It is not remarkable that self-righteousness and ideological fixation should be wedded to authoritarian attitudes, and that the temptation to abuse power should arise. What is interesting, what makes the point of contact a significant starting point for inquiry, what is interesting even about the vulgar—because wholly indiscriminate—attempt to turn Watergate into a reproach to liberal opinion, is that Watergate is evidence of a weakened capacity of our legal order to serve as a self-executing safeguard against this sort of abuse of power. The checks and balances of the government, the contrivance, in the words of the 51st *Federalist,* of "the interior structure of the government," so that "its several constituent parts may, by their mutual relations, be the means of keeping each other in their proper places"—this contrivance is working reasonably well. The inner structure was meant to insure accountability, and it is doing so. But it is accountability by crisis, accountability by trauma, accountability tending to shade into retribution. One would have expected that the legal order would have operated to prevent what we now know to have occurred. It is a first line of defense that has generally held: not always against plain theft, but effectively enough against self-righteous abuse of executive power in the service of ideological or moral ends. It has held in the past in this respect, making it unneccessary to reach the battlements and entrenchments of the constitutional checks and balances. It did not hold this time.

I come thus to the statement of a thesis. I do not pretend to explain Watergate or the Nixon Presidency. And I do not propose to understand, for fear that there may be some truth in the saying *tout comprendre, c'est tout pardonner.* Again, I am far from suggesting that Watergate was inevitable. My thesis is only—or at least the only explicit statement of it I am willing to make is—that much of what happened to the legal and social order in the fifteen years or so before Watergate was prologue. The scandals of corruption in our history had their climates, their prologues in war-profiteering and in general relaxation of standards. The Vietnam war has produced no major scandal or corruption. It and much that preceded it produced a moral fire storm, which was the prologue to Watergate.

In order to identify those aspects of recent history which I think came to a point of contact with Watergate, I must draw some distinctions concerning the position of conscientious objection and of civil disobedience in our legal order, as I see it. Our law has traditionally recognized a certain autonomy of conscience, and has therefore allowed certain conscientious objections, particularly to war, although not to war alone, as became happily evident when the Supreme Court in 1972 upheld the constitutional right of the Amish not to submit their young to organized education past the eighth grade. And even beyond the autonomy of conscience that the law is able to make allowance for within itself, the legal order may be said to countenance conscientious disobedience.

Much depends on the kind of law that is in question, the demands it makes of the individual, the foundation it has in shared values, and the kind of disobedience to it and its source. Frequently, however, the unlawfulness of disobedience to law on sincerely held grounds of conscience is not taken as conclusive against the legitimacy of disobedience. We often consider, rather, that disobedience raises a question about the law at which it is directed, a question not only about its effectiveness—that is obvious —but about its rightness or at least its utility.

In what I just said I have blurred a distinction, useful for many purposes, between conscientious objection and civil disobedience. Conscientious objection, as has been pointed out by many writers, among them notably Hannah Arendt and Ernest van den Haag, demands nothing more than exemption from a legal obligation. No further or broader challenge to a law inhers in conscientious objection. But as Hannah Arendt has written and as I have just implied, "conscientious objection can become politically significant when a number of consciences happen to coincide and the conscientious objectors decide to enter the marketplace and make their voices heard in public." There is then necessarily implicit a challenge to the law objected to, or at least the legal order perceives such a widespread manifestation of conscientious objection as a challenge to the law, and the objectors are assimilated to the ranks of civil disobedients.

As to civil disobedience, there is much conduct that bears its appearance and that in other, more unitary systems, which do not diffuse power and law-making authority as ours does, would indeed be civil disobedience. With us a great deal of such conduct is not. In our federation, there are laws within laws and laws above laws. Thus one system of laws which is valid and fully authoritative within itself may be called into question by appeal to another, generally superior system; and in some measure, it works the other way as well. It is possible, therefore, for men to behave in a manner which is lawful, but is not recognized as such by the legitimate authority in one or another place, and therefore constitutes defiance of that authority, and causes disorder; or in a manner that may turn out to be lawful, but that at the moment violates the positive law of a given place, also causes disorder, and what is more, cannot with assurance be assumed to prove lawful in the end. In a unitary system, behavior of this sort would carry every aspect of civil disobedience. But it is often invited by the many-tiered process of law formation that is characteristic of our system.

A general definition of civil disobedience, applicable to our legal order, would be the following: Civil disobedience is the act of disobeying formally binding general law on grounds of moral or political principle without challenging the validity of the law; or the incidental disobedience of general law which is itself neither challenged as invalid nor disapproved of in the course of agitating for change in public policies, actions, or social conditions which are regarded as bad on grounds of moral or political principle—all in circumstances where the legal order makes no allowance for the disobedience. This last qualification has to be added because the First Amendment is construed as making some allowance for the sort of incidental disobedience referred to in the second half of the definition.

In purpose if not in effect, civil disobedience differs greatly from conscientious objection. The effect of the coincidence of multiple consciences objecting to a law and the effect of civil disobedience may be the same. But conscientious objection is a withdrawal. Civil disobedience is ineluctably an attempt to coerce the legal order, an exercise of power in the sense in which Burke defined it: "Liberty, when men act in bodies, is *power.*" And it is not easy to make room for it, although I shall argue that our legal order does so. Thus not only the Hobbesian but the contractarian view of the nature and foundation of society can tolerate no civil disobedience at all. The contractarian view legitimates government as a compact among citizens, embodying the agreement of each to abide the judgment of all. The ends of government are substantially predetermined in the contractarian view, in that they are limited by timeless principles, the rights of man. Government is allowed some margin of error, but the premise is that it will normally act only in plausible pursuit of predetermined ends. If it should not, says Locke, the remedy is revolution, and there is a right to use force against the government. Short of the right of revolution, there is an absolute duty to obey. Rousseau held that the people, expressing themselves through universal suffrage, give voice to the general will, although he allowed that they might also not. The general will is the highest good, and when the people by majority vote give it voice, the individual owes absolute obedience, even unto death. If at times a minority has hold of the true general will it follows that absolute obedience is equally owed to it. This in fact, said Rousseau, only forces the individual to be free.

The latest contribution to contractarian theory, by Professor John Rawls, in his *A Theory of Justice,* is somewhat curious. It defines the general will—called justice as fairness—in more detail than Rousseau, and commits government to its effectuation. Like Rousseau, it then insists on popular sovereignty, modified only by some power in the judges to keep government within the limits dictated by the general will. And it posits a duty to obey. But it makes allowance, one may think inconsistently, for civil disobedience, defined as above, with the proviso that it be public and willing to accept punishment. Civil disobedience is allowed because, it turns out, justice as fairness—the general will—is not always readily ascertainable, the majority and the judges may be wrong, or less right than a protesting minority, and civil disobedience can play its role in helping the entire society decide what is right. In that event, it would seem, there is less to the prior detailed definition of justice as fairness than met the eye.

In the actual American legal order, ends are less permanently predetermined than by contractarian theory, faith in majoritarianism is less enthusiastic than Rousseau's, readiness to have recourse to revolution is not as great as Locke's, and there is little willingness to accept the righteous dictates of a minority possessed of the true general will. What is above all important is consent—not a presumed theoretical consent, but a continuous actual one, born of continual responsiveness. There is popular sovereignty, and there are votes in which majorities or pluralities prevail, but that is not nearly all. Majorities are in large part fictions. They exist only on election day and they can be registered on very few issues. To be responsive and to enjoy consent, government must register numerous expressions of need and interest by numerous groups, and it must register relative intensities of need and interest. Neither the vote nor speech—the latter, after all, an elite exercise—sufficiently differentiates needs and interests, or expresses intensity. Civil disobedience can often effectively do so. Hence it is that civil disobedience has accompanied so many of the most fruitful reform movements in American history. Hence it is that its legitimacy must be recognized.

But there must be limits, both to conscientious objection and to civil disobedience, limits to be stated not as positive law imposed by the enforcement machinery of the legal order, but as a moral obligation, a duty to obey. For use of the enforcement machinery of the legal order denotes the point at which it has broken down. The test of a legal order is its self-executing capacity, its moral authority. In an extraordinarily sustained experience of civil disobedience and conscientious objection on the part of at least three distinct, sizable groups in the society over a period of some fifteen years, which perhaps no other society could have endured without a change of regime—in this sustained experience, I shall suggest, the limits were often transgressed. The experience started with white Southerners in the mid-1950's; it was followed and overlapped by the civil-rights movement; and it ended with and was overlapped by the white-middle-class movement against the war, which bade fair for a while to take permanent shape as a movement addressing numerous other issues as well, from ecology up, down, and sideways to gay liberation. The limits, as I say, were transgressed, and in some measure, I am willing to suggest, Watergate is a replica of the transgressions.

A first and most easily stated limit was very clear to Lincoln when he opposed the *Dred Scott* decision. "We do not propose," he said, "that when Dred Scott has been decided to be a slave by the court, we as a mob will decide him to be free. . . . but we nevertheless do oppose that decision as a political rule which shall be binding." The line is thus drawn between the general law, the law of the land, as it is commonly called, enunciated in a judicial decision, or *mutatis mutandis* in legislation, and the judicial judgment addressed to the parties in an actual case. There is no moral duty always and invariably to obey the former. There is a moral duty to obey the latter.

This limit was transgressed repeatedly in the South during the 1950's and 1960's, by private and official persons, and by mobs who disobeyed or violated judicial decrees. It was transgressed as well by disruptive courtroom behavior on the part of the radical Left in the late 1960's, which amounted to the same thing, denoting as it did a rejection of the process and necessarily, therefore, of its results. Both kinds of transgression were perhaps more spectacular than numerous, but they told.

Another sort of limit has to do with means. Violence must be a monopoly of the state. In private hands, whatever its possible misuses by the state, it is always an unjust weapon. It is inadmissible, but was of course widely used and excused. Only the other day the historian Gabriel Kolko said of the man who planted a bomb in 1970 at the University of Wisconsin's Mathematics Research Center, which killed one person and wounded four: "To condemn Karl Armstrong is to condemn a whole anguished generation. His intentions were more significant than the unanticipated consequences of his actions."

Some nonviolent interference with the justified and lawful activities and expectations of innocent third parties is an inevitable concomitant of civil disobedience, and if contained and civil, is to be borne, subject to other limits to which I shall come in a moment. But when the interference is massive, when it is not civil, when it borders on violence or threatens it, when it is coercive not in its ultimate intent, as all civil disobedience necessarily is, but in its immediate impact, when its imposition is not of inconvenience but of terror, then it is unacceptable. And yet we saw quantities of it.

Additional limits, at least equally important, are much more difficult to state. One, also having to do with means, is suggested by the action of Daniel Ellsberg in using his position of trust to spirit out the Pentagon Papers, or the action of the unknown person who handed to Jack Anderson a transcript of a secret meeting on the India-Pakistan war at the White House presided over by Henry Kissinger. There is in such cases the question whether a legal obligation was breached. This was and remains a question in some doubt in both the examples I am discussing, which the aborted Ellsberg litigation did not settle. I assume, strictly for purposes of argument, that a legal obligation was breached, although in truth I believe it to be quite doubtful that there is on the books a statute that effectively renders illegal what Ellsberg, for example, did.

At any rate, these were acts of conscience taken against at least a privately formulated obligation. They were taken in conditions where conscience could have been satisfied in part by resignation.

Instead Ellsberg and the unknown person to whom I referred allowed their consciences to push them into affirmative action. That was not because as moral beings they could do no other. It was rather because they wanted to make others do otherwise than they were doing. Their actions, their own individual actions at the time they took them, moreover, not possibly their acts multiplied by the acts of thousands of others which in the aggregate might exert political pressure: their own acts, unaided by other independent consciences, had a different and greater impact than ordinary conscientious objection, I should say a coercive impact, lent them by the trust that had been reposed in the actors personally. These actors were not denying the legal order their own participation in its immoral activity, as they viewed it. They sought rather to coerce the legal order by destroying *pro tanto* the procedures by which it conducts its business.

I do not say that such acts can never be justified. Suppose Ellsberg had discovered evidence of plans to herd people into concentration camps and gas them, or evidence of treason? These, however, are examples of an extreme kind of moral outbreak activating the individual. My point is that impositional, coercive acts of conscience of this sort should require a much higher moral threshold than does passive conscientious objection, and I do not believe it was clear in either the Ellsberg or the Kissinger secret-meeting case that the threshold had been reached. Certainly the Vietnam war raised moral issues. But the secrecy of the Pentagon Papers did not raise the same ones, by any means, even though the mendacity of government is a serious matter. And it was self-deception to think that release of the Papers would solve the moral problem of the war. Anyone contemplating an impositional coercive act of conscience must recognize orders of magnitude among moral questions. An insufficiently differentiated exaltation of wrongs to the same moral level is quite entirely the same as, and no less dangerous than, moral blindness.

Just as there are circumstances when a breach of duty of the impositional sort committed by Ellsberg could be justified, so conditions arise when extralegal action by a President in the interest of national security are called for. Again, the threshold must be very high. But if challenged, such actions may in the proper circumstances be ratified as legal, if only from necessity, as the removal of Japanese Americans from the West Coast in 1942 unfortunately was. The principle of legitimation is the simple one once stated by

Justice Jackson: The Constitution is not a suicide pact. The President has the function at times, even the duty, to see that it does not become one. Lincoln discharged this duty. And even when not ratified by the institutions of the legal order—as the seizure of the steel industry by Harry Truman, or Lincoln's suspension of *habeas corpus,* or martial law in Hawaii in World War II, or domestic wiretapping by Presidents from Franklin D. Roosevelt through Nixon were not ratified—such actions are not necessarily condemned. But the threshold for taking them has in the past been enormously high. Legal norms have radiated with powerful force. In a paroxysm of paranoia, to state the case as indulgently as possible, the Nixon administration lowered the threshold. Early on, before Ellsberg, Mr. Nixon and his people may well have sorely abused what they regarded, not unjustly, as wiretapping authority legitimated by practice, and they at least contemplated other outrages, but it cannot be entirely a coincidence that Ellsberg's removal of the Pentagon Papers from the Rand Corporation was the occasion for creation of the White House plumbers unit, so called. Threshold for threshold.

I set aside the judgment made by a newspaper in publishing what Mr. Ellsberg spirited out. Here also careful discriminations are required, but they are not controlled and hardly affected, I think, by the provenance of the material. I would say only, touching this issue glancingly as I do, that short of the case—plans for concentration camps, treason, and the like—in which it is plainly justified, the more unjustified the breach of the government's trust in bringing the materials out, because their content is not such as to meet the high moral threshold required, the more justified and the easier the judgment of a newspaper in publishing them.

Returning to civil disobedience, let me restate, in approaching yet another limit, the grounds on which the legitimacy of civil disobedience can be rested. It is because on most issues we command no definite answers grounded in solid and generally shared values that we value an open, responsive, varied, and continual process of law-formation and provide numerous stages of decision-making, most of them provisional, and numerous opportunities for revision and resistance, including civil disobedience. But not only do the outcomes of the law-formation process, however provisional, count for something; what is more important, in the middle distance, and if also provisionally then over a much longer term, so that for a time they have a relatively enduring aspect, we do as a legal order hold some values, some principles, by which we judge the process and even some of its outcomes. Unless these are defended against coercive political action, there is no legal order, or at any rate, there is not this one. Therefore, the use of civil disobedience, not to redress grievances on the assumption of the continued operation of the system and by plausible appeal to its own principles, but against it, ought not be tolerated. Civil disobedience is one thing, revolutionary activity quite another, and the difference between them is told not only by their manner, but also by their objectives.

The distinction is rigorously drawn by Mr. Rawls in his *A Theory of Justice,* to which I referred earlier. The distinction was not drawn with anything like Mr. Rawls's rigor in the 1960's. Much of the disobedience of the late 1960's was aimed not at the government of the day, but at the system, and it opposed the system, not as flawed and perfectible, but as evil and abominable. The rhetoric was loud and it was reckless and vicious. It abandoned all pretense of allegiance, it acknowledged no restraint and no bounds. Yet it was often tolerated and even echoed by seemingly responsible opinion in the press, in the universities, and among political leaders. Cries of repression and of fascism, for example, were raised almost as soon as Mr. Nixon took office, and they were irresponsible and unfounded at the time, no matter how plausible they may now seem in retrospect. At the time, they were bound to have an effect on administration morale. Men who are loudly charged with repression before they have done anything to substantiate the charge are apt to proceed to substantiate it.

In a larger sense, toleration of this rhetoric and of disobedience with such aims undermined the moral authority of the liberal tradition in this country, which as Louis Hartz pointed out years ago is at once also the American conservative tradition, or at least the tradition that conserves the liberal American legal and political order. Hartz quoted the distinguished insight of Gunnar Myrdal, as he called it: "America is . . . conservative. . . . But the principles conserved are liberal and some, indeed, are radical." Liberalism has always been challenged from both flanks, and has always been a little anxious, since Jefferson, and like the Center in the third French republic, to make no enemies on the Left. It has historically been successful in coopting all but the revolutionary Left, moving far enough toward it to draw its sympathizers and outriders, but generally not so far as to be itself coopted rather than coopting.

To move too far is to lose moral authority, and that rather than numbers is the source of the liberal ascendancy in American politics, which safeguards the norms of the American legal order against the lawlessness and ultimate authoritarianism of radical movements. Liberalism embraced too much of the Left in the 1940's, and the result was the triumph for a moment of the radicalism of Joseph R. McCarthy. It embraced inexcusably much in the late 1960's. In this sense Watergate is to American liberalism as McCarthyism was.

Still another necessary limit of civil disobedience was transgressed. Like law itself, civil disobedience is habit-forming, and the habit it forms is destructive of the legal order. Disobedience, even if legitimate in every other way, must not be allowed to become epidemic. Individuals are under a duty to ration themselves, to assess occasions in terms of their relative as well as absolute importance. For disobedience is attended by the overhanging threat of anarchy. We did not ration ourselves, and those in authority in the universities in the late 1960's imposed no rationing. Coming as the third wave of massive disobedience movements in fifteen years, the demonstrations of the late 1960's, including the most peaceable and legitimate ones of all, carried the clear and present danger of anarchy. And their objectives were of course not restricted to stopping the war. They went on to ecology and to numberless other social and economic objectives.

The point may be put in another and more general way with reference not only to civil disobedience. In 1969, President Kingman Brewster of Yale charged a number of speakers about to appear at a Yale alumni seminar with addressing the subject, "What is happening to morality today?" My answer at the time, if I may quote myself, was: "It threatens to engulf us." The legal order heaved and groaned for years under a prodigality of moral causes, and if not broken, it is no wonder that it is badly bent. Vietnam, let us not forget, was not only a moral error, but for its authors, a moral urgency. The urgencies of "peace with honor," of the clean life, of patriotism—in a word, Watergate—were merely the last straws. It is ironic, but entirely natural, that "law-and-order" as a moral imperative should have clashed with the legal order.

The legal order, after all, is an accommodation. It cannot sustain the continuous assault of moral imperatives, not even the moral imperative of "law-and-order," which as a moral imperative has only a verbal resemblance to the ends of the legal order. No legal order can sustain such a bombardment, and the less so a federal constitutional order of separated and diffused powers. It is the premise of our legal order that its own complicated arrangements, although subject to evolutionary change, are more important than any momentary objective. This premise must give way at times, of course, to accommodate inevitable change. And change which is significant, as Justice Brandeis once wrote, manifests itself more "in intellectual and moral conceptions than in material things." But our legal order cannot endure too rapid a pace of change in moral conceptions, and its fundamental premise is that its own stability is itself a high moral value, in most circumstances the highest. The legal order must be given time to absorb change, to accommodate it to itself as well as itself to it. If the pace is forced, there can be no law.

The assault upon the legal order by moral imperatives wasn't only or perhaps even the most effectively an assault from the outside. It came as well from within, in the Supreme Court headed for fifteen years by Earl Warren. The judicial hallmark of Chief Justice Warren was that when some lawyer would be standing before him arguing his side of a case on the basis of some legal doctrine or other, or making a procedural point, or contending that the Constitution allocated competence over a given issue to another branch of government than the Supreme Court or to the states rather than to the federal government, the Chief Justice would shake him off saying, "Yes, yes, yes, but is it [whatever the case exemplified about law or about the society] is it *right?* Is it *good?*" More than once, and in some of its most important actions, the Warren Court got over doctrinal difficulties or issues of the allocation of competences among various institutions by asking what it viewed as a decisive practical question: If the Court did not take a certain action which was *right* and *good,* would other institutions do so, given political realities? The Warren Court took the greatest pride in cutting through legal technicalities, in piercing through procedure to substance. But legal technicalities are the stuff of law, and piercing through a particular substance to get to procedures suitable to many substances is in fact what the task of law most often is.

From within and from without, then, the legal order was bombarded by moral imperatives, and was reduced to submission time and again. The derogators of procedure and of technicalities, and other anti-institutional forces, rode high, on the bench as well as off. These were the armies of conscience and of ideology. If it is paradoxical that they were also the armies of a new populism, it is not a paradox to wonder at, for it has occurred often before, not least of all in Rousseau, who may be counted the patron philosopher of the time. The paradox, of course, is that the people whom the populist exalts may well, will frequently, not vote for the results that conscience and ideology dictate. But then one can always hope, or identify the general will with the people despite their votes, and let the Supreme Court bespeak the people's general will when the vote comes out wrong.

It has been a time of populism to the Left and populism to the Right, strongly encouraged by the Supreme Court. There was a powerful strain of populism in the rhetoric by which the Court supported its one-man, one-vote doctrine, and after promulgating it the Court strove mightily to strike down all barriers, not only the poll tax, but duration of residence, all manner of special qualifications, and even in some measure, age, to the enlargement and true universalization of the franchise. In this the Court led successfully. It became irresistible dogma that no qualification for voting made any sense. It didn't matter that you were a transient—the election is a snapshot, and wherever it catches you, you vote with no questions asked. No connection to place is relevant, there is no room for balancing interests and places, no need to structure institutions so that they might rest on different electoral foundations and in the aggregate be better able to generate consent. Every impediment, every distortion, including the electoral college, must go. All that matters is the people, told by the head.

Here the connection with attitudes that at least contributed to Watergate is direct. It was utterly inevitable that such a populist fixation should tend toward the concentration of power in that single institution which has the most immediate link to the largest constituency. Naturally the consequence was a Gaullist Presidency, making war, making peace, spending, saving, being secret, being open, doing what is necessary, and needing no excuse for aggregating power to itself beside the excuse that it could do more effectively what other institutions, particularly Congress, did not do very rapidly or very well, or under particular political circumstances would not do at all. This was a leaf from the Warren Court's book, but the Presidency could undertake to act anti-institutionally in this fashion with more justification because, unlike the Court, it could claim not only a constituency, but the largest one. This Presidency acknowledged accountability only at quadrennial plebiscites, but not to other, less plebiscitary institutions, and certainly not to irresponsible private ones, or to something called "public opinion," which is led and formed in mysterious ways, rather than being told by the head.

The accumulation of power in the Presidency did not begin with Richard M. Nixon, of course, but it reached heights made possible by the populism of the day. There was a time there, soon after the election of 1972, when Mr. Nixon gave the impression that he thought the American political process had taken place, so to speak, that it was over for a while, and that he could simply rule. We know again now that an election is the beginning as well as the culmination of a political process, and that the President, separate, independent, and critically important as he is, is part of the process, not its ruler. We were being led to forget, however, and had it not been for Watergate, conceivably we might have forgotten.

The Presidency of inherent powers, futurism, populism, and certainly moral urgency—these have too often been the vestments of liberalism in this century, though worn for the most part with a certain modesty. In the 1960's, the liberals, or large segments of them, consented to share these vestments, all but the first, with the radical Left, which adding several dashes of outrageous color, wore them immodestly. Diffusion of power, pragmatism, the relativism of values, gradualism, institutionalism, process, procedure, legality, technicalities—these were allowed to become the cloak of conservatism, indeed of reaction, and were not wanted on the voyage. Well, this cloak was not wanted in the White House either, we have learned. I don't know when Mr. Nixon caught the liberals bathing, but he did walk off with their clothes, and stood forth wearing the plebiscitary Presidency, his own futurism, and his own moral imperatives. We are all liberals, we are all conservatives, Mr. Nixon might have said, as for Jefferson we were all Republicans and all Federalists in 1800.

Watergate is the latest assault, the only one which was at once vicious and powerful, although other powerful ones were damaging, albeit not vicious—the latest assault in an age of assaultive politics. We cannot survive a politics of moral attack. I don't know how near a thing Watergate was, but perhaps it will be said that it was too near. We must resume the politics of what Burke called the "computing principle: adding, subtracting, multiplying, and dividing." The denominations to be computed are very often moral, to be sure. But few if any are absolute, few if any imperative. And the highest morality almost always is the morality of process, what Professor Paul Freund, speaking of Justice Brandeis's approach to issues, called "morality of mind."

The Danger of State Secrecy

THOMAS I. EMERSON

Secrecy has always been a crucial feature of the governmental process, but the expansion of government functions and the development of mass communications have given it new dimensions and made it a challenging issue of our day. Thus the American people and the whole world were taken to the brink of atomic war in the Cuban missile crisis, without knowing what was going on. In the U-2 affair, not only was the country unaware of the flights over Soviet territory but one of our most revered Presidents was caught in a flagrant lie. Cambodia was subject to extensive bombing for more than a year while the American people were told it was not happening and elaborate machinery was set up by the military bureaucracy to conceal the facts. Most recently, a massive network of deceit has been uncovered in the White House itself.

These are just a few of the shocking peaks of government secrecy; the day-to-day ramifications of secrecy permeate every level of government and create more pervasive and equally difficult problems. The effect of secrecy upon the operation of modern government is baleful and the task of controlling it is enormous. All that can be done here is, very briefly, to examine some of the basic philosophic and political considerations that underlie the use of secrecy in government, make note of some constitutional and statutory tools for dealing with the problem, and suggest some working rules for achieving a more just and effective mode of operation.

It long has been recognized that information is a source of power. The President controls foreign relations in large part because he alone has access to critical information about events in foreign countries and our responses to them. Similarly, the power of the executive branch to formulate an economic program, such as one to deal with the energy crisis, flows out of the massive volume of facts and

Reprinted by permission from *The Nation*. Copyright © 1974. Thomas I. Emerson, Linus Professor of Law, Yale Law School, is the author of *Toward a General Theory of the First Amendment* and *The System of Freedom of Expression*.

figures stored in the files of the bureaucracy. And the withholding of information from other participants in the governmental process is well understood to be a method of aggrandizing and in fact monopolizing power. Control of access to the factual material closes off public debate, eases the task of responding to criticism, and ultimately confirms the whole decision-making process to those who possess the crucial information.

As a general proposition, secrecy in a democratic society is a source of *illegitimate* power. This is so for a number of reasons.

In the first place, withholding of information by any part of the government is in direct conflict with democratic principles of decision making. Under our constitutional theory, the people are the masters and government is the servant, and it is incongruous that the master should be denied the information upon which to direct the activities of his servants. This is not just abstract theory. Regardless of how well the democratic process may work, regardless of the extent to which our mechanisms of government actually allow the ordinary citizen to participate in making choices, *no* rational choice can be made in the absence of adequate information.

Furthermore, under our constitutional system each branch of government has a part to play. For one branch to keep secret from another branch information it needs to perform its function, is to undermine the whole principle of the separation but coordination of powers. In the case of the legislative branch, the need for access to information possessed by the executive is virtually coextensive with that of the executive branch. In the case of the judicial branch, the need is less extensive but fully necessary in those areas where it exists.

Second, withholding information from citizens of a democratic society is unjust, morally wrong. We fully accept that when the government makes a decision about the fate of an individual, such as to confine him to prison or deprive him of his property, justice requires that he be afforded due process of law. And due process involves, as its most basic element, that the citizen be furnished all the information upon which the decision in his case is founded. What difference does it make whether the governmental decision at issue affects only a single citizen or many citizens collectively? There may be practical difficulties in establishing appropriate procedures in the latter case, but the issue of affording justice is the same. In other words, in our society the individual has a moral right to exercise control over his own destiny. It is the minimum price demanded by him, and owed to him, for bowing to collective authority.

Third, to the extent that information is withheld from a citizen the basis for government control over him becomes coercion, not persuasion. The citizen is given no rational ground for accepting a decision; he must submit to it as a matter of force. It is the obligation of democratic government to suppress the use of coercion and encourage the factor of acquiescence, but no such policy is possible when the operation of government is secret. Indeed, secrecy is the very mark of totalitarian government.

Fourth, secrecy is politically unwise. In the long run it leads not to support of government but to disaffection. One reason for this is that the concealment of information tends to engender anxiety, fear, panic, and extremism. It eliminates the possibility that the citizenry can face its problems on a rational basis and leaves room only for irrational response. Moreover, the disaffection thus aroused leads to suppression, and that in turn demands more secrecy. The process, as we are beginning to be aware, can accelerate.

Fifth, secrecy is totally inconsistent with the ultimate need for confidence in government that is essential to successful administration of public affairs and peaceful social change. Concealment of information by its nature leads to affirmative deception. In the end, however, much of the information will come out, partly by the passage of time, partly by leaks, partly by the efforts of a free press. The result is a credibility gap, one of the most ominous developments in modern government.

Broadly speaking, then, secrecy in government accompanies evil in government. There is, indeed, a symbiotic relationship—government wrongs are kept secret because they are evil; and evil is done because it can be kept secret.

Historically, no clear mandate for banning secrecy in government resulted from the work of the Constitutional Convention (indeed its own sessions were secret). The Constitution expressly provides that some operations of Congress might be kept from public view in that, while each house is obliged to keep and publish a journal of its proceedings, it is not required to publish "such parts as might in [its] judgment require secrecy." And President Washington refused on several occasions to provide Congress with documents which he determined should be withheld in the public interest. On the other hand, some provisions of the original Constitution were designed to eliminate secrecy in the workings of government. In voting on bills in each house, the "yeas and nays of the members . . . on any question shall, at the desire of one-fifth of those present, be entered on the journal." Similar provision for public accountability was made with respect to voting on the overriding of a Presidential veto.

Not until recent times, however, did a constitutional basis for open government begin to emerge. The applicable doctrines are derived mainly from modern ideas concerning the separation of powers, the First Amendment, and due process of law. Limitations are to be found primarily in the constitutional right of privacy. But despite some advance in these concepts, as yet only the bare outlines of effective constitutional doctrine can be discerned.

Separation of powers is normally conceived as prohibiting each branch of government from interfering with the work of another, but it can also be viewed affirmatively, in more modern terms, as including the right of each branch to receive from another such assistance as it needs to carry out its functions. As already noted, this would give the legislative branch virtually unlimited access to any information possessed by the executive branch, because the power of Congress to appropriate funds, to oversee the work of the executive branch, and to enact laws generally would give it a right of access to almost the entire spectrum of information held by the executive.

The principal constitutional limitation upon these powers, advanced by the executive branch historically and currently, has been the doctrine of executive privilege. More detailed treatment of the legitimate scope of executive privilege is reserved for later consideration. Here it suffices to say that while the doctrine has been relied on from time to time over the years (though the term "executive privilege" is a more recent coinage), the issues have ordinarily been settled in the political rather than the judicial arena, and usually by compromise. As a result, there is little constitutional law on the subject. The only court decisions which deal squarely with it are the rulings of the District and Circuit courts for the District of Columbia in the recent Watergate tapes case. Both those courts forcefully rejected the extravagant contention of Mr. Nixon and his lawyers that executive privilege allowed the President to withhold any information that he deemed required secrecy in the "public interest." The exact scope of executive privilege, however, remains undefined.

The main constitutional basis for the proposition that the operations of government should be open to the ordinary citizen lies in the First Amendment. Here again, the constitutional provision has been traditionally conceived as enforcing a negative—that the government shall not in any manner interfere with the right of individuals or groups to freedom of expression. Two additional features of First Amendment law, however, have recently begun to take shape, and both are directly related to the maintenance of open government.

The first deals with the right of reporters, scholars, and other gatherers of facts to have access to sources of information. Obviously any system of freedom of expression must recognize the establishment and maintenance of such a right. An untrammeled privilege to speak on a subject, but with no opportunity to obtain the relevant facts about that subject, guarantees but an empty freedom. The Supreme Court has dealt with this problem in only one case, involving the power of grand juries to compel newspaper reporters to reveal information obtained by them under a pledge of confidentiality. The Supreme Court recognized the basic constitutional right, agreeing that "news gathering" does "qualify for First Amendment protection," and adding, "without some protection for seeking out the news, freedom of the press could be eviscerated." But it refused to accept the specific First Amendment claim made in the case. Thus the general principle has been established but its application so far is limited.

The other development concerns what has come to be called the public's "right to know." The obverse of the right to speak, it embraces the right of persons to listen, to read, to observe; in short, to receive communications from others. The right to know implies, further, a right of access to the information necessary to enrich and make meaningful the basic guarantee. This right to know is a much more amorphous constitutional concept than the right to speak, and hence far more difficult to reduce to workable operating rules. Nevertheless it is fundamental to any system of freedom of expression that would meet the needs of a democratic society.

The Supreme Court first clearly acknowledged a constitutional right to know in a 1965 decision invalidating a federal statute that sought to impose restrictions upon receiving mail from abroad which had been designated by the government as "Communist political propaganda." In 1969 the Supreme Court, upholding the right of persons to read pornography in the privacy of their own homes, reaffirmed that "[i]t is now well established that the Constitution protects the right to receive information and ideas." And in the same year, in a case upholding the fairness doctrine for broadcasting, the Supreme Court declared that "[i]t is the right of the viewers and listeners, not the right of the broadcasters, which is paramount." Yet the Supreme Court, once again, has been loath to accord real substance to the right it has recognized in theory. In its most recent decision it declined to give any weight to the contention by a group of scholars that the government's refusal of a visa to a Belgian Marxist economist, who had been invited to lecture in the United States, violated their constitutional right to know.

The third possibility for invoking constitutional doctrine to bar secrecy in government grows out of an expansion of current concepts of due process of law. This ancient legal precept, first formulated in the Magna Carta, affirms that government decision making must follow procedures which the community recognizes to be just.

Due process has been applied most extensively to decision making by the judicial branch. And it is fair to say that, as a general proposition, it forbids the use of secret information in the judicial process. The basic rule in criminal cases is that, if the government refuses to reveal evidence upon which it relies, or withholds evidence known to be relevant to guilt or innocence, the court will dismiss the prosecution. No exceptions are permitted, even when national security is invoked as grounds for refusing to disclose. In civil cases the general rule is open to some exception. Thus, where a citizen sued the government for damages and sought information in the possession of the government, the Supreme Court held that the government might refuse to supply the information when national security would be jeopardized. On the other hand, where the government brings the civil action, the same rule as in criminal cases would seem to apply.

The requirements of due process also apply to decisions of the executive branch. In fact it is in the field of administrative law that the greatest expansion of due process has occurred. Here again, as in the judicial process, reliance upon evidence not disclosed to the parties is as a general proposition prohibited by due process concepts. Only in loyalty cases, where the government appeals to national security, have the courts wavered at all. Further, the right to compel disclosure of evidence in the possession of the government has steadily expanded.

Due process has had least application in the legislative sphere. Yet even here its concepts have been applied to the operation of legislative investigating committees.

The basic notions of due process, as already suggested, can clearly be extended to the use of secrecy in government operations. Decision making on a collective scale, it can be asserted, ought to follow the rules of fairness to the same degree as decision making that is directed against specific individuals or organizations. Access to all the facts, by all interested parties, is as essential to a just result in the one situation as in the other. The only difference is that in the individual case the facts are usually specific, whereas in the collective case they are general. This may make some difference in the form of rules necessary to implement the constitutional right, but it does not change the nature of the right asserted. One must concede, however, that the problem of government secrecy has thus far not been approached in these terms.

To complete the constitutional picture, it is necessary to consider the limitations imposed upon the obligation of the government to make information available to all citizens. As noted previously, these flow primarily out of the constitutional right of privacy. The right of privacy was first formulated by the Supreme Court in the Connecticut birth control case of 1965. Its parameters remain largely undefined, but the main concept is that the constitution recognizes with respect to each person a zone of privacy from which the government, its agents, and its laws are excluded. The zone of privacy derives from the right of a person to live as an individual, in respects to which he or she is not responsible to the collective, and intrusions by the collective are constitutionally forbidden.

It follows that some information in the possession of the government may not be publicly disclosed without violating the constitutional right of privacy. The information thus protected would involve mainly personal matters found in personnel files, loyalty dossiers, or investigative reports not matured into litigation. The drawing of a specific line between public and private matter might not be easy in individual cases, but it would occasion no more difficulty than many other lines drawn in the course of constitutional adjudication. The goal is simply to eliminate from the public forum material that is of legitimate concern only to the individual involved.

This sketch of a constitutional framework for open government suggests the possibility of developing fundamental constitutional principles into a mandatory protective structure. But that point has not yet been reached, nor does it seem imminent. Meanwhile, reliance must be placed upon the possibility of solving the problem through legislation.

The basic power of the legislature to eliminate or curtail secrecy in government through statutory enactment is not open to question. The legislative branch is authorized to make laws dealing broadly with the organization and operation of the executive and judicial branches. The only limits upon this power would arise from a constitutional claim asserted on the basis of executive privilege, a possibly similar claim urged by the judiciary, and claims of privacy advanced by individual citizens. The scope of executive privilege, as noted above, is uncertain, but it is unlikely that the courts would employ that doctrine to nullify in any substantial degree statutory directions that the executive furnish the legislature with specified materials. The other limitations would present minimal problems to an open system.

Unfortunately, the existing statutory structure is primitive and ineffective. The Freedom of Information Act, passed in 1966, starts out bravely by asserting that "[e]ach agency, on request for identifiable records . . . shall make the records promptly available to any person." Thereafter, however, the statute provides for nine exceptions which take away most of what was previously granted. One of these exceptions, for example, provides that the statute does not apply to matters that are "specifically required by Executive order to be kept secret in the interest of national defense or foreign policy." This removes all classified material from the operation of the Act. Furthermore, the Supreme Court has held that the courts have no power under the Act to review the executive decision as to whether material was properly classified or to force the executive to separate out classified from unclassified material embodied in a single document. In addition, the executive agencies have interposed serious administrative obstacles to the obtaining of information, even when it is rightfully available under the statute. State statutes, mostly providing for open meetings of legislative bodies, have made even fewer inroads on government secrecy.

The statutory scheme for eliminating government secrecy needs a substantial overhauling. That revision is not likely to come, however, until there is more general agreement on basic principles and more careful study of specific working rules. To that problem we now turn.

Remarkably little attention has been paid to the details of a system of nonsecret government. Discussion has centered around broad questions of whether executive privilege should exist, or has focused on the validity of executive privilege in a particular situation. Thus the development of a comprehensive set of basic principles and working rules has been slow to mature.

The underlying principle must be that decisions which the government makes without disclosing to all parties concerned the full information on which they are based cannot be considered a legitimate exercise of governmental power. The principle derives from the philosophical and political considerations set forth earlier. It means that any withholding of information in the governmental process must be an exception, expressly justified as such. The basis for making an exception must be that nondisclosure is unarguably essential to the performance of a proper government function. It is not sufficient that disclosure would simply make the function more difficult to perform or would change it in some way. Quite the contrary, it is to be expected that open operation of government, such as the deliberation of a legislative committee, might result in substantial change both in form and substance. Only where secrecy is inherent in a specific operation can it be justified.

Starting from these premises, one must define specific areas of exceptions. The first involves the advice privilege. It authorizes withholding information relevant to that part of the decision-making process which relies upon free and frank discussion with subordinate, coordinate, or superior officials. The justification is a sad but true reflection of modern bureaucracy—unless such an exchange of ideas, trying out of proposals, and general brainstorming is kept confidential, the whole process of reaching a reasoned decision is acutely impeded. This exception is most applicable to decision making in the executive branch, where the bureaucratic process is especially inhibited unless protection is afforded for new, experimental, or offbeat ideas. It is also applicable to some parts of the judicial process, particularly in connection with court conferences for decision making or in relations between a judge and his law clerk. The exception is least applicable to the legislative process, being limited, perhaps, to personal interchange between members of the legislature and to the relation of a member to his staff. Furthermore, in its application to all branches of government, the advice exception applies only to statements of opinion or ideas, not to matters of fact; it is not legitimately invoked with respect to discussions involving commission of a crime; and it requires the separation of privileged material from unprivileged, with only the former subject to nondisclosure.

A second exception relates to national security. The largest amount of government secrecy, administered mainly through the classification system, is based on that claim, and most of it is unjustified. There are few issues of national security which do not demand public discussion on the basis of all available information. It is inconceivable, for example, that in a democratic society such major decisions as the military buildup in Vietnam should be made by a few top government officials, to the total exclusion of the rest of the country. It should be noted that the Supreme Court, in holding that warrantless wiretapping was not justified as a matter of national security, has rejected the basic contention that reasons of national security authorize government operations in violation of constitutional principles.

The national security exception, therefore, should be limited to those situations where nondisclosure is clearly justified as a matter of immediate military necessity. This would confine the exception largely to information concerning the development of new weapons and actual tactical military operations. Acceptance of such limited exceptions would, of course, bring about a drastic change in methods of making decisions concerning national security matters. The burden of showing the need for broader exceptions, however, is difficult to meet.

A third exception must be devised for some aspects of foreign relations. This is probably the most troublesome area to define or keep within bounds. The complexities are many. Thus other countries may not adhere to our views or practices with regard to disclosure of matters of mutual concern; negotiations with foreign nations involve a bargaining process, a situation which raises special problems discussed hereinafter; and relations with other countries sometimes involve the use of procedures, such as espionage and counterespionage, which cannot be brought within the democratic principles upon which the theory of disclosure is premised. On the other hand, most of the information that has to do with foreign relations is of vital concern to the legislative branch and to the citizen. It is a safe assumption that much more information can be made public, without jeopardizing our foreign relations, than is now provided. The answer would seem to lie in framing exceptions in terms of those features which have just been noted as causing the major problems. Nondisclosure would not be justified merely because requested by another country: it would have to live with our policy. But secrecy would be permissible to the extent necessary to prevent revelation of bargaining positions, and protect espionage or counterespionage activities.

A fourth exception is justified where decision making is the result of a bargaining process and the disclosure of information at a premature stage would jeopardize the negotiations. Such a situation arises in collective bargaining with a union of government employees, in advance disclosure of a position of litigation, or in other procedures which involve development of fall-back positions. Under such circumstances the government should be entitled to the same advantages as its opponent, or a nongovernment bargainer. The withholding of such information, which in any case would be temporary, would seem permissible.

The fifth exception, already mentioned, concerns protection of the right of privacy and would extend to certain personnel, loyalty, and investigative files. Here the emphasis is upon the personal nature of the information. The material is normally not a matter of public concern, and nondisclosure would not seriously affect the conduct of public business.

A final word needs to be said about the administration of such a system of open government. Experience to date with the Freedom of Information Act has shown that two administrative matters are of prime importance. One involves the problem of separating secret from nonsecret material when both kinds are embodied in the same document or occur in the same conversation. This separation may pose some difficulties, including some cost, but it is essential that the effort to separate be pursued to the maximum degree possible. The other essential administrative requirement is that the decision of whether to disclose or keep secret must not be entrusted exclusively to the branch of government which possesses the information. A neutral arbitrator is imperative. In practical terms this means that the courts should have power to review all actions of the executive and legislative branches on these issues and to make final determinations on the basis of the applicable principles of law.

The above formulations, though only rough approximations, may point the way to the kind of legal structure that is necessary to maintain an effective system of open government. If we can succeed in this, we shall go far to make the exercise of government power legitimate and to encourage its use only in the degree necessary to solve our pressing problems. And we shall almost certainly make future Watergate disasters impossible.

3. Public Opinion

Watergate is one of those rare events that has the power to stir the sleeping giant, public opinion. It is apparent, as Kurt and Gladys Lang report, that public opinion dramatically registered the events of Watergate. Richard Nixon's Gallup popularity reached its peak in February 1973. Just after he was sworn in for his second term, having received 47 million votes, the President's popularity totaled 68 per cent. However, within nine short months the acting director of the FBI had resigned, the President's two top aides had resigned, John Dean had implicated the President in the Watergate cover-up, two former Cabinet officers had been linked to illegal campaign contributions, and the Watergate special prosecutor had been fired. Nixon's popularity melted to 27 per cent. By July 1974, that popularity shrank to its nadir, 24 per cent. Rocked by the disclosure of taped Presidential conversations, the White House transcripts, and impeachment proceedings in Congress, the majority of Americans were reportedly favoring the impeachment of the President of the United States.

The Langs consider how this shift in public opinion came about, focusing particularly on the impact of television coverage of the Senate Watergate hearings during the summer of 1973 and then the House Judiciary Committee proceedings considering articles of impeachment against the President in 1974. Under the weight of all this information, the Langs report, public opinion changed. By the end of the summer of 1973, almost as many people had changed their opinion as had not done so. Although the Langs found no evidence of massive shifts in opinion as a result of the televised Watergate hearings, the evidence indicates that the totality of Watergate coverage by the media did change opinions dramatically.

Under the impact of the electronic communications revolution, with most information now coming from radio and television, how have newspapers responded to the Watergate affair? Ben Bagdikian examines with dismay the contribution newspaper coverage of Watergate made, vis-à-vis television, to public awareness and understanding of the events. "The results are not reassuring if you assume readers need to know not just *what* happened, but also *why* it happened."

Democracy has always assumed public opinion a motive force for good government. In the final analysis of Watergate it was. Yet recovery from Watergate is not without problems. Throughout the two years of Watergate, approximately 40 per cent of the public dismissed the scandal as "just politics, the kind of thing both parties engage in." The press, for its handling of the story, has been criticized. Ben Bradlee, editor for the *Washington Post,* said that the press emerged from Watergate with a "black eye."

It is to the press's credit that it did break the Watergate story and pursue it to expose White House involvement. Robert Woodward and Carl Bernstein's book *All the President's Men* reveals how the press went about breaking the story. The Pulitzer Prize–winning reporters tell of their anguish in writing the story as they became mindful of White House involvement. They did not print raw, unsubstantiated charges, nor did they gobble up leaks. They worked diligently to confirm each new piece of information, kept copious records, and at times got cold feet at the prospect of printing a particular revelation. The book does, however, raise questions of ethics. Much of the information was obtained from anonymous sources, personal records, and even grand-jury contacts. Despite the substantive results in this case, what assurance have we that the media's public trust will be kept? Precisely because public opinion is an influential and sometimes even controlling factor in the conduct of politics in the United States, the standards and conduct of the news media, which so heavily shape the formation of that opinion, must be subject to continuous and close scrutiny.

Televised Hearings:
The Impact Out There

KURT AND GLADYS ENGEL LANG

Over the years, a kind of folklore has grown up which argues that massive shifts in public opinion take place as a result of television spectaculars, such as the Watergate hearings. Such a myth assumes that somewhere "out there," where the television picture ends up, lies a sleeping giant which, when roused, can be galvanized into action. Opinions change, action results (the theory continues) because a concerned audience absorbs the evidence and arrives at conclusions. There is the faith, shared by some senators on the Watergate panel, that thoughtful evaluation of the Watergate information will cause change. For example, our aroused sleeping giant will rethink the electoral process and will begin to question why such massive sums of money are needed to run a modern political campaign. He will also wonder about the kind of personal commitment to a candidate's election that causes breaking and entering, bugging, and "dirty tricks." As the hearings progress, this public will begin to express concern about the infringement on civil liberties that the investigations reveal. And perhaps, a thorough re-examination will begin of the kind of power that has been delegated to or usurped by the modern presidency.

Unfortunately, communications research generally shows that such hopes are very optimistic. Opinions change—but seldom that quickly or profoundly. Television is powerful—but coverage of any one event rarely produces sweeping transformations. The evidence now available indicates that Watergate *is* one of those rare events that has the power to stir the sleeping giant, to cause people to react—at least to the extent of changing some opinions. But the evidence at hand also indicates that the gavel-to-gavel TV coverage of the hearings

Reprinted by permission of the *Columbia Journalism Review*. Copyright © 1973. Kurt Lang is Professor of Sociology at the State University of New York at Stony Brook, where Gladys Engel Lang, his wife, is Professor of Communications in Social Sciences. They are the authors of *Politics & Television*.

played only a supplemental role—perhaps hastening shifts in the public mood that began before the hearings. Phase one TV coverage had far less effect on public opinion than the totality of Watergate coverage over one year, was far less influential than the continuous drama of the events themselves.

The relatively rare genus of fully televised public proceedings includes, in addition to Watergate, the Kefauver crime hearings in the early 1950's and the Army-McCarthy hearings in 1954. Researchers found that the changes which occurred solely as a result of televising the latter two hearings were incremental and subtle. After the Army-McCarthy hearings, for example, psychologist G. D. Wiebe undertook a study to find out if, as a result of the hearings, the public would be aroused to a "ringing reaffirmation of traditional liberties, and, correspondingly, to a mass rejection of Senator McCarthy for having encroached upon those freedoms in a bombastic and intemperate career which purported to expose Communist subversion." So Wiebe set up samples in two small cities in Maine and Kansas. The heart of Wiebe's thesis was that people would respond favorably to such statements as "It is wrong to assume guilt until innocence is proven," "It is wrong to require a man to testify against himself," "It is wrong to encroach on freedom of speech." In Wiebe's words, "The respondents did *not* talk about such values, either directly or by implication, often enough to justify reporting." Instead, Wiebe found that the hearings were seen in more personal terms, according to a kind of common sense. Wiebe found that people praised or blamed hearing participants by making such statements as "He sticks to his convictions, stands ready even if alone, in a good cause." This sort of reasoning was offered *both* by viewers who sided with McCarthy and those who sided with his opponents. Wiebe found that few on either side changed their minds as a result of viewing the hearings.

Another study by Wiebe, this on the impact of the Kefauver hearings, shows that most of those who watched were outraged by the revelations of crime and corruption. But, despite their arousal, Wiebe concluded that few viewers responded by considering pressures for legislative remedies or any other individual actions.

Our own study of the Kennedy-Nixon debates reveals that only very subtle changes followed that TV event. Most debate viewers did not, we found, try to judge who carried the day on which issue. Nor did they themselves carefully weigh the issues debated. Rather, the big effect of the debates was that people came to believe, for the first time, that Kennedy *acted* like a president, that he had a "presidential image."

Studies also show that although attentive viewers receive a good deal of new information, what they absorb is always filtered through what they already know and are capable of understanding. Our own study of the 1952 party conventions found at least two interesting mechanisms at work. Before the televised events began, we asked a sample of viewers to characterize their thoughts about what they were about to see. Some said they were about to see "backroom politics" in action; others thought it would be a "heroic drama" played out between the principal actors or candidates; others thought they would see "representative democracy" in action while still others took a more sinister view, that everything would be settled ahead of time. (At least some viewers with this attitude were reacting to "information overload," that is, because they could not absorb the enormous amount of information which was thrown at them in a relatively short space of time, they tended to fall back on the notion that it was all settled ahead of time anyway.) In almost every case, people's views of what happened after the convention were strongly influenced by what they thought *would* happen before they watched the event. When something happened on the convention floor, it was always viewed in the context of what the viewer perceived would happen before the convention began. An even more interesting outcome of the study was the discovery that many viewers are so intimately involved with the TV picture that they tend to react spontaneously and unreflectively to what they see. They forget that what they are seeing is a highly selective picture of an event, believing instead that they are actually experiencing the event. Because we all tend to put more stock in events actually experienced, the belief that TV is authentic experience makes it possible for viewers to reinforce their prejudices while at the same time believing they have increased their political expertise.

Definitive answers about the impact of the Watergate hearings won't be available until researchers have finished current studies. But, based on some 20 studies of the first phase of the Watergate hearings with which we are acquainted—and on the nationally published polls—we can draw some tentative conclusions.

The impact of all Watergate information on public opinion has had dramatic impact. A glance at the opinion polls shows, for example, that as public awareness of Watergate grew, so the

President's popularity declined. And indeed, in a study of media credibility, Professor Alex Edelstein at the University of Washington has come up with what he calls some remarkable findings. During interviews with a sample of 600 people in June 1973, Edelstein found an unusually large number (compared to previous social science studies) who said they had changed their opinions. "There was almost as much change of opinion as there was stability" between the time people first heard about Watergate and June 1973, Edelstein reports.

Based on Nielsen ratings, we know that the phase one Watergate audience exceeded all normal expectations. The best estimate of total exposure to the live daytime coverage (and evening rebroadcasts by the Public Broadcasting Service) is some 30 hours per television home. By early August, a Gallup survey revealed that close to 90 per cent of a national cross-section of the population had watched some part of the hearings. But this audience was far from a sleeping giant, a mass of unformed opinion. Long before the hearings began, the public had been forming judgments about the June 17 break-in. Even as early as September 1972, some 52 per cent had heard or read about the incident. Then, an overwhelming majority (75 per cent in a Gallup Poll) labeled the break-in "mostly politics," the kind of political skulduggery common in campaigns.

But, beginning on March 23 with James McCord's letter to Judge John J. Sirica, events began to snowball. The President admitted he had been "misled" about the existence of the Watergate cover-up. John Ehrlichman and H. R. Haldeman resigned—as did Attorney General Richard Kleindienst—and John Dean was fired. All of these events occurred before the hearings began; in a sense, they set the stage by creating an interested audience, familiar with the names and events, and ready now to follow the televised hearings. By mid-May, almost everyone knew about Watergate and a majority was now taking it quite seriously—that is, viewing it as more than "just politics." A Gallup Poll taken between May 11 and 14 said the 96 per cent who had read or heard about Watergate represented "one of the all-time high awareness scores recorded for a major news development." So by the time the hearings began, the audience was composed largely of those who already had opinions about the Watergate affair in general and about the President's responsibility in particular.

Nonviewers (and those who watched the hearings infrequently)

differed markedly from viewers—in their politics and, more significantly, in their attitudes about a citizen's relationship to government. Every study we have consulted has discovered convincing
evidence that Republicans and anyone else who voted for the President in 1972 were more often nonviewers, more likely to feel that
there was too much coverage of Watergate and that the hearings
"weren't good for the country." Conversely, a study being conducted
by David LeRoy at the Florida State University Communication Research Center found that voting for McGovern in 1972 was the best
predictor of viewing.

Yet, the people who didn't watch the hearings did not necessarily think the President was innocent. If he was guilty, to para-
phrase presidential adviser Melvin Laird, many people apparently
didn't want to hear about it. In fact, LeRoy's Florida study seems
to indicate that people who "never watched" the hearings were
almost as likely as those who did watch to believe that the President
had prior knowledge of both the break-in and the subsequent
cover-up. In other words, nonviewers were a lot more likely to
have voted for Nixon, but only a bit more likely than viewers to
believe him innocent. A possible explanation for this seemingly
contradictory attitude lies in the fact that nonviewing is also associated in general with a deep-rooted distrust of politics and politicians.
Social scientists have found that such a "plague on both your
houses" attitude has been endemic in American political life for
some time. It's a convenient way for people to avoid uncomfortable
ambiguities. Our own Watergate study on Long Island shows
generalized distrust (revealed by such comments as "All politicians
are corrupt" or "The only crime the Republicans committed was
getting caught") to have been especially typical of nonviewers with
no party identification who voted for Nixon in 1972.

Much has been made, however, of the belief that the immoral
and illegal methods used by some members of the Committee for
the Re-election of the President could cause viewers to become
disillusioned with the whole political process (the sleeping giant
theory, again). A Harris Poll taken in mid-July has been read as
evidence that Watergate together with the impact of live nationwide television promoted cynicism. The poll showed that 69 per
cent of the adults questioned agreed with the statement that "dirty
campaign tactics exist among Republicans and Democrats . . .
[with] the Nixon campaign people no worse than the Democrats
except that they got caught at it." The same question asked in

June showed 64 per cent of the respondents agreed. But before clucking too loudly about the harm televised Watergate did to respect for politics in general, we should note that the magnitude of the change is not overwhelming—public cynicism about the conduct of political campaigns was already high. We should also remember that between the campaign and the start of the hearings, both Gallup and Harris polls showed marked upswings in the public's belief that Watergate was a "serious matter" rather than "just politics." Most important, as we said above, cynicism and distrust are as much a *cause* of nonviewing as a result of viewing. People who don't care about politics because they distrust it rarely show much interest in media coverage of politics. Some studies now under way of Watergate, phase one, tend to support this long-standing generalization.

If you did watch the hearings, your basic attitudes probably had a good deal more to do with how you responded to Watergate in general and to Mr. Nixon in particular than did the information presented on the tube. Sidney Kraus and his associates at Cleveland State University in their Watergate study have been focusing on "trust." They see people as trusting more in "government," or in "leaders," or in "other people." Kraus's first results show that those viewers who register a high degree of "trust in government" tend to take a more tolerant attitude toward punishing the President than those who emphasize "personal trust."

Our own modest study of students on Long Island tends to confirm Kraus's findings about trust and vindictiveness. Among viewers who voted for Nixon, the desire for punitive steps (such as impeachment) was most common among Democrats who felt personally betrayed. Again, basic attitudes had a great deal to do with shaping response to the televised hearings. Professor Alex Edelstein's study of a community in southwestern Washington provides even more evidence for this assumption. At the end of June (after John Dean's testimony), Edelstein asked his respondents a series of questions about what they had believed when they first heard of Watergate, and what they believed as of June. While only 36 per cent said that events had confirmed all their initial beliefs, 82 per cent said they held to at least one of their first perceptions.

To say, though, that basic attitudes played a major role in shaping responses to the televised Watergate hearings is not the same thing as saying that no change in views occurred as a result of the gavel-to-gavel coverage. A glance at the opinion polls conducted between the beginning and the end of phase one shows that opinions were shifting—at least about the President's involvement. Coverage undoubtedly accelerated the decline in the President's popularity—a decline which was already in progress when the hearings began and which his August speech temporarily reversed. Our Long Island study found that the viewers who were most likely to change their minds (concluding that Mr. Nixon had advance knowledge of the break-in) had voted for Humphrey in 1968 and for Nixon in 1972. (We should not mistake this finding for evidence of mass conversions due to the coverage. For one thing, a great deal of viewing was probably motivated by partisan convictions. By the time the hearings began, the group without an opinion about the President's involvement was not very large. If you were convinced the President was innocent, you probably didn't watch the hearings much or at all.)

Even those who approached the hearings feeling they already knew everything about Watergate were hit with a tremendous amount of information, some of it hard to absorb. At the beginning of the hearings, Watergate meant only a bungled burglary at the Democratic National Headquarters. By the time phase one ended, in August, Watergate had become an umbrella under which were gathered such disparate elements as the break-in at Daniel Ellsberg's psychiatrist's office, the "enemies" list, the political use of income tax audits, the White House taping of conversations, and other events. And indeed, changes occurred in the public's perception of Watergate's meaning. Alex Edelstein's study found that approximately two-thirds of the respondents said some of their beliefs had changed between the time they first heard about Watergate and the end of June. When asked what views had changed, the greatest number, 42 per cent, listed their views on the nature of the problem (for example, "Watergate is a bigger problem than I thought it was;" "At first I thought it was just some two-bit burglary, but now I realize it's more serious"). Our own study shows that people's responses to queries about the Watergate revelations point to "shock" and "amazement." And when asked what they were most shocked about, respondents said they were amazed at how far the administration was prepared to move against individuals in pursuit of its own ends.

Seventy-seven per cent of the respondents (not all of them viewers) in a special *Time*-Yankelovich survey taken near the end of phase one agreed with the statement that Watergate "shows how

even the privacy of ordinary citizens is being threatened these days."
However, we should not misread this high agreement as evidence
of a revival of concern for general principles of civil liberties (remember the McCarthy study). Rather, our own data suggest that
people are much stronger in their personal condemnation of public
wrongdoing when they can clearly visualize personal harm being
inflicted on them or people like themselves. Watergate had begun
as an impersonal wrong, a break-in at the headquarters of the
Democratic National Committee; as the hearings progressed, the
acts that were revealed became more personally threatening. The
more people felt personally threatened, the more aroused and punitive was their response.

If there were no massive shifts in public opinion caused by televising the Watergate hearings, there is evidence that, over a longer
period of time, public opinion changed, and changed dramatically.
Studies like the one Alex Edelstein [did] for the ANPA News
Research Center on media credibility in Longview, Washington,
suggest the magnitude of the change. For example, when Edelstein
made his survey at the end of June, he asked people if, after they
first heard about Watergate, they found anything hard to believe
about it. While 21 per cent of his respondents said they found
nothing hard to believe, a whopping 64 per cent said there was at
least one thing they found hard to believe about Watergate at first,
and another 15 per cent said they could find two or more things
about Watergate hard to believe. When asked what the main thing
was they found hard to believe, 42 per cent said they found the
Watergate events, like the break-in and burglary, hard to believe;
another 25 per cent said they couldn't believe Nixon officials were
involved; interestingly enough, only 12 per cent said they found
the media hard to believe and only 10 per cent said they couldn't
believe Mr. Nixon was involved. Edelstein asked his respondents
to describe their thinking about Watergate in detail. As a result,
he elicited, on the average, four facts about Watergate from each
respondent. He found that people said they had changed their minds
about two Watergate facts, on the average, between the time when
they first heard about it and the end of June 1973. As far as Edelstein is concerned, such change is proof that what was happening
was a "process of education" whereby people received new information and, based on that new information, changed some of their
opinions. As we mentioned, Edelstein found that the greatest number of people (42 per cent) changed their minds about the nature

of the problem (for example, "Watergate is a more important kind of problem than I first thought it was"). Thirty-one per cent changed their minds about the President's involvement, 27 per cent changed their minds about the involvement of other top Republican officials, and only 7 per cent changed their minds about the media. (Edelstein believes, incidentally, that the media never were on trial during phase one of Watergate.)

All of this leads Edelstein to conclude that a process was involved between June 1972 and June 1973. "Things were happening. What we end up with is a portrait of a community evaluating its beliefs and disbeliefs about Watergate. This story was probably repeated over and over again throughout towns in America. People were making very pragmatic judgments about Watergate based on their experiential capacities."

Undoubtedly, then, the sleeping giant is stirring—not primarily as a result of the gavel-to-gavel coverage, but stirring nonetheless. Where the movement will take us, if anywhere, is a question that must elude, for the present, both sociologists and journalists.

Newspapers:
Learning (Too Slowly) to Adapt to TV

BEN H. BAGDIKIAN

Stanley Karnow, one of the country's leading journalists on foreign affairs, is only forty-eight years old, but when it comes to
American television he's Rip van Winkle, suddenly awake to a
massive change in his native land. He left the country after gradu-
ating from Harvard in 1947, at which time there were only 16,000
television sets in the entire United States. He was abroad almost
continuously for 25 years thereafter—for *Time* magazine, for the
Saturday Evening Post, for the *Washington Post*—a period when
television was saturating American households. During his expa-
triation, Karnow never saw a national political convention; he read
about them in the Paris *Herald Tribune,* the mailed editions of the
New York Times and the newsmagazines. In 1971 Karnow returned
to Washington and the following year saw his first television convention session. The next morning he walked into the *Post* news-
room and told a colleague, "I just had a crazy experience. I saw
the convention on television for the first time in my life. It's incredible; for the first time I didn't have to read the morning paper."

Karnow, now resigned from the *Post* and writing books and
magazine articles, says, "I guess it was old stuff to everyone else,
but for me it was a completely new experience. Now I find myself
attracted to sidebars and analysis in the papers if they're any good.
But I don't need the paper any longer to tell me what happened."

The first round of Watergate hearings should have been a similar
awakening for many other people: when television completely cov-
ers a visible event, it changes the function of printed journalism
—from the traditional announcement that something has happened
(which, of course, is still needed) to the added task of *explaining*
the event.

The impact of television on news has been creeping into print

Copyright © 1973 by Ben H. Bagdikian. Reprinted from the *Columbia
Journalism Review* by permission of the Sterling Lord Agency, Inc. Ben H.
Bagdikian is National Correspondent of the *Columbia Journalism Review.*

consciousness for a long time. It was preceded by radio's killing of the "Extra" edition. Even the start of World War II did not prompt many publishers to order an "Extra," because broadcasters had already carried the message, with the familiar preface: "We interrupt this program." The biggest visible news breaks in the 1950's and 1960's became known before the papers could hit the street. When President Kennedy was shot in Dallas in 1963, 44 per cent of the American population knew it within 15 minutes, 62 per cent within 30 minutes, and 90 per cent within an hour, according to studies made by communications professor Bradley Greenberg.

This new fact of journalistic life has dawned on many readers, but Watergate demonstrated that many newspaper editors still don't take it seriously. A study of 20 U.S. afternoon dailies shows (if this random selection is representative) that most papers approach a completely televised event as though readers know nothing about it, and, worse, as though readers don't *need* to know more than the eyewitness details seen on TV.

Some papers studied, usually the largest ones, did try to tell readers what they might wish to know *because* they had seen the hearings. But most papers did not. Most of the papers carried only straight news accounts, with no analysis or background.

There may be unjustified complacency within the printed-journalism field. After all, 62 million papers continue to be sold every day. And the extensive televising of Watergate could be dismissed as a unique event. Yet the ultimate significance of the television coverage for printed journalism was far greater. It provided an example of what may happen to printed journalism when a technical development—cable television—takes hold in coming years. Unless most of the projections about cable are wrong, within ten years the home viewer will routinely have access to video coverage of Congressional hearings, state legislatures, city councils, school and zoning boards—all of which are now staples of print journalism.

The latest figures show 7 million homes—11 per cent of all TV homes—are already connected to cable. Projections are that by 1980 or shortly thereafter practically all urban and suburban homes will be so connected. The FCC has told cable operators to include at least 20 channel connections to each home and to reserve channels for public access and for government activities. Within five years there will be 20 channel systems in the top 100 television markets, which include 87 per cent of all television—and newspaper—households. Some current systems provide 40 channels, and a few have 62 channels. The spectacular audience for TV coverage of Watergate was a dramatic omen for print editors.

There wasn't much excuse for editors to miss the point. TV's success was symbolized by the page one banner headline in *Variety,* the show-biz paper, for August 8: ERWIN & CO. SOAKING THE SOAPS. Translation: the weekly ratings by A. C. Nielsen of the daytime programs on commercial network for the week July 9 to 13 showed that Senator Sam Ervin's Watergate hearings had more viewers than the soap operas, the most popular daytime programs. That week the witnesses were John Mitchell, former Attorney General and former director of the 1972 Nixon campaign, and Richard Moore, White House legal tactician.

At the start of the hearings, when the minor spear-carriers were testifying, all the networks carried each session. The morning ratings for each network then averaged 7.0, which meant 4,500,000 television homes (and about that same number of adults) were tuned to each of the three networks. In the afternoon, about 5,200,000 adults per network seemed to be watching.

As of June 6 (witness: Hugh W. Sloan, Jr., former treasurer of the Committee to Re-elect the President), most sessions were carried by one network only; the afternoon sessions averaged ratings of 9.0, or 6 million adults and 700,000 teen-agers.

These figures do not include the early evening network news shows, which broadcast key portions of the testimony (as President Nixon bitterly observed). The networks claim their early evening newscasts reach 23,770,000 television homes in almost all of the nation's 209 markets, for a possible total adult audience of 50 million. Nielsen says that network news reaches 81 million adults sometime during each week. In a 1965 study, NBC claimed that radio news reached approximately 92 million adults each day.

To all of this must be added the extraordinary experience of public television with Watergate. Watergate was probably the most important thing that has happened to noncommercial public affairs reporting since its founding. The hearings established public television as a realistic alternative to commercial broadcasting in the minds of an important new audience.

At first some of the 237 affiliates of public TV did not carry the nightly replay of the day's hearings, but soon 92 per cent were broadcasting them. The reluctant stations no doubt recalled the administration's criticism of public television; their controlling boards include local establishment types reluctant to lend their facilities to embarrassing national news (as the White House knew when it kept pushing for strictly local, nonnetwork public television). But the noncarrying affiliates were soon deluged with demands to carry the hearings, and most acceded. In the first two weeks of Watergate coverage, the public network asked for letters of comment; it received 75,000 letters (98 per cent approving), and then had to rescind its request because staff members couldn't handle the flood of correspondence.

The ratings for public television in the evening are usually less than 1 per cent (1 per cent means 650,000 homes or about 1,300,000 evening viewers). During Watergate, ratings tripled and quadrupled. For example, on May 25 (witnesses: John J. Caulfield, former New York policeman, then an assistant director for criminal enforcement in the Department of the Treasury; Anthony T. Ulasewicz, another former New York policeman, then aide to Caulfield, and hearing comic; and Gerald Alch, former attorney for plumber activist James W. McCord, Jr.) the average of ratings for eight U.S. cities surveyed was 3.1. If that average held for all affiliates, the public television audience could have totaled at least 4 million viewers. By August 1 (witness: H. R. Haldeman, former White House chief of staff) one public television affiliate alone, WNET in New York City, had a 7.6 rating, the highest it ever garnered and one that could have meant a million viewers in that metropolitan area alone.

James Karayn, president of the National Public Affairs Center for Television (NPACT), says Watergate gave local affiliates confidence in running controversial public affairs. It showed that programs could reach beyond the highbrow viewers. It also brought in $1,500,000 in donations, two-thirds of the donors saying that this was the first time they had ever watched noncommercial television.

Curiously, while television is always quick to announce a triumph over printed news (and vice versa), commercial network executives had mixed emotions about their Watergate success. They kept reminding everyone in sight that each network was suffering losses of at least $100,000 per day of Watergate coverage. As *Variety* said in its lead story about the spectacular audience: "Television has a new smash hit, but for the first time ever the industry was too stunned and embarrassed to drum it up. In fact, there's little doubt that the vast majority of network and stations execs wish it would go away."

The Ratings

Following are the A. C. Nielsen average audience figures for the top ten sponsored daytime TV programs during the week of July 9 to 13.

	Rating [1]	Share [2]
Watergate (NBC)	10.7	37
Let's Make a Deal	10.0	34
Watergate (ABC)	9.6	33
Split Second	9.5	33
Newlywed Game	9.4	32
Girl in My Life	9.4	32
As the World Turns	9.2	31
Watergate (CBS)	9.1	34
All My Children	9.1	32
Days of Our Lives	8.8	29

[1] The "rating" is the percentage of total existing TV households (65 million) tuned to a particular program.

[2] The "share" is the percentage of turned-on sets that are tuned to a particular network at a specific time. (Because, among other factors, many households have more than one set, "share" is considered the more pertinent competitive figure.)

Yet, it didn't go away. Millions of people are addicted to the daytime serials, and the networks were not happy to think that, after Watergate, the addicts might kick the habit. After all, Sam Ervin would be center stage for only a few months, but Procter & Gamble is on camera forever.

The Newspaper Advertising Bureau claims that 77 per cent of U.S. adults (eighteen and over) read—or skim—at least one newspaper per day. If the claim is accurate, more than 100 million people see a daily paper—more than the 81 million people (eighteen and over) who see network news sometime during the week, according to Nielsen, or the 50 million who may watch each evening.

Whatever the total audience figures for television news—30 or 50 or 80 million people—or for the Watergate hearings in full—10 or 15 or 20 million—the fact remains that, before the next day's paper came out, most people interested in the news knew the essential facts. But this apparently mattered little to most newspaper editors.

A sample of 20 dailies was selected to see how many gave their readers only straight news on Watergate and how many added analysis, background, interpretation or other explanatory material designed to help the reader better understand the complex developments.

The sample was weighted in favor of finding more sophisticated coverage. First, the study was restricted to afternoon papers (including a few all-day papers). Since these papers go to press early in the day, they plan overnight pieces that almost inevitably tend to be interpretive or to provide background information. Only the larger papers were examined, further weighting the sample toward those papers most likely to have local talent for interpretation and insight in writing and editing. There are 1,441 afternoon papers in the country but only 324 with circulations of 25,000 or more; it was from these larger papers that every tenth was selected. The *Standard Rate and Data* listing of afternoon papers by size was used, and where the tenth paper was not available for scrutiny in the Library of Congress collection, the next larger paper in the collection was chosen.

A period of 12 days during the hearings, July 17 through July 28, was selected for study; most of the afternoon papers did not have Sunday editions, so 11 editions were available for most of the 20 papers. Among the possible total of 220, only 5 editions were missing from the Library's collection.

The results are not reassuring if you assume readers need to know not just *what* happened, but also *why* it happened, what it may mean and how it affects citizens. Most newspapers failed to do precisely what print can do best: provide thoughtful, analytical discussion about the significance of events. Some papers were simply silly as they tried to present something beyond televised Watergate, relying on bizarre features typical of the elder Hearst. Others settled for the extra dimensions offered by syndicated columnists (editorials and regular columnists weren't counted in this study).

Generally, the five biggest dailies in the sample (*Detroit News, St. Louis Post-Dispatch, Buffalo Evening News, Minneapolis Star,* and *Sacramento Bee*) did well by their readers. Among them, 37 issues included analytical or interpretive pieces; only 17 did not. They presented a total of 262 columns of straight news on Watergate compared to 104 columns of analysis and background.

The next five in size (*Indianapolis News, Ft. Worth Star-Telegram, Grand Rapids Press, Flint Journal,* and *Youngstown Vindicator*) did less well as a group: 30 issues with analysis and 21 without, and 182 columns of straight news compared to 48 columns of analysis.

The next five in size (*Ft. Wayne News-Sentinel, Jacksonville*

Journal, Manchester Union Leader, Wilkes-Barre Times-Leader-News Record, and *Erie Daily Times*) did less well than the second group. They had 18 issues with analysis, 34 without; 121 columns of straight news and only 28 columns of analysis.

The smallest five papers (*Lincoln Evening Journal, St. Joseph News-Press, Waterbury American, Montgomery Alabama Journal,* and *Tampa Times*) perhaps did slightly better: 22 issues with analysis and 32 without; 118 columns of straight news and 31 columns of analysis.

In general, the larger papers did better, both in total amounts of analysis and background, which might be expected of fatter papers, but also in the proportion of analysis to news. The largest five papers averaged one column of analysis for every two and one-half columns of straight news; the smallest five, one column of analysis for every four columns of straight news. Since the sample omitted papers smaller than 25,000 in circulation, it can be imagined how little analysis was presented by the 1,248 papers under 25,000, which are 70 per cent of all dailies, or the 1,117 afternoon papers, which are 77 per cent of all PM's. While these papers represent only 20 per cent of the total U.S. daily circulation, they are usually the only papers in their communities. Thus, if Watergate is any measure, something like two-thirds of all newspaper communities probably get negligible amounts of interpretation or background information with their news.

There were some happy exceptions among the smaller papers. The *Tampa Times,* for example, presented analysis on 7 of the 10 days the paper was examined, with almost a third of its Watergate space devoted to interpretive and background pieces. This performance was better than that of the *Minneapolis Star,* except that the *Star,* a larger paper in size, had more columns of straight news on the hearings.

Among the ten larger papers, the tenth, the *Youngstown Vindicator,* had eight issues with analysis and only three without, better than most other papers in this category.

The quality of the analysis and interpretive pieces varied greatly, of course, but in general it seemed to parallel the *quantity* of such material offered by the paper. It seems fair to assume that, if a paper devotes a generous portion of its space to analytical pieces, the paper takes the subject seriously enough to write or select pieces carefully.

There was no scarcity of interpretive and background pieces available to editors. Notable as sources were the *New York Times* news service and the *Los Angeles Times–Washington Post* news wire; although both standard wire services filed background pieces regularly, the quality was usually not up to that of the supplementary services.

The *Detroit News,* while tending to be conservative in its analyses, did offer a variety, carrying *Washington Post* background stories as well as pieces by James Burnham of the *National Review.* It ran one Op-Ed essay (distributed by the *New York Times* service) written by Richard Nixon when he was admitted to the New York bar, and another, which appeared in a number of other papers, by Nick Thimmesch criticizing the *Washington Post* for alleged "McCarthyism."

The *Minneapolis Star,* while providing a smaller quantity of analysis, did try some imaginative approaches. It published excerpts from George Orwell's *1984,* along with editorial-page staff pieces under a standing head, JUDGING THE LAW. Subjects included executive privilege and other legal issues that arose in the daily hearings.

The *Indianapolis News* ran the Thimmesch piece—and, for 4 days, a series of articles on Martha Mitchell, headlined THE MOUTH THAT ROARED.

The *St. Louis Post-Dispatch* was the heaviest of all the afternoon papers in analysis, both in frequency (10 out of 12 issues) and in space (37 columns, far more than any other paper in the sample). It began an inside section with the title "News Analysis" and ran several useful interpretive pieces there and elsewhere. It was notable for having staff capability to produce such pieces. It also used its syndicated services; for example, a piece on the Harding scandals that was distributed by Editorial Research Reports.

The *Manchester Union Leader* had the worst record of all 20 papers in number of days and amount of space for noneditorial analytical pieces. For purposes of this study, a story presenting itself as straight news was counted as such, which caused some problems in studying the *Union Leader.* The Manchester paper is usually awkward to categorize in terms of analysis, interpretation, and news, since its publisher, William Loeb, has passions that run through them all. His page-one editorials, while not counted as analysis, do spread a certain tone to the rest of the news around them. For example, when someone falsely representing himself as Treasury Secretary George Shultz phoned Senator Ervin to say the presidential tapes would be delivered to the committee, Loeb ran a page-one editorial with the headline: HOAXTER BEATS HUCKSTER. It was an attack on Senator Ervin, in which Loeb called the committee's chairman "Senator Claghorn Ervin" and said, "Anyone that stupid has no business being a U.S. Senator!"

(It was the *Manchester Union Leader* that first carried, during the 1972 primaries, the hoax letter accusing Senator Edmund Muskie of making a derogatory reference to French-Canadians as "Canucks." Since the *Union Leader* made so much of the letter without confirming its authenticity or even the existence of the letter-signer, an unkind observer might have remarked that anyone that stupid has no business being a newspaper publisher.)

The Wilker-Barre paper on July 18 ran an analytical piece saying that the Nixon wiretaps were *not* a violation of the law, while the Manchester paper on the previous day had run a headline stating: FCC SPOKESMAN SAYS PHONETAPS WERE ILLEGAL. As the contradiction illustrates, interpretive pieces do give play to differences of interpretation. That is inevitably the strength and the danger of interpretive journalism. Different views do illuminate events more fully, but the danger of doctrinaire presentations exists because of many papers are local monopolies. Unless editors vary the analytic viewpoints they print, local readers may get stuck with one narrow analysis.

The prize for Background Shlock must go to the *Ft. Wayne News-Sentinel*. On July 21, the day after testimony by Robert C. Mardian, the former head of the internal security division of the Department of Justice and a major CRP aide, and by Gordon Strachan, a former assistant to H. R. Haldeman, the *News-Sentinel* carried no straight news on Watergate at all; it did, however, run a banner across the top of page one—in blue ink—referring to Jeanne Dixon, the syndicated fortune teller: SEER SAYS NIXON TO SURVIVE WATERGATE. On the same day, the paper carried an interview with Robert Welch, head of the John Birch Society, playing up Welch's assertion that Nelson Rockefeller planned Watergate and that Richard Nixon wanted to be the first President of the World.

This proves, if anything, that there is a continuing need for straight news in print. It suggests that too many editors still underestimate their readers. It also indicates that producing good analysis and interpretation demands higher standards for editors and reporters, standards of intellectual discipline, honesty, and knowledge in depth.

Analysis need not terrify editors who fear that reporters' personal judgments will leak into the paper. A great deal of the need can be met by logically arranging information—including previously reported information—to help readers understand what is at issue.

For example, one puzzle of Watergate was conflicting testimony, which most papers merely labeled as conflicting. Yet there was much they could have done—as did the newsmagazines and a few dailies—to clarify the contradictions.

The July 19 testimony of Robert Mardian offered an ideal occasion for telling readers, in factual terms, who was contradicting whom on what events. One could, after a time, list the major contradictions: Did the then Attorney General, John Mitchell, approve of the Watergate burglary and its budget? Did he participate in the attempt to use the CIA as a cover? Did he order the destruction of the "Gemstone" bugging files?

In his testimony, Mardian contradicted his former friend and superior, Mitchell, on a number of points. He differed with Frederick C. LaRue, former aide at CRP, who had preceded him on the stand; he contradicted John Dean, who said Mardian had received FBI reports on its Watergate investigation; and he disputed testimony of Maurice Stans that Mardian was involved in concealing some campaign funds.

It would have been helpful, for example, merely to juxtapose conflicts in testimony. Jeb Stuart Magruder, former deputy director of CRP, swore before the committee on June 14:

"Mr. Mitchell flew back that Monday [two days after the Watergate burglary] with Mr. LaRue and Mr. Mardian. We met in his apartment with Mr. Dean, Mr. Mardian and myself. . . . One solution was recommended in which I was to, of course, destroy the Gemstone file. . . . It was generally concluded that that file should be immediately destroyed."

LaRue, July 19: "As I remember, there was a response from Mr. Mitchell that it might be a good idea if Mr. Magruder had a fire."

Mardian, July 19: "No such discussion took place in my presence."

A similar context could have been provided for Dean's earlier testimony: "I reported at one point in time to Mr. Mitchell and Mr. Mardian [prompting] Mr. Mardian, as I recall, to suggest that the CIA might be of some assistance in providing support."

Mardian: "I do not recall that conversation."

The presidential taping of telephone and other conversations in his various offices raised questions of propriety, wisdom, and legality. The wire services moved stories on the legal question, but the stories were usually ambiguous and led to differing headlines in different papers. What was needed was background on the law, the FCC regulations, the telephone company's rules, and court precedents on tapping, eavesdropping, and other kinds of surveillance.

Few papers made clear, for example, that while it is legal for one party to a two-party telephone conversation to tape the conversation, there are two ways to do it and that the White House, whichever way it did it, violated the rules. One device for recording a conversation is an induction coil, usually a suction cup on the telephone, requiring no direct wired connection to telephone lines. This is a violation of American Telephone and Telegraph Company regulations, which are part of its tariff filed with the Federal Communications Commission; thus, the FCC requires the telephone company to terminate service on any telephone which uses such a device. If the recording is made by a direct wire connection—as apparently in the White House—this, too, is subject to AT&T Tariff No. 263, which requires that a tone be emitted every 15 seconds during the taping. Even the connecting device, the black box with the tone in it, cannot be installed without telephone company approval. The company must terminate service to any phone user who persists in violating the rule (a rule insisted upon by the FCC in 1948). These rules apply to all interstate calls and most localities, including the District of Columbia. It would have been news to thousands of people who use induction coils that they are risking loss of telephone service.

Or, to take another example, few papers considered the difference between executive privilege—the right to maintain secrecy for presidential conversations with aides—and separation of powers—the requirement that the executive, judicial, and legislative branches of government do not encroach upon one another.

During the studied period, John Ehrlichman testified that J. Edgar Hoover had refused to approve of the plan proposed by presidential aide Tom Huston for gathering intelligence by conducting burglaries, eavesdropping, infiltration, and other activities. It was one of several opportunities for papers to bring up some previously reported—and relevant—facts. Instead, Hoover's refusal to approve the Huston plan was praised, and it was suggested that Hoover was either a civil libertarian or a stickler for following the rules. Yet in 1971, the FBI offices in Media, Pennsylvania, were burglarized by a political group that mailed memoranda from the files to various newspapers. The memoranda and reports were authenticated. They showed that Hoover had for years been ordering the FBI to do exactly the things included in the Huston plan. Yet, when Hoover's action became an issue during the Watergate hearings, the press failed in one of its major obligations to its readers —to have a memory.

Papers can also do some inquiring of their own to follow up on testimony. It seemed to pass unnoticed that the Marine Commandant, General Robert E. Cushman, former deputy director of the CIA, testified that he had been liaison man for Richard Nixon when Nixon was vice president, advising him, among other matters, on the early stages of preparation for the Bay of Pigs invasion of Cuba by the CIA. At that time, Cushman knew E. Howard Hunt, then deeply involved in the CIA invasion preparations, and later chief adventurer of the White House plumbers. Did Vice President Nixon also know Hunt during the 1950's? And if so, could that have contributed to Hunt's involvement in the plumbers' group? Could that tell us anything about presidential prior knowledge?

Unfortunately, no one on the committee asked about the Nixon-Cushman-Hunt relationship in the 1950's. Neither, apparently, did the press.

When the White House spoke bitterly about the prejudicial effect of the hearings and their coverage, leading to public condemnation in the absence of a legal trial, the press, by way of adding a larger context to such complaints, might have recalled Mr. Nixon's pretrial condemnations of Charles Manson and Angela Davis, J. Edgar Hoover's pretrial condemnations of the Berrigan brothers, even Spiro Agnew's broadsides aimed at whole classes of people. In their anger, apparently, White House officials forgot that Constitutional rights apply to out-groups as well as in-groups.

Where papers cannot do original reporting—like interviewing General Cushman or checking archives that might show past personal connections—they can, sometimes with just a telephone call, consult academic authorities on such matters as separation of powers, executive privilege, privacy in telephone communications, and Fourth Amendment protection against search and seizure. Few papers, even very small ones, lack nearby libraries and academic centers that might help in discussing basic Constitutional, legal, and historical questions.

Even without television and the prospect of cable, there is a need for more analytical and interpretive writing in newspapers. And, if cable broadcasts of every important national and local hearing will be available to concerned citizens within a decade, then newspapers should worry now about what they will be saying to readers the day after. There is always a great deal to be said, as a few papers demonstrated during Watergate. But to say it, papers will need to appreciate what is happening to news technology and the political intelligence of citizens, and they will need to cultivate journalists who are knowledgeable and perceptive enough to have something useful to say about what the public has seen and heard.

4. Political Parties and Elections

Richard M. Nixon was re-elected President of the United States in 1972 with the largest popular vote ever recorded—47 million. In a very real sense, the election was a mandate for him. Not until well after the election did the nation learn of all the campaign irregularities. However, the election of 1972 means more than campaign abuse. The issues of Watergate signal, as both Irving Horowitz and Theodore White observe, a changing method of conducting Presidential elections. With the creation of the Committee to Re-elect the President (CREEP), staffed as it was with managerial and political novices and run from the White House, a new approach to Presidentical politics was inaugurated. White suggests that the two-party system was being abandoned, and agrees with Aaron Wildavsky that the coalitions formed during the Depression were breaking apart; party loyalties no longer claimed the support they once had. "By 1972," White reports, "the parties had changed in character so fundamentally as to be almost unrecognizable, even to men who had made party politics their life study."

Since 1952, the Democratic party had captured the White House only twice. However, a Republican majority did not appear to be emerging. Ticket-splitting was a phenomenon of the 1970's. To Richard Nixon and the men of CREEP, political parties seemed superfluous to the task at hand, which was securing an electoral mandate for Richard Nixon. What they failed to perceive is that 47 million votes may be a mandate, but to what? Without a party, without Congress, without a legislative program or formulations of alternative points of view, it must be a hollow mandate. Electoral victory became more important than responsibility.

Clinton Rossiter once remarked that there is "no democracy without politics, no politics without parties." Horowitz, in his article, sees as the principal consequence of Watergate the growing intensity of interparty and intraparty conflict. In apparent emulation of Europe, America is moving toward polarized parties, with cleavages between and among Republicans and Democrats running deep. CREEP raised almost $70 million, but little of it reached the GOP's

Congressional or state candidates. The Republicans, it would seem, were excluded from the Presidential campaign. The Democrats, at the same time, were splitting apart, with a leftist ideological wing supporting George McGovern; yet they failed to develop a programmatic alternative to the policies of the administration. Political parties and brokerage politics were the victims of the 1972 election.

The Nixon Presidency has passed; the transition to Gerald Ford has been effected. The mandate of 1972 lies in pieces; CREEP is gone. But the impact of Watergate provides its own mandate for parties, indeed the nation, to come to grips with media, money, mobility, and computers in the conduct of party politics. The task is for parties to give their constituents accountability, the essence of democratic politics.

There is also the mandate to clean up campaigns. The stakes are democratic elections responsibly conducted. Presently before Congress are a number of reform bills intended to correct many of the campaign abuses. The basic areas of reform under consideration are

1. *Public financing.* Proposals differ regarding full versus partial public financing and whether Congressional races should be added to Presidential campaign support. It is hoped public financing will cut down campaign bankrolling.

2. *Campaign spending.* The major proposals set restrictive limits on amounts candidates for national offices may spend for their campaigns. From $60,000 for Senate races to $20 million for Presidential campaigns, limits are proposed to control the cost of elections.

3. *Campaign contributions.* Greatly restricted is the amount any individual or organization may contribute to any candidate or party within a year. Cash contributions are limited to $100 a year.

4. *Financial disclosure.* All campaign income and expenses would be made public as required by the Campaign Spending Act of 1971. Candidates would be required to disclose sources of personal income, net worth, and so forth.

5. *Enforcement.* Serious consideration is being given to the creation of an independent Federal Election Commission (FEC) to enforce campaign laws and prosecute violators.

The Europeanization of American Politics

IRVING LOUIS HOROWITZ

Watergate is more than a historic event in American politics. It is an apocalyptic event in American morality. It represents a benchmark to the abrupt termination of a two-hundred-year-old age of innocence, empirical confirmation that Providence has abandoned America for parts as yet unknown. Textbooks on law and political science have been filled with an equilibrium model of how the United States works: checks and balances between executive, legislative, and judicial branches of government; an everlasting stasis between the two political parties; a firm belief in the responsiveness of federal authorities to vox populi. Indeed, the foresight of the founding fathers, the authors of the Federalist papers such as Madison, Jay and Hamilton, was enough to make one believe in miracles. But there was one great fly in the ointment. The founding fathers of the Constitution predicated everything, and staked everything, on the belief that those who rule, although chosen by the people and hence not always brilliant, would at the very least be honest. And it is the age of the politician as an honest man in the Montesquieu sense of *l'esprit des lois* that came crashing down with Watergate.

The Federalists were thoroughly aware of the dangers in any concentration of powers in the hands of a single charismatic leader. But in their writings and in their age it was the prospect of too much power in the hands of the legislative branch that was of paramount concern. They feared that in this "first new nation" it was a legislative majority that would become unhinged and threaten the rights of the minority. And they had ample evidence from the inherited European systems of this sort of "mobocracy." Being men of property only reinforced this sensibility to legislative constraint.

The issue was how to increase the powers of the Presidency to counterbalance the presumed potency of the legislative branch. The

Reprinted from *Commonweal* by permission of Commonweal Publishing Co., Inc. Copyright © 1974. Irving Louis Horowitz is Professor of Sociology and Political Science at Rutgers University, Director of *Studies in Comparative International Development,* and Editor-in-Chief of *transaction/Society.*

idea of a single President rather than a plural Presidency was debated. It prevailed on the basis of yet another assumption: the
existence of a judicial electoral college comprised of leading citizens.
What in effect took place was an early break with the utilitarian-
enlightenment premise that major decisions should not be made by
one man acting in isolation, but by a collective body of elected
officials. Most institutions, from corporations to voluntary agencies,
are run on the premise of checks and balances generated by plural
executive leadership. The primary exception of note to this pluralism is the American Presidency. And with the concomitant rise of
expertise replacing electoral officials in the decision-making roles,
the Presidency became not just largely independent of legislative or
judicial controls, but insulated from such constraints. The growth
of the "imperial Presidency" coupled with the decline of legislative
capacity for autonomous action was thus the constitutional backdrop
to unchecked power, otherwise known today as corruption in government.

It is not that American politics is any more corrupt or dishonest
than it ever was; this is a debatable position. Rather, it is that the
evidence of corruption has been so sharply presented by the mass
media that even the most duncelike devotee of American political
mythology can no longer escape awareness of political corruption.
Rather than leading to universal morality, mass politics has led
down the slithering path of selective pragmatism, a word that has
become a euphemism for collective immorality. But since this is a
change in the perception rather than the reality of American politics,
the real issue becomes: Why now? What has happened to compel
a lifting of the shades, to reveal a cracked windowpane behind
which the exercise of politics is conducted as the impromptu use of
raw power, simply to retain government office?

One convenient fiction is that the Senatorial hearings, and the
subsequent revelations of the Cox review commission, reveal an
autodidactic learning and healing process. It is asked more in desperation than in certainty: where else in the world would such
revelations of corruption in high places have taken place, and
beyond that, if revealed, have not shaken the nation to its roots
and foundations? Yet, Presidential authorities fought these special
Senatorial hearings tooth and nail; withholding support, information and, finally, openly confronting and challenging the legitimacy
of the Ervin subcommittee to hold public hearings altogether. And
the Cox commission, the executive counterpart of a Congressional

committee, once it got close to the connection between Presidential policy and economic manipulation, was overthrown in a frightful putsch, a one-day takeover that involved a Federal Bureau of Investigation seal-off of the Cox commission offices that frightened even the more ardent supporters of the President.

The idea that the Watergate revelations are an unmixed blessing represents sophism. It assumes, somewhat grotesquely, that only a state organ in a condition of total corruption can elicit the real health of the body politic. This is a sort of bourgeois equivalent to the vulgar Trotskyist "theory" that the worse things are in the present, the better must they get in the future. Such forms of explanation as offered by the legion of Presidential advisers and apologists are, in effect, not explanations at all, but panegyrics and hyperbolic nonsense. The plain truth, as everyone recognizes with a sigh of relief, is that the fascist timetable, coming in the form of nervous nativism, has been seriously derailed, if not permanently stalled by the Watergate hearings. At least in its elitist variety, the fascist threat to suspend civil liberties and to equate criticism with subversion and opposition with antipatriotism has been profoundly weakened. That this in turn has led to a serious lacunae, a state of suspended political animation in which power itself appears to be exercised in a vacuum, is a deeper outcome of the Watergate revelations. In other words, the consequence of Watergate was a derailment of one classic form of the fascist timetable which in turn led to a power vacuum clearly attested to by the current paralysis which characterizes United States foreign policy from the Middle East to Southeast Asia.

To illustrate this paralysis, it would be difficult to imagine a nation as powerful and imperial in its pretensions as the United States bowing so meekly to the wishes of Saudi Arabian oil ministers, did there not exist a real crisis in United States foreign policy. In this sense, the Arab oil embargo was fortuitous in its timing. It corresponded precisely with a paralysis in the United States's internal affairs. As a result, if for no other reason than to have breathing space to restore the confidence of its public, American foreign policy is at an all time low ebb with respect to bellicosity and belligerence. Whether this has happened as a result of Arab intransigence or Soviet planning is less significant than the simple fact that under conditions of domestic intranquility the imperial eagle has turned into an international pigeon. As a result, the United States may be compelled to deal harshly and even punitively with internal dissension. It is, after all, far simpler to manage internal threats from unemployed laborers or disenfranchised minority groups than to respond to overseas threats from "Third World" sheikdoms which nonetheless have the capacity to call upon Second World bolsheviks.

Watergate has thus served to reinforce already widening tendencies toward neo-isolationism; toward an intense turning within, no less than turning inward. The rise of spiritualism, psychologism, healing, and all sorts of "superstitious" beliefs from palm-reading and astrology to devil worship reveals a sure-sighted collapse of any willingness (even if we presume the capacity) of America's political rulers to risk a world war on the say-so of a President who has proven himself to be less than candid. The recent Congressional passage over a Presidential veto, of a measure limiting the war-making powers of the executive office, that is, the Commander-in-Chief, is an indication, not only of a breakdown of confidence in the Presidency of Richard M. Nixon, but a collapse of moral verve and belief in the ability of the United States to win wars, and not simply engage in them.

The principal consequence of Watergate is that it reflects the growing intensity of inner-party and intraparty conflict in the United States. In the past, the structure of American party politics was best described as a matter of shadings and nuances between fundamentally similar organizational types; whereas in the post-McGovern reform period, the gaps between the two parties have become much sharper, calling into question fundamental premises about who governs, the nature of state responsibility for the welfare of the poor, the obligations for a full-employment society, and even the racial, class, and sexual composition of the party leadership itself. More than that, as the present halfway Keynesian house began to show its cracks, the need to move beyond welfarism became paramount. Hence, a polarization process commenced, with the dominant wing of the Republican party embracing a doctrine of law, order, respect for leaders, continued high military expenditures, in short the verities of what Lasswell long ago identified as the Garrison State. The Democrats, for their part, became acutely aware of the theme of social injustice: the rights of black minorities and the outrageous iniquities against majorities like women.

Coming into the 1970's, the competing philosophies of the two parties could be summarized as follows: for the Republicans, the main purpose of citizenship is service to the state; for the Democrats, the main concern of the state is service to its citizens. This classic dichotomy, with roots that go deep in Western political thought, became the substance of the 1972 elections that at times was disguised by differences in personal styles. As the party of power, the Republicans were not about to risk everything in exchange for an "alien" McGovern philosophy that must have seemed to the likes of Nixon, Ehrlichman, Haldeman, Magruder, *et al.* a veritable assault on 200 years of the American way of life. In this sense, Watergate was but one incident in the ongoing struggle between conservatives and radicals, all of whom ostensibly accepted the confines of American social structure. But in the polarized party analysis of what is right and wrong with the American structure, a cleavage between Democrats and Republicans was revealed that was as deep as, if not deeper than, what exists throughout the European political system.

A major reason that worldwide opinion on Watergate has been aroused is the intrinsic appreciation of the extent to which American politics, in the past said to have been providentially guided toward eternal consensus, has become Europeanized. Europeans are familiar with crisis in governmental confidence, dismissal of leading political officials for corruption and dishonesty in the conduct of duty and the cynical manipulation of public office and public trust for private gain. The shock of recognition for the American public was that the American political system is not exempt from the laws governing any other parliamentary regime. In fact, Providence took this moment to abandon America to its own devices, a condition of being adrift that is well known in Western European capitals suffering under a feeble tradition of parliamentary cretinism and executive corruption.

The reason that Watergate became a postelectoral rather than pre-electoral scandal is first and foremost the huge power of the Republican party apparatus to delay any real investigation of the break-in of the Democratic party headquarters until the elections were well out of the way. The clever if transparent rationale is that to have done otherwise would have turned the investigation into a political football. But a second factor, perhaps equally necessary for the scandal to remain buried for so long, is the strange capacity of the Democratic party to engage in self-deception. In part, this was a consequence of the bitterness of the conservative factions of the party which lost out to its radical wing. But even such an erstwhile figure as Gary Hart, Senator McGovern's campaign manager, barely mentions Watergate as a factor in his book-length review of the 1972 campaign. However, when the elections were held, and the Presidential landslide became apparent (even in the face of stiff popular resistance to Republican party candidates at Congressional and statewide levels), then the full recognition of how this landslide was manipulated and managed by the Presidential advisers, if not the top man himself, became painfully clear. Only then, in the aftermath of the dirty tricks campaign which isolated and defeated Muskie and Humphrey, and which took the full measure of Senator Eagleton, did the attitude of the Republican high command to the Democratic party—conceiving it as the Enemy and not simply the Opposition—become manifest. Only at this point, too, late in time to reverse the Nixon landslide, did the Democratic party mobilize and articulate its concern over the future of democracy, no less than over the future of the party system as such.

A special tragedy in the Watergate aftermath is the inability of the American Left (presuming such a beast actually exists) to seize the moment to put a reasonable series of options before the American public. At a time when the need for fundamental political and economic reforms loomed large, when the American people could see concretely structural weaknesses in the American system of government, all the literary Left is able to come up with is a series of empty and tendentious platitudes about the evils of American capitalism. Just as the Right saw Watergate as a purifying agent within the World's Greatest System, the Left saw the same event as evidence that this is the World's Worst System.

As one shrewd political scientist, Edward Schnier, remarked recently in *transaction/Society,* the Watergate affair pointed up the weakness of a Left that was strictly ideological and lacking utopian capacities, that is, a Left which could criticize but not construct alternatives. If any evidence for this judgment were needed it is the Left's tragic inability to mobilize a single demonstration, spark a single mass form of protest, or launch an impeachment movement. Instead, what occurred was the strange spectacle of moral indignation being registered by the stranded Republican minority, and political capital being made by the frustrated Democratic party majority. The Left remained outside and above the battle: taking two steps backward into abstraction as the American people struggled to take one step forward into specificity.

The Watergate hearings and their revelations on matters ranging from a rage against isolated antiwar protestors to extremely shady and sharp tax practices have compelled Americans to confront a condition of political venality that can no longer be dismissed as the ravings of the radical fringe. But in the near-total silence of the Left, the impulse to reform gives way to the instinct of self-preservation. In this sense, Watergate is not a revolutionary spectacle of Marxian proportions, in which an exploiting economic class and its state machinery give way to mass uprisings and a new radical leadership as they did in the Bolshevik and Maoist revolutions. Rather, we witness a bizarre spectacle of Hobbesian proportions in which the ruling elite and state authority as such are rendered helpless by inner-party strife and intraparty rivalry.

Watergate has not elevated the Democratic party to virtue, nor relegated the Republican party to vice. Yet, there is a dangerous precedent set in which the holders of state power are unwilling to abide by the premises and principles which have governed the United States for nearly 200 years. The present circumstances seem attuned to the English and French revolutions, in which aristocratic elites displayed precisely a collapse of class nerve and moral verve that created a leadership vacuum in which disenfranchised groups were compelled to seize power. The present intranquility derives not so much from any doubt as to the authenticity of a crisis in the American Leviathan, but rather how this crisis will be resolved in the long pull of time, and what social forces will be unleashed capable of moving us beyond this malaise. The practical issue becomes: will the United States talk Left and move Right, and thus create a climate for a flourishing fascism, or will it be capable of restoring national confidence based upon an international cleansing or purge (there are no pleasant palliatives to describe the question of impeachment or removal of a President from high office) of the present holders of authority. Only one fact is certain: the present politics of centrism cannot be sustained amidst a climate of corruption and crisis.

As a result of this desultory performance on the part of the ideological Left, the Watergate affair threatens to be reduced to simply a matter of Republican party strategy, that is, conservative decision-making concerning the advisability or inadvisability of going with the President for the Congressional and state elections of 1974, and the Presidential elections of 1976, or moving toward a solid front behind Gerald Ford, the new Vice President. The choice becomes a conservative one: to "brazen it out" with Nixon or "ride the new wave" with Ford. But either determination leaves the Left at the starting gate, without a program and without a vision. Thus, however important Watergate may be in relation to the structure of power in America, the absence of an organized Left with a historic vision and mission to capitalize on such an event means that this event becomes part of a deepening cycle of cynicism and antipolitics in America. It feeds rather than destroys the revolutionary myths. It leads to a Hobbesian rather than a Marxian series of responses to the political turmoil. This means that those who praise order when they really worship terror have the most to gain by a scandal which in its origins and evolution should have held out the promise of a democratic response to terror.

Events, even important ones, are not self-evident in their political consequences. The tragic inability of the Left to capitalize on Watergate means that, at best, the reform wing of the Democratic party will emerge with a newly born strength; at worst, Watergate will lead to a new style of fascism—less Platonic, less elitist, but no less dangerous or virulent, since fascism also has been known to come in populist packages, wrapped in slogans celebrating integrity and integration. In short, Watergate does not alleviate the fear and trembling. Watergate proves that, even in America, politics does not stand still and that constitutions are not made for all eternity. However, Watergate also makes plain that the velocity of social change and political corruption may lead to something worse no less than something better. An era of turmoil may give birth to new beginnings, but it may also stir up ancient evils. This is a time for careful searching rather than careless celebrating, itself not a small lesson that Americans are finally beginning to understand.

The Making of the President—1972

THEODORE H. WHITE

What history had to settle remained all through the campaign of 1972 difficult to define, for the American people were seeking clear yes-and-no answers in an age of political transition. The postwar world was cracking up, and the settlements of the great war against Fascism which had left America master of the globe twenty-five years before were now as obsolete as the Treaty of Versailles or the Peace of Westphalia. A world power shift was going on, comparable to that of the 1840's and 1850's, when China had first been recognized by the Western powers as prey, when the 500-year war between England and France was fading to memory, when new entrants in the power world—Germany, Russia, America—were making their weight felt, when the old ideas of legitimacy and authority were dissolving under the acids of Marxist doctrine, American experience, industrial-technological innovation. So, too, now in 1972 a global power shift was going on.

Power relationships, when they change, crunch people who have no idea where the crunch and hurt come from, who cannot understand what has made them fat or now drives them from their homes. This was what was happening to Americans in 1972—the world was pressing on them, and pressing their politics at home, too, into strange new shapes. The changing world required a concentration of power in the President's hands greater than ever before to negotiate the perilous and delicate passage between two world eras. That concentration of power was changing the office of the Presidency at home as abroad. . . .

The change was easiest to see overseas, and there Richard Nixon led in understanding it. The world of 1945–1950 was a world of American design; except for Russia, which was to be contained,

From *The Making of the President—1972* by Theodore H. White. Copyright © 1973 by Theodore H. White. Reprinted by permission of Atheneum Publishers, New York. Theodore H. White is a journalist noted for *The Making of the President* series. His *The Making of the President—1960* won the 1962 Pulitzer Prize.

no balance or restraint limited either America's power or America's generosity to deal with that world as it wished.

By 1972, however, that postwar world was dead and awaited burial. The United States had in the 1950's encouraged the Common Market of Europe as a counterforce to Russia; now, not only was the Common Market a power force in its own right, but England, America's closest ally, had cast its lot in with Europe, not America. The trading system America had designed was totally obsolete—America could no longer both sustain and drain the free economies of the world, setting the rules by its own power. America had financed the recovery of Germany and Japan—but by 1972 recognized them as its chief trading rivals. America had pegged the world to gold in 1944—but now gold, man's oldest measure of value, had been erased as a measure of value by the United States itself. The postwar map had been sponged and its lines redrawn. Africa was almost entirely free. Pakistan, that artificial state, had broken apart. Despite continuing Arab hostility, the state of Israel was now sovereign and seemed both secure and permanent. Martial lines of settlement were elsewhere subsiding into uneasy but peaceful political acceptance—East and West Germany were negotiating their own way into the future, North and South Korea had begun to talk. Most of all, the Soviet Union and China were joining the world dialogue. The Russians had closed the missile gap; and, given parity in missiles, the Russians were finally talking to America about their most vital common interest: how to strike a balance of nuclear terror.

Anywhere one looked at the globe, it presented a fresh aspect for which no coherent doctrine existed. Not only was it a fresh globe —it was a thriving, prosperous globe. People lived better, ate better, slept better, survived longer over more of the world's surface than ever before. America had been more responsible for this global prosperity than any other country. It had created this new world out of self-interest—but the genuine goodwill and generosity that went along with its self-interest could not be denied. Yet both American self-interest and American goodwill were now checkmated by the world they had created.

Japanese and Russians, for example, were eating better than ever before in their history, but, like Americans, wanted more. Their ships and trawlers looted the oceans of the world for fish, ravaging the seabeds within twelve miles of American shores, Atlantic and Pacific. Japanese, who paid almost four dollars a pound for medium-grade beef, and Russians, who wanted millions of tons of grain to produce more meat, were competing with the American housewife at the supermarket for hamburger and steak. Hundreds of millions of previously illiterate people around the globe had been taught to read and write—and their appetite for the paper on which to print the words was shooting up the price of every American newspaper at home. What was happening in distant lands reached into every American family budget, pocketbook, and holiday plan.

Energy, for example. Americans had multiplied by six their consumption of electric energy since the end of World War II, fouling their skies as they did so. They had also multiplied by four times their use of gasoline in automobiles. There was now no longer enough oil in the world as the civilization of wheels spread from America to Europe and Japan. The great world reserves of oil lay in the rickety principalities of the Middle East, whose accumulation of gold and dollars could now threaten the U.S. currency and the personal welfare of ordinary Americans. In every suburb of America or deep-center city, the energy crisis intruded itself. It intruded itself on those muggy days of August when the air-conditioning failed to work, on those subzero days in winter when the oil truck, short of supplies, failed to deliver fuel. The end of the postwar world abroad was at hand from coast to coast, whether Americans realized it or not.

The world abroad, as much as anything, had provoked the end of the era in American politics at home, too. The sharpest of these provocations was, of course, the Vietnam war, undertaken by a President without consent of Congress, without lust for territory or profit, in the name of a cause once honorable but ossified to dogma —and conducted with mindless stupidity. The war had provoked millions of Americans to ask why their sons should be sent to war without consent or apparent cause, and die in strange lands. What was politics all about? "Why am I in politics," a Wisconsin Democratic county chairman had asked me as early as 1967, "if they're going to take my boys and send them off to a war I don't believe in, and I can't do anything about it?"

But more than just the Vietnam war was pressing on American politics. Great ideas were changing. The idea of a free-enterprise economy, for example, was changing. That principal idea had fostered America's industrial power. It had been reconditioned in the Roosevelt revolution when the New Deal had insisted on supervising the investment process. It was now in the early 1970's changing again—the government was being asked to stand between the producer and the consumer as arbiter on wages and prices, on quality and value. The orthodoxies of the postwar world were trembling—the Keynesian theories of economics, the social workers' theorems of the Great Society were demonstrably inadequate. So, too, were engineering theories, planning theories, finance theories. The government had built highways which destroyed cities and ruined railways and public transportation; the government had financed suburbs with cheap credit and strangled the cities that lived inside their ring; it had pumped in education to create an elite without responsibilities; it had accepted, in noble, high conscience, the revolution of civil rights—but dumped its burdens on cities unable to sustain the burden; it had liberalized the immigration laws of the country—and overwhelmed, with a new absorption problem, cities already strained to the breaking point by the civil-rights revolution.

The politics of 1972 writhed under the strain of the thinking required, so coarsely translated on the stump or the airwaves. The rhetoric remained the same, but the country the rhetoric described was different. The climate of life had changed—from the irritable file at the airline gate where electronic eyes scanned your body for guns, to the supermarket where you studied the fine print on packages and tried to puzzle out which detergent or bug-killer you as a good citizen should buy. It was a period of passage in culture and response. The draft was over, thank God, after thirty-two years of conscription. The birth rate was down to its lowest point in American history—but was that good or bad? The privacy of grand juries, whose traditional secrecy was so essential to the protection of innocents under accusation, had been torn open by an enthusiastic press—whose own essential privacy of sources and reporting was, on the other hand, being challenged by the government. Labor unions, within government and outside it, were demanding the right to interrupt essential processes of service and survival with the same impunity with which they had won the right to interrupt the production of shoes, shirts, and automobiles. Values were changing.

Even without the crunch on Americans from outside, there would have been a vast disarray of ideas in American civilization as the postwar world came to its end—what the New Deal had established thirty years before as the values of humanity and what the Great Society had tried to put into institutional practice had run out of vitality, at home as abroad.

There was, thus, a turning point, which had not yet reached a clarity of options. No country moves forward more by ideas than America. And one of the problems of 1972 was that the idea system had become clogged by its own excessive outpourings. American intellectuals had written the Constitution, engineered the turn-of-the-century reform, provided Franklin Roosevelt with his blueprints of reorganization, armed America with marvels of technology during the Second World War. They had been rewarded with a gush of approval, with an outpouring of funds, private and public, that had all but choked off fresh ideas—like a garden overseeded and overfertilized. The American idea system poured out paper after paper, study after study, learned investigation after learned investigation on the race problem, the urban problem, the environmental problem, the television problem, the violence problem, the identity problem, until clear thinking was suffocated by the mattress of scholarly investigation.

The problems came to their most acute edge for those who enjoyed, or aspired to, power. Richard Nixon was a President who repudiated most of the intellectually fashionable ideas of his time. Abroad, with the help of Kissinger, and with the authority Presidents traditionally enjoy in foreign affairs, he could work out his own ideas—with a clarity of vision and so tenacious a grip on reality that history must mark him among the great foreign-policy Presidents of the United States.

But at home, the use of power was more complicated.

Thus, irony: Richard Nixon campaigned in 1972, as he always had, against central power, against the idea of the omnipotent President doing his will from Washington. He was for returning home power to the people in their communities. But in practice he took to himself more personal power, delegated to more individuals of his staff the use or abuse of that power, than any other President of modern times. Faced by a hostile Congress, a hostile intellectual world, a hostile vanguard of the press-television system, a recalcitrant party of his own and a Democratic Party committed by definition to opposition, he abandoned all the old conventions of party politics.

His campaign was, therefore, a personal campaign and, above all, a campaign of issues. It was a campaign that never invited Americans to judge his use or manipulation of power, but only its apparent end results and its stated direction. He personally stood above detail, above the nitty-gritty of political mechanics. Mao Tse-tung would have approved of his long view. Americans overwhelmingly responded to Nixon's presentation of the issues—they chose his directions, freely and openly, as against the directions offered by George McGovern. And though McGovern tried, gallantly and eloquently, to turn national debate to a consideration of the style of power itself, he could not score the question through on the minds of people. That was left for the press to do later: to pose the question of internal power within the Nixon administration, and of how the President had let that power be used, and abused, to defile the laws of the country and the political process itself.

None of the changes that marked the end of the postwar world at home and abroad could fail to affect the vehicles of American power—the two great parties of tradition, the Republican and Democratic parties. By 1972 the parties had changed in character so fundamentally as to be almost unrecognizable, even to men who had made party politics their life study. The parties no longer controlled loyalties as they once had; the parties no longer delivered responses as they once had; the parties no longer related to government as they once had.

The process of degradation in American national politics had been going on, of course, for years before 1972. Election after election, from 1960 on, had seen the process increasingly polluted by money. A two-party total of $24,000,000 had been spent for the Presidential candidates of 1960. The sum had risen to $37,500,000 in 1964, to $100,000,000 in 1968, and substantially more than $100,-000,000 in 1972. Election trickery and deception had always been part of American politics—but beginning in 1964, in the Johnson campaign against Goldwater, trickery, espionage, counterdemonstration had first begun from the White House itself, condoned then by many because it was practiced against Goldwater, whom they despised. By 1972 the Nixon campaign had lifted trickery to the level of crime. The first mild and jocular adversary demonstrations planned against Goldwater by the White House in 1964 had by 1968 become a cult of politics controlled by no party, and of themselves escalated to riot in the street, maturing in the violence of conspirators seeking to hit and influence the national election process at its most vulnerable. The stage of politics was changing as television became its most important platform of action. Politics, in response, was planned increasingly for dramatic and visual effect. All the while, too, education, joining television, was freeing more and more millions of Americans from unquestioning obedience to past tradition, their union begetting what has been called the age of ticket-splitting.

America had not been born with a party system; the founding fathers had feared parties as the greatest possible danger to the republican system they envisioned. The party system had grown up in the first third of the nineteenth century as a way for people with common interests to band together to make power do what they wanted done. But the parties now, as the dying postwar world bequeathed the unbelievably complicated problems of this age of passage, were unable to perform the functions for which people had once intended them.

The transformation of the Democratic Party was a conscious one, as we shall see, although its consequences were completely unpredictable at the beginning of 1972.

The Republican situation was worse—the party was simply allowed to decay so completely that it played no role whatsoever as a national party in the national election of 1972. Both national parties as they presented themselves to the American people in 1972 had come, by no one's design, to reflect the wills and the personalities of two individual candidates. The candidates' personal staffs were responsible not to what their parties stood for but to what they thought their candidates stood for. Neither campaign represented more than what its candidate said, or wanted, or permitted. Thus there came about, on the Democratic side, the buffoonery of the Eagleton affair. And, on the Republican side, something incomparably more disturbing—the felony of Watergate. . . .

The Watergate affair is inexplicable in terms of older forms of corruption in American history, where men broke laws for private gain or privilege. The dynamics of its irrationality are compounded further by stupidity. The men involved were involved at a moment, in 1972, when history was moving their way. They were trying to speed it by any means, fair or foul. By so doing perhaps they wrecked their own victory. And that, as history may record, compounds their personal felonies with national tragedy.

For it would be no less than national tragedy if men came to regard the election of 1972 as fraud; or attempted to reverse the verdict of the people at the polls on the technicalities of a burglary, in a spasm of morality approaching the hysterical.

The view of the 1972 election as fraud is comforting to many who, intellectually, have been unable to accept the proportions of the 1972 vote. Watergate has, curiously, restored their faith in the American people. The people had, according to this theory of fraud, simply been hoodwinked, bamboozled, tricked into a giant mistake. According to this theory, the people could be rehabilitated and forgiven for what they had done—had they known the truth, they would have turned Richard Nixon out.

Of all the ironies of 1972, this could become, if accepted, the greatest.

There have been four American campaigns in living memory in which the issues were clearly stated—the Roosevelt campaigns of 1932 and 1936, the Goldwater-Johnson contest of 1964, the McGovern-Nixon contest of 1972. All others have been contests of personalities or of party organization. If anything, the election of 1972 was an invitation to the American people, eloquently expressed by both candidates, to consider the use of power in their country. Americans had lived through a postwar world where impatience of power had led either to questionable result or to disaster. Vietnam had been explained to them first as a war in a high cause where, with the investment of several battalions of American troops, a quick mop-up could be effected in a few months against ragged guerrillas—and with a few more troops, the war would be over by Christmas . . . 1965, 1966, 1967. The great cause of civil rights had also been simply explained, its rallying cry "Freedom Now!" "All deliberate speed" had been the judicial formulation, but the accent had been on speed; and the rush had brought results as much of sorrow and agony as of brotherhood and hope. The Russians had been ahead of us in the race to the moon, we were told, which was true; and so, with all the speed and impatience of American power, the rush to the moon was on, with what large benefits no one can yet perceive.

The Republican campaign of 1972 was explained to me by many of its own participants and leaders, but several of the explanations that echo longest in memory come from the defeated of the headquarters of George McGovern. "The Republican Party is the place where people vote when they want to go slow, and I think they want to go slow now," said veteran Ted Van Dyk, McGovern's chief speechwriter, in late October. Much later young Pat Caddell added, "America is not a place in geography, it's an idea. Watergate fouled up the idea."

Between them, they spanned the giant irony. The idea that prevailed in the election of 1972 was that the power should go slow. Go slow abroad, go slow in the cities, go slow with power wherever it interfered with how a child grew up, where she went to school, or where he was sent to die. The election itself was a dull election in the reporting, a refutation of drama, as if the American people were spitting in the wind of history, demanding of time that it stand still. Richard Nixon promised them that—a curb on power. And then, once he was elected, the Americans learned that his administration had been guilty of the grossest abuse of power.

Yet the people had spoken their will. All the dirty tricks, all the dirty money, all the devices known and still to be revealed were as nothing compared to the massive exposure that television and the press—"the system"—gave to what the candidates thought, said, actually did. Reform of national election laws has been overdue for twenty-five years, to make them conform to the new shape of the new America. But no reform yet suggested could have affected the outcome in 1972.

The Americans were for slowing the pace of power, and they chose Richard Nixon.

They would not be ready to march again, or vote again in counterlandslide, until the ideas to make them march or vote had matured wherever they might mysteriously be making themselves ready. For the moment, all the old ideas of the postwar world were dead—and America, which was born of ideas, was an intellectual wasteland. Its most eloquent accepted political thinkers were largely advocates of dead partisan causes; its *avant-garde* thinkers had lacquered over outworn dogmas with new phraseology; the primitive thinkers who opposed them had forgotten, or could not express, the values that had given strength to their tradition. It is characteristic of an age of passage, as a country moves from one set of crumbling ideas to another yet undefined, that palace politics reaches maximum power; goals cease to be national goals and become administrative.

Thus, a man like Richard Nixon must envy a man like Harry Truman.

Truman came to power at a time of crisis, with a country unified behind him, its purpose clear—to destroy Fascism. So, too, were its purposes at home clear to Harry Truman—to eliminate the pestilence of unemployment, to give the black people equal access with whites to American opportunity, to endow and reward education, to make it possible for ordinary people to build and own their own homes. Truman was an amateur in foreign affairs, and his first two years of learning resulted in the needless tragedy of American enmity with China, the awkward intervention of America in a third world it did not understand. But, at least at the beginning, Truman was in no doubt either of his purpose or of his moral authority as President, and I remember best of all the stories I have heard from or about Presidents one that Dr. Robert Oppenheimer told me.

Oppenheimer was the prime creator of the atom bomb. This knowledge haunted him. He, Dean Acheson, David Lilienthal, and others had wanted to share the secrets of nuclear power with other nations. The White House resisted. Oppenheimer asked to be received by President Harry Truman, who had dropped the bomb which killed so many. Oppenheimer had never met a President before.

As I heard the story from Oppenheimer, a few weeks before he died—the great scientist already gaunt, his throat seared with the red glaze of radiation where the cancer was being treated, knowing the end was coming—we talked of the relation of thinkers to power, of intellectuals to national decision. He recalled that when he saw Truman he had pleaded as persuasively as he could for Presidential approval of the Oppenheimer-Acheson-Lilienthal plan. Truman asked why Oppenheimer seemed so agitated by the problem, why he seemed so upset. Oppenheimer recalled that he held out his two hands and said, "Mr. President, I have blood on my hands." Truman paused, reached in his pocket and pulled out a handkerchief. Then he said, "I'm the President. I dropped the bomb. Take my handkerchief and wipe the blood off your hands."

A President can absolve, pardon, or wipe guilt from any citizen's hands when national goals are clear enough—as Truman did, offering absolution to Oppenheimer. A President can even deny liberty —as Abraham Lincoln did during the Civil War when he suspended *habeas corpus*, or Franklin Roosevelt when he interned the Japanese of California in 1942. But when there are no overriding national goals, when purposes and directions for the next era are still shaping, then the democratic process itself becomes vital. There can then be no absolution for anyone who has tampered with the supreme need of a passing time—that the process be kept fair and open, that the process proceed without fear, so that new men can think through what the problems of the new era are and what choice of solutions may be offered.

The Americans stand, thus, in the presence of not one but two mandates.

There is, as I write, the current mandate of Watergate—that the process be kept clean. It reads that no one—not the President, nor his staff, nor anyone using their names—may abuse the law. That mandate spreads far beyond palace politics. It requires that Americans recognize that impatience in any form of power, whether expressed in street riot, demonstration, or government espionage, be recognized as the begetter of crime against the democratic process. It requires that the press, too, recognize the limitations on its power —a recognition that the privacy essential to government is equivalent to the privacy essential to newsmen's sources. But the beginning of the current mandate is pointed at the President: that he purge, at whatever cost in affection or personal loyalties, those who defiled the process of law which he promised to uphold. "The abuse of greatness," said Shakespeare, "is when it disjoins remorse from power."

But then there is the governing mandate—of the election.

Americans have a propensity for reinventing a past in order to serve the needs of the present, for rewriting history to prove a contemporary point. Yet if there is a purpose to history, it is to make men conscious of what in the past can be useful for the present—for, after all, the past shaped the present, and an amnesiac nation is as helpless as a wanderer in the streets.

This second mandate, that of the people speaking at the polls in 1972, closed a generation.

Rudely but compellingly, every thirty or forty years, the ideas of one generation become the prison of the generation that follows. The more powerful the idea, the more confining the imprisonment. The idea of compromise with slavery had been accepted in American politics in 1820 as imperative for saving the Union. By 1860 such compromise had frozen politics so completely that it could be released only by the Civil War. The creative domestic ideas of Abraham Lincoln during that war opened new horizons. The war Congresses of the 1860s sought to open the plains by giving a free hand to the railroads, free soil to the settlers, all the while encouraging industry in the cities and new thinking leadership by vast land grants to universities. Thirty years later all these ideas had succeeded—and the horizons had shrunk. Their success had left the settlers of the plains victims of the railroads, the unorganized workers the prey of industrial brutality, the beauty of the country despoiled. So thirty years later came the political upheaval of the 1890's—inspirited by the intellectual and political leadership of the land-grant colleges the same ideas had so casually endowed.

We live, similarly, at the end of a generation, when the ideas of hope and grandeur that moved the decades of the 1930's and 1940's, having achieved their triumphs, imprisoned new thinking. Those ideas increased the power of the state beyond the experience of any previous generation—the power of the state to make war or make peace abroad, to create suburbs with federal credit, or destroy cities with federal roads and tax burdens, to broaden education and opportunity, to command the deployment of children in schools, to heal and to build. The extrapolation of those ideas by George McGovern frightened too many Americans; too many had been hurt along that road. The majority wished to pursue those ideas no further now; the Democratic Party, which called itself the party of the future, had become, in their eyes, the party of the past. They turned instead to Richard Nixon, affirming the change of direction he declared he was giving to government—a restraint on the power and reach of the federal state into daily life. However his use of the power of state may be defined in the months or years to come, this restraint on power and its excess was what the majority voted for. For this time, they preferred to live their own lives privately—unplagued by moralities, or war, or riots, or violence. In the alternation of the sequences of American history, in the cycle between poetry and pragmatism, in those generational shifts of mood characteristic of the adventure in democracy, certainly the ideas of the minority who voted for McGovern would come into their time again. Those ideas still stirred in the spirit of the nation. But until those ideas had new form, new shape, new perspective, the majority of Americans would not be called out to march in their cause. Such was their mandate in 1972.

5. The Presidency

The limitation of executive power is one of the major issues raised by Watergate. The devices of executive control that led Arthur Schlesinger, Jr., to label the Nixon Administration an "imperial presidency" are now familiar. The Special Investigation Unit (plumbers) was created to deal with the executive branch. Impoundment, the pocket veto, and executive privilege were techniques employed to challenge the traditional comity between the executive and Congress. Will the resignation of Richard Nixon put an end to executive abuse of power? Will the new administration restore the Constitutional balance of power? At issue is the degree to which Watergate is symptomatic of the nature of the Presidency rather than a particular problem of the Nixon Administration.

Accepting the stewardship theory of the Presidency (according to which the President can do anything not specifically prohibited by the Constitution) and pressing for social action in the face of a recalcitrant Congress, America came to believe in initiative on the part of the President as chief administrator, chief legislator, leader of his party. "How to make those powers work for *him*," Richard Neustadt wrote on Presidential power in 1959. "My theme is personal power and its politics; what it is, how to get it, how to keep it, how to use it." In his present article, Professor Neustadt looks at the constraints operating on the Presidency, how they operated during the Truman Administration, and what the lack of both propriety and prudence did to Nixon's White House.

The Presidency is a potent mix of institutional power and individual personality. Presiding over eleven departments and a Presidential establishment of six thousand advisers, assistants, and staff, the office demands skill, stamina, a grasp of public opinion, a sense of humor, and a sense of history. Because of the urgency of foreign and domestic problems, there was widespread approval of a strong Presidency. Until Watergate, little attention, and even less criticism, was given to this expanded role of the Presidency. Now, however, many reforms are being proposed.

One group of reforms would strengthen Congress. For example

tightening of purse strings and toughening of confirmation-of-appointments and of impeachment laws are suggested as means to revitalize checks and balances. Senator Sam Ervin and historian Henry Steele Commager both see a stronger Congress as the means to control Presidents. Other reforms stress restructuring the office of the Presidency. Reforms advanced range from the six-man executive suggested by Barbara Tuchman to instituting parliamentary votes of no confidence.

Although he finds that the Nixon Administration attempted to "transform the presidency of the Constitution into a plebiscitary presidency," Arthur Schlesinger, Jr., believes in a strong Presidency and calls for restraint in reforming the office. Discussing various reform proposals, he suggests why, rather than structural change, the most efficient means of reform and control lie in politics. And he points out that, ultimately, should normal political means fail to redress a violation of Constitutional balance, the Founding Fathers designed a remedy for such "great and dangerous offenses"—impeachment.

While the issue of impeachment has become moot, the issue of executive power remains. The debates over structural reform and the balance of political power among the branches of government deserve our attention. Even though Nixon is gone, the nation must address itself to the broader issue of Presidential power, the expanded Presidency. Equally important is the analysis of constraints of the Presidency—Cabinet, press, party, Congress, and so on. However, before any Constitutional comity between branches can be restored, the internal operations of the Executive branch must be re-examined in terms of the democratic process.

The Constraining of the President

RICHARD E. NEUSTADT

The White House was once—and will be again—a great place for a young man to work. I did it myself and have never been sorry. Fate was kind and my age was right: It was Harry Truman's White House, and I worked for Charlie Murphy—Charles S. Murphy, to give him his due. He was the President's Special Counsel, successor to Clark Clifford in that post and one of Truman's senior aides. Working for Murphy and with him for the President was a fine experience, as unlike Egil Krogh's or Gordon Strachan's as day from night. A story illustrates what made it so, and the story is a starting point for looking at the Presidency now, by light of Watergate.

In December, 1950, at the wrenching turn of the Korean war, amidst Chinese attack, American retreat, renewed inflation, fears of World War III, Truman met at the White House with the Congressional leaders of both parties. Their meeting in the Cabinet room was largely symbolic, underlining events; it was an occasion for briefings, not actions. Soon after it broke up, a White House usher came to Murphy's office with a memorandum found under the Cabinet table. This was a document of several pages addressed by the staff of the Senate Minority Policy Committee to Senators Robert A. Taft and Kenneth S. Wherry, the Republican leaders. Some of his assistants were with Murphy at the time, and we fell upon it with whoops of joy. As I recall, one of us read it aloud. It dealt with the contingency (which had not arisen) that the President might use that meeting to seek pledges of bipartisan support for the Administration's future conduct of the war. This, the memorandum argued, ought to be resisted at all costs. By Easter recess the war could have taken such a turn that Republicans might wish to accuse Truman of treason, and they should be free to do so. The term "treason" fired in me and my associates an outrage we

© 1973 by The New York Times Company. Reprinted from the *New York Times Magazine,* by permission. Richard E. Neustadt is Professor of Government at Harvard University. He served as a Consultant to President Kennedy, 1961–1963, and is the author of *Presidential Power.*

wanted the world to share. With the loyalty of subalterns, more royalist than the king, we cried, "Get it copied . . . show it to the President . . . leak it to the press!" Murphy smiled at us, took the memorandum from us, sealed it in an envelope, summoned a messenger and sent it by hand to Senator Taft. End of story.

Murphy's conduct showed propriety—indeed, for me defines it—so that much recent White House staff behavior simply shocks me. His conduct also showed prudence. He worked in a White House where seniors had constant incentive to contain themselves and restrain the young.

The Presidency as we know it now took shape in Franklin Roosevelt's time, the product of Depression, war, the radio, and Presidential personality. Truman inherited and consolidated. In terms of personnel, both military and civilian, the federal government during his later years was roughly the same size as it is now. (The great growth of civilian public service since has been at state and local levels.) In constitutional and statutory terms, the Presidency's formal powers then were much what they are now. Like President Nixon, Truman fought undeclared war, imposed price controls, presided over a great turn in foreign policy, sought changes in domestic policy, and championed "executive privilege." But if, in these respects and others, Presidential powers are substantially unchanged, what has changed is a set of inhibitions on their use.

Formal powers stay about the same, but their conversion into actual power—into making something happen—takes place with less restraint than formerly. If the Nixon regime felt itself under siege in 1971, so did Truman's in 1951. Yet there were no do-it-yourself White House horrors. Had propriety not barred them, prudence would have done so.

Almost surely, Watergate's effect upon the Presidency will be to prop up old incentives for restraint, restoring White House prudence to something like its former state. Such a prop is artificial and cannot last forever, but it should hold good for years to come. Score one for Watergate! In that perspective it is not a tragedy—far from it.

So the modern Presidency's past and prospects are bound up with the questions: What was prudence made of? What became of those ingredients! And on what terms does Watergate restore them?

A generation ago, our system's formal checks and balances were strongly reinforced by an array of informal constraints on White House conduct. Some were external, imposed on the White House, equally affecting President and staff. Others were internal, products of his operating style, affecting the staff more than him. External constraints reflected his dependence upon men whom he could not control for work he wanted done. Such men were found in many places, but let me single out three: the Congress, the party, and the Cabinet. As for internal constraints I shall single out another three: his schedule, press conferences, and the staff system.

THE CONGRESS

Those men on whom the President depended were his "colleagues" in the quite specific sense that while he needed them, their power did not stem wholly from his. To need is to heed, or at least to listen. Truman had one such set of colleagues on Capitol Hill: the Speaker of the House, the House and Senate floor leaders, and the committee chairmen. As the modern Presidency emerged before and during World War II, it was assumed that those posts would go to men of the same party as the President. So it had been for all but four years since the turn of the century. So it remained in Truman's time for six years out of eight. Under FDR and Truman this assumption was built into governmental practice, not least at the White House, where it moderated tones of voice, promoted consultation, and preserved respect, at least for working purposes. Speaker Sam Rayburn and the floor leaders met Truman every week. They were colleagues together: At Rayburn's wish they met alone, no staff—and no recordings.

While all the posts of power on the Hill were manned by men who shared the President's party label, Truman could not do what he did in 1948 and in effect run against Congress, lambasting it for a "do-nothing" record he himself had forced on it by seeking bills he lacked the votes to pass. But that was the 80th Congress, elected two years earlier with Republican majorities in both Houses. Truman could not turn as sharply on an institution led by Rayburn. Nor would he have wanted to. Nor could his staff. Family quarrels were of a different quality than conflict with the rival clan.

And even as he rose to the attack in 1948, Truman carefully walled off from party battle what he took to be the cardinal field of foreign relations, including European policy, and especially the Marshall Plan. Under the aegis of Senator Arthur H. Vandenberg, the Congressional Republicans did likewise. For limited purposes, the Truman-Vandenberg connection linked the White House to Republican leaders as closely as ever to Democrats.

In 1954, Truman's successor, General Eisenhower, faced the re-

verse situation when the Democrats regained control of both houses
of Congress. He then faced it continuously for six years. Eisenhower
was a national hero, consciously so, and only lately become a Republican. He joined Rayburn and the latter's protégé, the new Senate
Leader Lyndon Johnson, in a loose but comfortable connection.
Over a wide range of issues this served much as Truman's with
Vandenberg.

What Truman had for two years and Eisenhower for six, Nixon
now has had for more than four, with no prospect of change:
Congress organized by the other party. But Nixon, despite intermit-
tent caution in his first term, seems not to have wanted special
connections of the sort his predecessors threw across the party breach
between themselves and Congress. And after his triumphant re-
election, he immediately tried a reverse twist on Truman's warfare
with the 80th Congress. Truman had made demands that Congress
would not meet, and cried "do-nothing"; now Nixon made budget
cuts that Congress would oppose, and readied taunts of "fiscal irresponsibility." In such a game the negative makes for even less
restraint than the affirmative. Truman wanted the program he
requested but lacked votes and did not get it. Nixon no doubt
wants to keep the cuts he made, and wields the veto. Until scandal
overtook him I think he was winning hands down—and he is not
defeated yet. In all events, little remains of a once-strong constraint.

THE PARTY

Twenty years ago, both parties were what they had been since
Andrew Jackson's time: confederal associations of state parties
grouped together for the sake of Presidential nominations and cam-
pagins. The state parties, in turn, consisted of some relatively standard parts: city machines, court-house gangs, interest-group leaders,
elective officeholders, big contributors. Stitching them all together
nationally every fourth year was a task for party regulars assembled
in convention. Barons strongly based in interest groups or regions
or machines collectively had power to decide, or at least veto, and
their number at a given time was never very large. Perhaps 50 or
100 men—buttressed, of course, by aides and friends and clients—
were crucial to each party's nomination and campaign, crucial in
convention and in canvassing and funding. And they were a known
circle, shifting over time but usually quite easy to identify at any
moment.

As with Congress, Truman was linked in stable fashion to the party leaders by a common interest: the Presidential succession. Such a relationship constrains one politician's staff in dealing with another politician, and even more so when, as was usually the case with Truman, he needed more help than he could give. Gallup Poll approval of his conduct fell to 32 per cent in 1946 and then as low as 23 per cent in 1951, eight points below Nixon's low last August. Not coincidentally, in 1946 Truman was requested by the Democratic National Committee *not* to campaign for Congress. In 1948 the railroads withdrew credit and his famous whistle-stop tour almost stopped for lack of funds. In 1952 Governor Adlai Stevenson of Illinois persistently evaded his embrace, insisted on a draft, refused a White House build-up. The party barons out in states and cities may have liked the President and felt some kinship for him, but few if any were prepared to die for him, and none, so far as I know, were content to work through staff in lieu of him. Like Rayburn, they preferred to deal, and to be known to deal, and to be known to deal directly. In Truman's situation their preferences mattered a lot.

As organizations our two national parties have never been twins. But insofar as both shared features of the sort I have described, both are now changed almost beyond recognition. TV and jet aircraft, primaries and ticket-splitting join with education, affluence, and population shifts to outmode old customs and weaken old fiefdoms. We have left the age of barons and entered the age of candidates. Its hallmarks are management by private firms, exposure through the tube, funding by direct-mail drives as well as fat-cats, and canvassing by zealous volunteers.

For the Republican party nationally, 1964 exposed the passing of the old regime; for Democrats the year was 1972. Nixon in a sense is our first President to deal with party ties wholly in terms of the new conditions. Watergate sheds light on how his White House dealt. What it shows is an inordinate concern for raising money, coupled with a campaign organization run by White House aides. The Committee for the Re-election of the President was wholly independent of the Republican National Committee; it remained in existence after the campaign. Perhaps coincidentally, the White House planned that after the election those aides and others should fan out all over town, taking up sub-Cabinet posts or civil service supergrades in every major agency. Much of this actually happened last winter; it was the most determined such effort by any Administration in memory.

Why grab so much money? Why carry on CRP? Why scatter

subalterns all over the place? Likelier than not the answer lies in sheer momentum, in doing what comes naturally (and to excess, as was typical of the Nixon staff). But possibly they are related. It is conceivable these three developments were part of a scheme for dominating not only the Administration, but also the Republican succession. In an age of candidates, could White House-controlled bank accounts combined with White House–controlled agencies provide a substitute for defunct party baronies? As hopefuls crowded the primaries in 1976, could these assets have given the power of decision or veto to the White House staff? In any event, the setting does not make for much constraint!

THE CABINET

Truman's Cabinet officers were his appointees, for the most part, but rarely his creatures. Some of them (not many) had party standing of their own, linked to a faction of those old-style barons. Some bureau chiefs (a lot) had the equivalent in links to leading Congressmen and vital interest groups. Everyone, regardless of his standing, owed a duty to the statutory programs he administered, and so to the Congressional committees that controlled their life blood: laws and funds. Since the "Compromise of 1789"—when Congress took the power to create departments, leaving the Presidents the discretion to dismiss department heads—it had been recognized in practice, if not always in words, that "executive" agencies of all sorts were subordinate at once to President *and* Congress, a triangular relationship that left them with two masters who could frequently be played off against each other. J. Edgar Hoover's practice of this art in 1971 seems newsworthy today but would have seemed the norm for any self-respecting bureau chief in 1951 or earlier, the period when Hoover perfected his technique.

So it was in Truman's time, and so with variations it appears to have remained. But the variations are important. They suggest that Nixon's White House up to now has rarely felt the full constraint shared mastership used to impose. That Nixon's aides thought otherwise—as their extraordinary memoranda show—hints at either ignorance or paranoia.

Viewed from a distance, two changes stand out. As of, say, 1970 compared with 1950, most Cabinet officers seem less important to the President, while bureau chiefs appear less certain of Congressional support against the President, or anyway less likely to invoke

it. The latter change reflects what may have been a passing phase
—much of Washington heeds the dictum "never hit a man unless
he's down," and Nixon, like Truman before him, has become vulnerable. Or maybe it reflects a downward shift of levels for Congressional support deep into program management, and well below
the bureau chiefs, almost out of sight. And possibly the change is
greater than it would be if party ties helped connect committees to
agencies. But if this change is hard to pin down, the Cabinet change
is not.

The low estate of most contemporary Cabinet posts reflects reduced White House dependence on departments as well as increased
dependence of departments on each other. Twenty years ago the
President relied on Cabinet members for a great deal of the staff
work now performed inside the White House. President Eisenhower was the first to pull into the White House the detailed work
of lobbying with Congress for Administration bills; Truman had
mostly kept it out. And the hiring and firing of agency officials
below Cabinet rank is now centralized as never before. Whatever
its purpose—partisan or managerial or both—the fanning out of
Nixon aides last winter into agencies reflects unprecedented White
House planning and initiative in lower level appointments. Initiative once rested mostly with department heads; they usually won
their contests with the White House staff. (It has been only a dozen
years since Kennedy's Defense Secretary rejected out of hand a
White House proposal for Secretary of the Navy, none other than
Franklin Delano Roosevelt Jr.)

In Truman's years, moreover, a department head could look
down at his bureaus, out to their clients, and up to subcommittees
on the Hill without having to think hourly about other departments. A bailiwick was still a bailiwick. For many department heads
this is no longer true. I once worked closely with the head of the
housing agency that preceded HUD. I do not recall that he gave a
thought to the Federal Security Agency, the forerunner of HEW.
But there was then no Model Cities Program.

Since President Johnson got his chance to put through Congress
a whole generation's worth of Democratic programs—many stem-
ming from Truman proposals stalled since the 1940s—new endeavors
have entangled departmental jurisdictions in such a web of overlapping statutes, funding, staffs, and clientele that no one moves
without involving others, often painfully. I gather it is even hard
to stand still on one's own. In dealing with the consequences, bu-

reaus are important, and so are Presidential staffs; the bureaus can operate, albeit on a narrow front, while the staffs can coordinate, at least in terms of budgets. Department heads are often poorly placed to do either. Their positions often are at once too lofty and too low.

Johnson once wanted supermanagers to rationalize his programs as they built them up. Nixon called for supermanagers to rationalize those programs down, and build up revenue-sharing. From either standpoint, Cabinet posts seemed cramped in White House eyes. In addition, the incumbents were cramped for time. New programs conferred on most departments new relationships with more Congressional committees than before. These Cabinet members still were in position to testify. So they did, over and over. It took a lot of time. But it added little to their weight at the White House. And Ehrlichman condescended.

Down the drain went still another set of Presidential colleagues —and constraints.

THE SCHEDULE

As for internal constraints on Truman's Presidency, the first derived from his operating style. He was accessible beyond contemporary belief. Following Roosevelt's peacetime practice and a long Presidential tradition, HST stood ready to see any member of Congress, granting 15-minute interviews to anyone who asked, if possible within 24 hours of the asking. The same rule held for Cabinet and sub-Cabinet officers, heads of lesser agencies, and governors of states—these among others. His days were chopped up into 15-minute segments, morning and afternoon. He managed to include not only those who wanted to see him but also those he wished to see. He was available to staff early and late. And he met weekly, in addition, with the legislative leaders, the Cabinet, the National Security Council, and the press—all this on top of ceremonies and aside from reading, late into the night.

Those 15-minute interviews, on the callers' business, at their option, took a large amount of time—no mean constraint—and also follow-up, which constrained his staff all the more, as Truman, like Roosevelt before him, usually met his callers alone. Inefficiencies resulted, and waste motion. But at the same time, this President was personally exposed, day in and [day] out, to what a lot of people wanted from him; he learned what they cared about, believed, hoped, and feared. And constraining or not, I think Truman liked the flow. He found in it large compensations.

Eisenhower, by contrast, chafed under it, found it intolerable, channeled off all he could to his aides. Until his heart attack in 1955, members of Congress complained, and so did Cabinet members and others. Afterward, acceptance set in. Before President Kennedy took office he was warned (to his discomfort) that he would be pressed to resume Truman's custom. But this did not occur. Washington had accepted the Eisenhower custom. Kennedy and Johnson were as free as has been Nixon to receive or put off whom they chose. Their choices were very different from his. But their freedom to make them eased his choice of relative isolation.

THE PRESS

Twenty years ago, another internal constraint derived from White House press relations, above all from the press conference as a regular weekly undertaking. These were no longer the intimate affairs of Roosevelt's time, with reporters crowded compatibly into the Oval Office; by Truman's second term they had become big-scale affairs in larger quarters, less educative for the correspondents, less fun for the President. But they still served many other functions, communications functions *within* government, connecting our peculiarly separated branches, as well as informing the public. Regular press conferences gave the White House staff a chance to put the President on record unmistakably with Congressmen or bureaucrats or interest groups or partisans who could not be convinced at second hand. They gave those others chances to check up on the assertions of the staff. They gave the President himself a chance to reinforce or override the claims made in his name by staff and everybody else. They gave him, finally, opportunities to puncture myths and gossip.

Truman did not always turn these chances to his own account. Sometimes he backed into unintended promises, disclosures, or embarrassments. Thus press conferences constrained him. But I think they constrained others more, not the least his staff. At any rate, whatever pain they caused, those regular press conferences offered all concerned, the President included, compensations not obtainable from any other source. This we found out after Johnson impaired them by irregularity, still more after Nixon virtually shut them down. By Johnson's time, of course, press conferences had come to be live television shows. He reacted against the risks to his own image and his programs inherent in exposure through an entertainment medium, where many things besides words are conveyed to many publics viewing as a passive audience. Endowed with different style and temperament, Kennedy had faced those risks with relish. Not Johnson, and not Nixon. Seeking to safeguard their public relations, these Presidents backed out of regular press conferences; in the process—inadvertently perhaps—they impaired their internal communications.

THE STAFF

The last constraint I want to mention arose from Truman's staff system, which as its central feature made him his own chief of staff. He chaired the morning staff meeting; he parceled out assignments; he watched the White House budget; he approved new staff positions. He dealt directly, one by one, with all but junior aides; he allowed few of these, kept an eye on them, and made sure that in meetings they saw a lot of him. He was immersed in detail, and it all took time. Thereby he was constrained. His aides, though, were also constrained—by him.

In this and other respects Truman followed rather closely, although not very consciously, the pattern FDR had brought to Presidential staffing in his second term. Roosevelt's pattern had four features; he clung to them consistently, and so did Truman. First, the President, and only the President, was the chief of staff. Second, there was a sharp distinction between "personal" and "institutional" staff. The latter worked in such places as the Budget Bureau, with a mandate to think always of the Presidential office apart from personal politics. The former, the White House staff per se, would think about the President's personal interests, while he could weigh both views and choose between them. Third, personal staff meant only those who helped the President to do what was required of him day by day, manning his schedule, drafting his speeches, guarding his signature, nursing the press corps, or, during the war, dealing with Stalin and Churchill. "This is the White House calling" was to mean the President himself or someone reliably in touch with him. Roosevelt cared devoutly for the symbolism of that house. All other aides were "institutional," to be kept out of there and off that phone. He overlapped staff duties, reached out to departments, pored over newspapers, probed his visitors, and quizzed his wife. Not only was he chief of his own staff, he also was his own director of intelligence on happenings in his Administration. Except when they embarrassed him, he looked upon press leaks as adding to his sources.

The Rooseveltian pattern has had a curious history over the years. It evolved under Truman and then was abandoned by Eisenhower. The General could not abide it and thought it wrong in principle. Rather than immersion he sought freedom from detail and built a bigger staff than Truman's to relieve him of it. He made someone else his chief of staff, and created a swirl of secretariats to serve committees of Cabinet members. In reaction, Kennedy scrapped most of that and consciously restored the Rooseveltian arrangement, adapting as he went but following all its features. Johnson adapted further, but with less care as he grew more and more immersed in his war. Nixon evolved a different pattern that somewhat resembled Eisenhower's, but with a marked change in its means for tackling policy. Committee secretariats became substantive staffs, with initiative and discretion independent of Cabinet members. A much larger White House staff resulted. Seeking freedom for himself, Nixon left its management to others.

Thus in the more than 30 years since the White House staff became a major feature of our government, we have alternated between two contrasting patterns for its composition and control. Numbers tell part of the story. In 1952, civilian aides with some substantive part in public business numbered 20. In 1962, the number was the same. In 1972, it seems to have been somewhere between 50 and 75 (depending on how one counts the third-level assistants). Moreover, the alternation follows party lines; the contrasting patterns have almost become matters of party philosophy. At least they are matters of party experience, handed down through the political generations from old cadres to the young. When a Haldeman eloquently testifies on the philosophy of Nixon's system, Democrats scoff. Republicans did likewise at the lack of system in Roosevelt's arrangements, to say nothing of Kennedy's. It naturally is harder now for Democrats than for Republicans to think Nixon could genuinely, if wishfully, not know—and then be cramped in finding out about—the cover-up of Watergate. Students of the Eisenhower Presidency are less skeptical.

A staff system that liberates the President to think frees staff men from his watchful eye. The price he pays for liberty comes in the coin of power. So we have seen with Nixon since last March. This always worried Roosevelt.

It is a matter of coincidence, I think, that even as the old constraints of prudence slackened, the White House staff fell under the control of senior aides so lacking in propriety as those we saw this summer on our television screens. Men like these are the opposite of Truman's Counsel, Murphy. Not everyone who ever served in the White House met his standard. But few if any ever fell so far below it as those Nixon aides. Men of their extraordinary impropriety have not been found there before, at least not in such numbers. Their like might not have been there under Nixon, or not so many of them, had he won the Presidency eight years earlier, succeeding Eisenhower. Even in 1969 they did not have the place all to themselves, but had to share it for a while with seniors of a different sort, men who were old hands at governing, experienced downtown and tempered by long contact with the Hill. Murphy's sensitivities owed much to the flavor of Congress—especially the Senate (where he himself had been a legislative counsel) and most especially the Senate of the old Southern ascendancy, exemplified by Senator Richard Russell. (In 1951, Russell's masterful performance in the chair of the MacArthur hearings caused the General to fade away, no harm to the Republic, and set a high standard for Senator Ervin.) But in Nixon's White House those most respectful of the Hill's old flavor did not long survive a contest with the masters of new-style campaigning. Zealous for their chief, the winners packed the place with second- and third-level men of their own mind, magnified his wishes by their own means, and wound up blighting the bright prospect of his second term.

Excess now has bred its own corrective. Watergate puts new life into old constraints, or, more precisely, it assures a set of temporary substitutes. If the White House is forced into continuous give-and-take, this after all is what the Constitution intended. If the give-and-take sometimes degenerates into sheer nastiness, that will reflect the way it all began, in White House zealousness. Near-term results are predictable. If he wants, Nixon can have a limited connection with the Congressional leaders, though at a higher price than formerly. Where he does not, stand-offs will ensue, with each side using assured powers to harass the other. Budget cuts and vetoes will be countered by withheld appropriations or rejected confirmations. Bargains will be struck, *ad hoc,* on relatively even terms, a process hardly conceivable six months ago. At the same time there will be fresh support by subcommittees for pet programs, and vice versa, no matter what the White House says or wants. Caught in between, department heads will drift toward their subordinates regardless of the White House, or subsist increasingly in lame-duck isolation. Some Cabinet officers will probably emerge as major figures in their own right. And while the President himself cannot now be expected to change operating styles, the senior aides now near him, and particularly those inflicted on him, should be quite able to do so in the direction of caution. Their accessibility compensates a little for his isolation.

If these predictions* are borne out, the three and one-half years remaining for this President—assuming, as I do, that he fills out his term—will be neither easy nor tidy; in domestic terms they will produce more noise and less redirection than he wanted, and in foreign terms they will produce less movement than he hoped. But he would have faced some shortfall even if Watergate had not happened. The failure of Phase Three to keep down prices, and the failure of bombing in Cambodia to bring "peace," assured that opposition would revive on the Hill and in the press.

The modern Presidency is a sturdy vehicle. Hardship and untidiness are frequently its lot. But at worst a President retains his formal powers. These put him at the center of the legislative process, the administrative process, national politics, foreign relations; combined they make him central to the news. Accordingly, so long as he has time ahead, there will be men in every part of Washington who are mindful of his wishes because they in their own jobs have need of him in his. Until his last appointment, his last budget, his last veto, his last summit, he cannot sink to insignificance in government; his office will uphold him. As for changes in the office of the sort now being argued both in Congress and the courts—limiting impoundment, or his use of force abroad, or claims to executive privilege—each dents the Presidency at an outer edge, narrowing discretion, reducing flexibility, but strikes no vital spot. What is vital to the office is that combination: processes, politics, peace, and the news. Within our government the combination is unique, and so confers unique advantages. These remain.

(The Nixon proposal for a single six-year Presidential term is in a different category. It would change the Presidency's central core, to my mind, for the worse. We now have, in effect, an eight-year term subject at midpoint to an opposition audit reviewed by the

---

* Made in October 1973—Eds.

electorate and then a vote of confidence without which he retires. The required re-election at midterm is one of the most democratic features of the office and adds to its legitimacy in a system of popular sovereignty. Removal of this feature to protect us from its possible corruption is a frivolous proposal for a President to make, especially when his regime has been the most corrupt. Nixon, I hope, was not serious.)

The Supreme Court last interfered with Presidential powers in 1952 when Truman was denied authority to seize the nation's steel mills. But the Court managed not to say it never could be done again in any circumstances. On the contrary, the artful spread of concurring opinions left the future relatively open. The Presidency is limited only a little. This is the likeliest outcome again when current issues reach the highest court. The net result may be to make some future Presidents work harder, under more restrictions, conciliating more, and forcing issues less than Nixon chose to do in his first term—or Truman at the time of the steel seizures. The Presidency won't be flattened by that!

To write of Truman is to recall the trouble and the pain associated with his Presidency: the pain of the Korean war and those interminable truce talks; the pain of domestic reforms deferred, of foreign developments blighted; the pain of MacArthur, and McCarthy; the China charges; the corruption charges; the list goes on and on. But where is that pain now? The young know nothing of it; the old have long since put it out of mind. A few of us would gladly show our scars, but we have no viewers except for historians, and not even many of them. Truman never captivated the campuses. And so I predict it will be with our current trouble. At the same time, though, short-term results have a way of shedding light on problems for the more distant future.

If the value of Watergate is great as a temporary renewer of old constraints, it is not unqualified. We now are in a period of antipolitical politics, with journalists and politicians playing to their own sense of successive, cumulative, public disillusionments. Watergate feeds the mood. When such a period descended on us in the early 1950s we got Eisenhower for President, the hero-above-politics. Since we lack heroes nowadays, the next time could be worse. Moreover, the renewed constraints on Nixon cannot last forever. Watergate's effects will wear off over time, perhaps by his successor's second term (taking us no farther than 1984). As this occurs the weakened state of old constraints will be exposed once more: the parties gone beyond recall, the Congress mortgaged to ticket-splitting, the Cabinet frayed by overlapping jurisdictions, the dependence of all the rest on the President's own style.

But separated powers still define our system, so new colleagues, bringing new constraints, may replace the old, and some of the old may revive. What happens in our parties is especially important. We may face perpetual disarray, a dire prospect. But renewal is by no means inconceivable. For instance, big-state governors, linked to professional managers and money, may revive party baronies in the guise of perpetual candidacies. Reagan and Rockefeller may be precursors. As part of the same vision, or perhaps quite separately, cadres of volunteers funded by direct-mail drives may come into existence state by state to man elective party posts and staff campaigns, substituting, in relatively stable fashion, for old-style machines. "Favorite sons" may come to have renewed significance. The national convention may again become the place for interstate negotiations (especially if the TV networks cut back live coverage). A President, like others, then negotiates again.

If national parties revive, this makes it the more likely that Congress and the White House will some day be run again by men with the same party label. A President then will welcome back old colleagues. As for executive operations, residual price and wage controls—an incomes policy with some sort of club in the closet—may well join revenue-sharing and resource regulation as likely long-term features of the federal scene. White House attention may be focused on them in the future, along with defense and diplomacy. If so, no matter what becomes of traditional Cabinet posts, the President will gain new executive colleagues: corporation officials, union leaders, governors, mayors.

Even the traditional executive positions may again turn more collegial from a President's standpoint than most of them were six months ago. Much depends upon the evolution of relationships with Congress. Senator Walter F. Mondale recently has urged, as one of several new checks on the White House, a televised Senate question period for Cabinet officers. This is an old proposal, but with the new addition of television, no small matter. Such appearances would distance Cabinet members from the President and so make them more important to him, in the very act of making them perform independently. But television is not without risk. While distancing them, it might also diminish them—and the Senate along with them—especially if viewers were to compare Senate sessions with, say, the press conferences of a JFK. The tube is a two-edged sword; thus, so is Mondale's scheme. But it suggests how readily the future may be open to some changes in the status of traditional Cabinet posts.

In short, I think it possible that 20 years from now constraints upon a President will be at least as strong as 20 years ago. While we wait for the emergence of new colleagues or a welcome-back to old, we have little to depend on by way of these informal checks and balances, except constraints of the other sort, those of operating style. Then the man's methods alone define the sense of prudence he may call to the support of his own sense of propriety. All is subjective, turning on him, much as it was until lately with Nixon.

But for a while Watergate supervenes. Nixon's successor, I predict, will not be tarred by it. Indeed he probably will be its beneficiary, winning as a "Mr. Clean." Almost surely he will pledge to make himself accessible and to rein in his staff. So did Nixon five years ago, but the next President will have more need to be serious about it, and more reason, and he may well possess a temperament more suited to the task. Voters, I suspect, will shun secretive types. God willing. they will welcome humor. At worst we should get prudence with a pretense of propriety. At best we will get the genuine article.

The Runaway Presidency

ARTHUR M. SCHLESINGER, JR.

I

"The tyranny of the legislature is really the danger most to be feared, and will continue to be so for many years to come," Jefferson wrote Madison six weeks before Washington's first inauguration. "The tyranny of the executive power will come in its turn, but at a more distant period." On the eve of the second centennial of independence, Jefferson's prophecy appears almost on the verge of fulfillment. The imperial presidency, created by wars abroad, has made a bold bid for power at home. The belief of the Nixon Administration in its own mandate and in its own virtue, compounded by its conviction that the Republic has been in mortal danger from internal enemies, has produced an unprecedented concentration of power in the White House and an unprecedented attempt to transform the presidency of the Constitution into a plebiscitary presidency. If this transformation is carried through, the President, instead of being accountable every day to Congress and public opinion, will be accountable every four years to the electorate. Between elections, the President will be accountable only through impeachment and will govern, as much as he can, by decree. The expansion and abuse of presidential power constitute the underlying issue, the issue that Watergate has raised to the surface, dramatized, and made politically accessible.

In giving great power to Presidents, Americans have declared their faith in the winnowing processes of politics. They have assumed that these processes, whether operating through the Electoral College or later through the congressional caucus or still later through the party conventions, will eliminate aspirants to the pres-

Adapted from Chapter 11 of *The Imperial Presidency*, by Arthur M. Schlesinger, Jr. Reprinted from *The Atlantic Monthly*, copyright © 1973. Arthur M. Schlesinger, Jr. is Albert Schweitzer Professor of Humanities at City University of New York. Among his many books are the three volumes of *The Age of Roosevelt*, *The Age of Jackson*, and *A Thousand Days: John F. Kennedy in the White House*.

idency who reject the written restraints of the Constitution and the unwritten restraints of the republican ethos.

Through most of American history that assumption has been justified. "Not many Presidents have been brilliant," James Bryce observed in 1921, "some have not risen to the full moral height of the position. But none has been base or unfaithful to his trust, none has tarnished the honour of the nation." Even as Bryce wrote, however, his observation was falling out of date—Warren G. Harding had just been inaugurated—and half a century later his optimism appears as much the function of luck as of any necessity in the constitutional order. Today the pessimism of the Supreme Court in an 1866 decision, *ex parte Milligan,* seems a good deal more prescient. The nation, as Justice Davis wrote for the Court then, has "no right to expect that it will always have wise and humane rulers, sincerely attached to the principles of the Constitution. Wicked men, ambitious of power, with hatred of liberty and contempt of law, may fill the place once occupied by Washington and Lincoln."

The presidency has been in crisis before, but the constitutional offense that led to the impeachment of Andrew Johnson was trivial compared to the charges now accumulating around the Nixon Administration. There are, indeed, constitutional offenses here too —the abuse of impoundment and executive privilege, for example; or the secret air war against Cambodia in 1969–1970, unauthorized by and unknown to Congress; or the prosecution of the war in Vietnam after the repeal of the Tonkin Gulf Resolution; or the air war against Cambodia after the total withdrawal of American troops from Vietnam. But these, like Andrew Johnson's far less consequential defiance of the Tenure of Office Act, are questions that a President may more or less plausibly insist lie within a range of executive discretion. The Johnson case has discredited impeachment as a means of resolving arguable disagreements over the interpretation of the Constitution in advance of final judgment by the Supreme Court.

What is unique in the history of the presidency is the long list of potential *criminal* charges against the Nixon Administration. The investigations in process suggest that Nixon's appointees were engaged in a multitude of indictable activities: at the very least, in burglary, in forgery, in illegal wiretapping, in illegal electronic surveillance, in perjury, in subornation of perjury, in obstruction of justice, in destruction of evidence, in tampering with witnesses, in misprision of felony, in bribery (of the Watergate defendants), in acceptance of bribes (from Vesco and ITT), in conspiracy to involve government agencies (the FBI, the CIA, the Secret Service, the IRS, the Securities and Exchange Commission) in illegal action.

As for the President himself, he has denied that he knew either about the warfare of espionage and sabotage waged by his agents against his opponents or about the subsequent cover-up. If Nixon knew about these things, he obviously conspired against the basic processes of democracy. If he really did not know and for nine months did not bother to find out, he is surely an irresponsible and incompetent executive. For, if he did not know, it can only be because he did not want to know. He had all the facilities in the world for discovering the facts. The courts and posterity will have to decide whether the *Spectator* of London is right in its harsh judgment that in two centuries American history has come full circle "from George Washington, who could not tell a lie, to Richard Nixon, who cannot tell the truth."

Whether Nixon himself was witting or unwitting, what is clearly beyond dispute is his responsibility for the moral atmosphere within his official family. White House aides do not often do things they know their principal would not wish them to do—a proposition which I and dozens of other former White House aides can certify from experience. It is the President who both sets the example and picks the men. What standards did Nixon establish for his White House? He himself has admitted that in 1970, till J. Edgar Hoover forced him to change his mind, he authorized a series of criminal actions in knowing violation of the laws and the Constitution—authorization that would appear to be in transgression both of his presidential oath to preserve the Constitution and of his constitutional duty to see that the laws are faithfully executed. In 1971, as he has also admitted, he commissioned the White House plumbers, who set out so soon thereafter on their career of burglary, wiretapping, and forgery. "From the time when the break-in occurred," he said of the Watergate affair in August, 1973, "I pressed repeatedly to know the facts, and particularly whether there was any involvement of anyone in the White House"; but two obvious sources—John Mitchell, his intimate friend, former law partner, former Attorney General, head of the Committee for the Re-Election of the President, and Patrick Gray, acting director of the FBI itself—have both testified under oath that he never got around to pressing them.

He even, through John Ehrlichman, asked the Ellsberg judge in the midst of the trial whether he would not like to be head of the FBI. And he continues to hold up Ehrlichman and Haldeman as models to the nation—"two of the finest public servants it has been my privilege to know."

Nixon, in short, created the Nixon White House. "There was no independent sense of morality there," said Hugh Sloan, who served in the Nixon White House for two years. "If you worked for someone, he was God, and whatever the orders were, you did it. . . . It was all so narrow, so closed. . . . There emerged some kind of separate morality about things." "Because of a certain atmosphere that had developed in my working at the White House," said Jeb Stuart Magruder, "I was not as concerned about its illegality as I should have been." "The White House is another world," said John Dean. "Expediency is everything." "No one who had been in the White House," said Tom Charles Huston, "could help but feel he was in a state of siege." "On my first or second day in the White House," said Herbert Porter, "Dwight Chapin [the President's appointments secretary] said to me, 'One thing you should realize early on, we are practically an island here.' That was the way the world was viewed." The "original sin," Porter felt, was the "misuse" of young people "through the whole White House system. They were not criminals by birth or design. Left to their own devices, they wouldn't engage in this sort of thing. Someone had to be telling them to do it." Gordon Strachan told of his excitement at "being twenty-seven years old and walking into the White House and seeing the President"; but, when asked what word he had for other young men who wanted to come to Washington and enter the public service, he said grimly, "My advice would be to stay away."

This is not the White House we have known—those of us, Democrats or Republicans, who served other Presidents in other years. Appointment to the White House of Roosevelt or Truman or Eisenhower or Kennedy or Johnson seemed the highest responsibility one could expect and therefore required higher standards of behavior than most of us had recognized before. And most of us look back at our White House experience, not with shame and incredulity, as the Nixon young men do, but as the most exhilarating time in our lives. Government, as Clark Clifford says, is a chameleon, taking its color from the character and personality of the President.

Moreover, Nixon's responsibility for the White House ethos goes beyond strictly moral considerations. In the First Congress, Madison, arguing that the power to remove government officials must belong to the President, added, "We have in him the security for the good behavior of the officer." This makes "the President responsible to the public for the conduct of the person he has nominated and appointed." If the President suffers executive officials to perpetrate crimes or neglects to superintend their conduct so as to check excesses, he himself, Madison said, is subject to "the decisive engine of impeachment."

II

The crisis of the presidency has led some critics to advocate a reconstruction of the institution itself. For a long time people have felt that the job was becoming too much for one man to handle. "Men of ordinary physique and discretion," Woodrow Wilson wrote as long ago as 1908, "cannot be Presidents and live, if the strain be not somehow relieved. We shall be obliged always to be picking our chief magistrate from among wise and prudent athletes,—a small class."

But what was seen until the late 1950s as too exhausting physically is now seen, after Vietnam and Watergate, as too dizzying psychologically. In 1968 Eugene McCarthy, the first liberal presidential aspirant in the century to run against the presidency, called for the depersonalization and decentralization of the office. The White House, he thought, should be turned into a museum. Instead of trying to lead the nation, the President should become "a kind of channel" for popular desires and aspirations. Watergate has made the point irresistible. "The office has become too complex and its reach too extended," writes Barbara Tuchman, "to be trusted to the fallible judgment of any one individual." "A man with poor judgment, an impetuous man, a sick man, a power-mad man," adds Max Lerner, "each would be dangerous in the post. Even an able, sensitive man needs stronger safeguards around him than exist today."

The result is a new wave of proposals to transform the presidency into a collegial institution. Mrs. Tuchman suggests a six-man directorate with a rotating chairman, each member to serve for a year, as in Switzerland. Lerner wants to give the President a Council of State, a body that he would be bound by law to consult and that, because half its members would be from Congress and some from the opposite party, would presumably give him independent advice. Both proposals were, in fact, considered and rejected at the Constitutional Convention.

Hamilton and Jefferson disagreed on many things, but they agreed that the convention had been right in deciding on a one-man presidency. A plural executive, Hamilton contended, if divided within itself, would lead the country into factionalism and anarchy and, if united, could lead it into tyranny. When power was placed in the hands of a group small enough to admit "of their interests and views being easily combined in a common enterprise, by an artful leader," Hamilton thought, "it becomes more liable to abuse, and more dangerous when abused, than if it be lodged in the hands of one man, who, from the very circumstances of his being alone, will be more narrowly watched and more readily suspected." With a single executive it was possible to fix accountability. But a directorate "would serve to destroy, or would greatly diminish, the intended and necessary responsibility of the Chief Magistrate himself."

Jefferson had favored a plural executive under the Articles of Confederation, and, as an American in Paris, he watched with sympathy the Directoire of the French Revolution. But these experiments left him no doubt that plurality was a mistake. As he later observed, if Washington's Cabinet, in which he had served with Hamilton, had been a directorate, "the opposing wills would have balanced each other and produced a state of absolute inaction." But Washington, after listening to both sides, acted on his own, providing the "regulating power which would keep the machine in steady movement." History, moreover, furnished "as many examples of a single usurper arising out of a government by a plurality, as of temporary trusts of power in a single hand rendered permanent by usurpation."

The question remains whether the world has changed enough in two centuries to make these objections obsolete. There is, of course, the burden-of-the-presidency argument. But is the presidential burden so much heavier than ever before? The scope of the national government has expanded beyond imagination, but so too have the facilities for presidential management. The only President who clearly died of overwork was Polk, and that was a long time ago. Hoover, who worked intensely and humorlessly as President, lived for more than thirty years after the White House; Truman, who worked intensely and gaily, lived for twenty. The contemporary President is really not all that overworked. Eisenhower managed more golf than most corporation officials or college presidents; Kennedy always seemed unhurried and relaxed; Nixon spends almost as much time in Florida and California as in Washington, or so it appears. Johnson's former press secretary George Reedy has dealt with the myth of the presidential work load in terms that rejoice anyone who has ever served in the White House. "There is far less to the presidency, in terms of essential activity," Reedy correctly says, "than meets the eye." The President can fill his hours with as much motion as he desires, but he also can delegate as much "work" as he desires. "A president moves through his days surrounded by literally hundreds of people whose relationship to him is that of a doting mother to a spoiled child. Whatever he wants is brought to him immediately—food, drink, helicopters, airplanes, people, in fact, everything but relief from his political problems."

As for the moral and psychological weight of these political problems, this is real enough. All major presidential decisions are taken in conditions of what General Marshall, speaking of battle, used to call "chronic obscurity"—that is, on the basis of incomplete and probably inaccurate intelligence, with no sure knowledge where the enemy is or even where one's own men are. This can be profoundly anguishing for reasonably sensitive Presidents, especially when decisions determine people's livelihoods or end their lives. It was this, and not the work load, that did in Wilson and the second Roosevelt. But is the sheer moral weight of decision greater today than ever before? Greater for Johnson and Nixon than for Washington and Lincoln or Wilson or FDR? I doubt it very much.

If there is an argument for a plural executive, it is not the alleged burden of the presidency. The serious argument is simply to keep one man from wielding too much power. But here the points of Hamilton and Jefferson still have validity. The Council of Ten in Venice was surely as cruel as any doge. One wonders whether a six-man presidency would have prevented the war in Vietnam. It might well, however, have prevented the New Deal. The single-man presidency, with the right man as President, has its uses; and historically Americans have as often as not chosen the right man.

The idea of a Council of State has more plausibility. But it works better for foreign than for domestic policy. A prudent President is well advised to convoke ad hoc Councils of State on issues of war and peace. Kennedy added outsiders to his Executive Committee during the Cuban missile crisis, and it was an ad hoc Council of

State in March, 1968, that persuaded Johnson to cease and desist in Vietnam. But, as an institutionalized body, with membership the ex officio perquisite of the senior leadership of House and Senate— that is, of the men in Congress who in the past have always been inclined to go along with Presidents—it could easily become simply one more weapon for a strong President. As Gouverneur Morris said at the Constitutional Convention, the President "by persuading his Council . . . to concur in his wrong measures would acquire their protection for them."

Above all, both the plural executive and the Council of State are open to the objection that most concerned the Founding Fathers— the problem of fixing accountability. In the case of high crimes and misdemeanors, who, to put it bluntly, is to be impeached? The solution surely lies not in blurring responsibility for the actions of the executive but in making that responsibility categorical and in finding ways of holding Presidents to it.

III

The other change in the institution of the presidency under discussion runs in the opposite direction. The idea of a single six-year presidential term is obviously designed not to reduce but to increase the independence of the presidency. This idea naturally appeals to the imperial ethos. Lyndon Johnson advocated it; Nixon has commended it to his Commission on Federal Election Reform for particular study. What is more puzzling is that it also has the support of two eminent senators, both unsympathetic to the imperial presidency, Mike Mansfield of Montana and George Aiken of Vermont—support that gives it a hearing it would not otherwise have had.

It is not a new idea. Andrew Jackson recommended to Congress an amendment limiting Presidents to a single term of four to six years; Andrew Johnson did the same; the Confederate Constitution provided for a single six-year term. Mansfield and Aiken now press their version on the ground, as Mansfield says, that a six-year term would "place the Office of the Presidency in a position that transcends as much as possible partisan political considerations." The amendment, says Aiken, "would allow a President to devote himself entirely to the problems of the Nation and would free him from the millstone of partisan politics."

This argument has a certain old-fashioned good-government

plausibility. How nice it would be if Presidents could be liberated from politics for six years and set free to do only what is best for the country! But the argument assumes that Presidents know better than anyone else what is best for the country and that the democratic process is an obstacle to wise decisions. It assumes that Presidents are so generally right and the people so generally wrong that the President has to be protected against political pressures. It is, in short, a profoundly antidemocratic position. It is also profoundly unrealistic to think that any constitutional amendment could transport a President to some higher and more immaculate realm and still leave the United States a democracy. As Thomas Corcoran told the Senate Judiciary Committee during hearings on the Mansfield-Aiken amendment, "It is impossible to take politics out of politics."

But, even if it were possible to take the presidency out of politics, is there reason to suppose this desirable? The electorate often knows things that Presidents do not know, and the nation has already paid a considerable price for presidential isolation and ignorance. Few things are more likely to make Presidents sensitive to public opinion than worrying about their own political future. Moreover, if public opinion is at times a baneful influence, what else is democracy all about? The need to persuade the nation of the soundness of a proposed policy is the heart of democracy. "A President immunized from political considerations," Clark Clifford told the Senate Judiciary Committee, "is a President who need not listen to the people, respond to majority sentiment, or pay attention to views that may be diverse, intense and perhaps at variance with his own."

The Mansfield-Aiken amendment expresses distrust of the democratic process in still another way—by its bar against re-eligibility. If anything is of the essence of democracy, it is surely that the voters should have an unconstrained choice of their leaders. "I can see no propriety," George Washington wrote the year after the adoption of the Constitution, "in precluding ourselves from the service of any man, who on some great emergency shall be deemed universally most capable of serving the public."

IV

Oddly, the crisis of the imperial presidency has not elicited much support for what at other times has been a favored theory of constitutional reform: movement in the direction of the British parliamentary system. This is particularly odd because, whatever the general balance of advantage between the parliamentary and presidential modes, the parliamentary system has one feature the presidential system badly needs now—the requirement that the head of government be compelled at regular intervals to explain and defend his policies in face-to-face sessions with the political opposition. Few devices, it would seem, are better calculated both to break down the real isolation of the latter-day presidency and to dispel the spurious reverence that has come to envelop the office.

In a diminished version, applying only to members of the Cabinet, the idea is nearly as old as the Republic itself. The proposal that Cabinet members should go on to the floor of Congress to answer questions and take part in debate, "far from raising any constitutional difficulties," as E. S. Corwin once observed, "has the countenance of early practice under the Constitution." The Confederate Constitution authorized Congress to grant the head of each executive department "a seat upon the floor of either House, with the privilege of discussing any measures appertaining to his department," and Congressman George H. Pendleton of Ohio, with the support of Congressman James A. Garfield, argued for a similar proposal in the Union Congress in 1864. In his last annual message, President William Howard Taft suggested that Cabinet members be given access to the floor in order, as he later put it, "to introduce measures to advocate their passage, to answer questions, and to enter into debate as if they were members, without of course the right to vote. . . . The time lost in Congress over useless discussion of issues that might be disposed of by a single statement from the head of a department, no one can appreciate unless he has filled such a place."

In the meantime, the young Woodrow Wilson carried the idea a good deal further toward the British model, arguing that Cabinet members should not just sit voteless in Congress but should be actually chosen "from the ranks of the legislative majority." Instead of the chaotic and irresponsible system of government by congressional committees, the Republic would then have Cabinet government and ministerial responsibility. Though Wilson did not renew this specific proposal in later years, it very likely lingered in the back of his mind. On the eve of his first inauguration he noted that the position of the presidency was "quite abnormal, and must lead eventually to something very different." "Sooner or later," the President must be made "answerable to opinion in a somewhat more informal and intimate fashion—answerable, it may be, to the Houses whom he seeks to lead, either personally or through a cabinet, as well as to the people for whom they speak. But that is a matter to be worked out."

Wilson never found time to work it out. Today there appears to be little interest in reforms that squint at parliamentarianism. This may be in part because the parliamentary regimes best known in America—the British and French—have themselves moved in the direction of prime-ministerial or presidential government and offer few guarantees against the Vietnam-Watergate effect.

V

The problem of reining in the runaway presidency centers a good deal more at the moment on substantive than on structural solutions. Congress, in other words, has decided it can best restrain the presidency by enacting specific legislation in the conspicuous fields of presidential abuse. The main author of this comprehensive congressional attack on presidential supremacy, well before he assumed the chairmanship of the Senate Select Committee investigating Watergate, has been Senator Sam Ervin of North Carolina.

The Republic owes a great deal to Sam Ervin. No one for a long time has done so much to educate the American people in the meaning and majesty of the Constitution (though his Constitution seems to stop with the ten amendments adopted in 1791; at least he does not show the same fervor about the Fourteenth and Fifteenth amendments as he does about the First and Fourth). For most Americans the Constitution has become a hazy document, cited like the Bible on ceremonial occasions but forgotten in the daily transactions of life. For Ervin the Constitution, like the Bible, is superbly alive and fresh. He quotes it as if it had been written the day before; the Founding Fathers seem his contemporaries; it is almost as if he has ambled over from the Convention at Philadelphia. He is a true believer who endows his faith with abundant charm, decency, sagacity, and toughness. The old-fashioned Constitution—"the very finest document ever to come from the mind of men"—could have no more fitting champion in the battle against the imperial presidency.

But Ervin is concerned with more than the vindication of the Constitution. His larger design is to establish a new balance of constitutional power. Congress itself, Ervin thinks, has negligently become "the chief aggrandizer of the Executive." The restoration of the Constitution, he believes, requires the systematic recovery by Congress of powers appropriated by the presidency. The bills designed to constrain presidential war powers are, in his view, a confused and sloppy application of this strategy; he has little use for them. His own approach, direct and unequivocal, is expressed in the bill in which he proposes to give Congress absolute authority to veto executive agreements within sixty days. Congress never had, or even seriously sought, such authority before. While the provocation is real enough, the bill, if enacted, would give Congress unprecedented control over the presidential conduct of foreign affairs.

A leading item on Ervin's domestic agenda is executive privilege. This question has been historically one of conflicting and unresolved constitutional claims. In the nineteenth century, while insisting on a general congressional right to executive information, Congress acknowledged a right, or at least a power, of presidential denial in specific areas. It acquiesced in these reservations because they seemed reasonable and because responsible opinion saw them as reasonable. But what Congress saw as an expression of constitutional comity, Presidents in the later twentieth century—Nixon above all —have come to see as their inherent and unreviewable constitutional right.

Ervin, in response, has introduced a bill requiring members of the executive branch summoned by a committee of Congress to appear in person, even if they intend to claim executive privilege. Only a personal letter from the President could warrant the claim, and the bill gives the committee the power to decide whether the presidential plea is justified. In the words of Senator William Fulbright, it places "the final responsibility for judging the validity of a claim of executive privilege in the Congress, where it belongs."

A presidential thesis in violation of the traditional comity between the two branches has thus produced a congressional answer that would itself do away with what has been not only a historic but a healthy ambiguity. For one hundred and eighty years the arbiter in this question has been neither Congress nor the President nor the courts but the political context and process, with responsible opinion considering each case more or less on merit and turning against whichever side appears to be overreaching itself. The system is not tidy, but it encourages a measure of restraint on both sides and has avoided a constitutional showdown. Now absolute presidential claims have provoked an absolute congressional response. Would this really be an improvement? Would Ervin and Fulbright themselves twenty years earlier have wanted to give Joe McCarthy and his committee "the final responsibility" to judge whether executive testimony could be properly withheld?

Next on the Ervin agenda stands the restoration of congressional control over something it has thought it had anyway—the power of the purse. This means a solution of the problem of presidential impoundment. Impoundment existed before Nixon, but no previous President used it to overturn statutes and abolish programs against congressional will. For Nixon, impoundment is a means of taking from Congress the determination of national priorities.

The courts have been more willing to grasp the nettle of impoundment than they were, at least at the start, in the case of executive privilege. In decision after decision this year, judges have declared one aspect after another of the impoundment policy illegal. No judge has accepted Nixon's claim that he has a "constitutional right" not to spend money voted by Congress. One judge calls his use of impoundment "a flagrant abuse of executive discretion." "It is not within the discretion of the Executive," says another, "to refuse to execute laws passed by Congress but with which the Executive presently disagrees." The decisions are, however, as they should be, constructions of specific statutes and stop short of proposing a general solution to the impoundment controversy.

Though the courts have rallied splendidly, it is not really very satisfactory to have to sue the executive branch in every case in order to make it carry out programs duly enacted by Congress. But Congress itself has found it hard to make a stand on the Constitution. For Nixon has changed the issue with some success from a constitutional to a budgetary question. Impoundment, in other words, is alleged as the only answer a fiscally responsible President can make to insensate congressional extravagance. Sam Ervin derides this proposition. "Congress," he says, "is not composed of wild-eyed spenders, nor is the President the embattled crusader against wasteful spending that he would have you believe." The figures bear Ervin out. Congress, for example, cut more than $20 billion from Administration appropriation requests in Nixon's first term. Congress and the presidency roughly agree on the amount of money government should spend but disagree, as Ervin puts it, "over spending priorities and [the President's] authority to pick and choose what programs he will fund." Impoundment, says Ervin, has to do not with the budget but with the separation of powers.

It is a political fact, fully recognized by Ervin, that anti-impoundment legislation will have to be accompanied by new evidences of congressional self-control in spending. Ervin is personally a budget-balancer anyway. So his impoundment bill includes a spending ceiling. The bill, as passed by the Senate in 1973, also has certain eccentricities for a constitutional fundamentalist. After a clear statement in Section 1 that impoundment is unconstitutional, subsequent sections say that nevertheless the President is authorized to commit this unconstitutional act for periods up to seventy days. Thereafter impoundments not covered by the antideficiency acts (which permit the executive to impound funds not required to achieve the purpose of a statute) must cease unless Congress specifically approves them by concurrent resolution. The House, on the other hand, is quite willing to let impoundments stand unless specifically disapproved by one house of Congress. Both bills legitimize impoundment, but, where the House would place the burden on Congress in each case to stop impoundment, Ervin would place the burden on the President in each case to justify impoundment.

VI

In one area after another, with the concealed passion and will of a deceptively relaxed personality, Ervin is moving to restore the balance of the Constitution by cutting the presidency down to constitutional size. However, his is the Constitution not of Abraham Lincoln but of *ex parte Milligan*. "What the framers intended," he says, "was that the President . . . should be merely the executor of a power of decision that rests elsewhere; that is, in the Congress. This was the balance of power between the President and Congress intended by the Constitution." The "ultimate power," Ervin says, is "legislative."

It is hard to know how literally to take the Ervin scheme. If it sounds at times like an effort to replace presidential government by congressional government, it must be remembered that the Ervin proposals have been provoked by an attempt to alter the nature of the system. Ervin and his colleagues are fighting to protect Congress from the plebiscitary presidency, not to frustrate the leadership of a President who recognizes his accountability to Congress and the Constitution. Yet, if taken literally, the Ervin scheme is a scheme of presidential subordination. Where presidential abuse of particular powers has harmed the country, those powers are now to be vested in Congress. Pursued to the end, the Ervin scheme could produce a national polity which would be almost as overbalanced in the direction of congressional supremacy as the Nixon scheme is in the direction of presidential supremacy.

The Ervin counterattack thus runs the risk of creating a generation of weak Presidents in an age when the turbulence of race, poverty, inflation, crime, and urban decay is straining the delicate bonds of national cohesion and demanding, quite as much as in the 1930s, a strong domestic presidency to hold the country together. For Sam Ervin is of the pure Jeffersonian school, like the old Tertium Quids who felt that Jefferson and Madison, in building up the presidency and seeing the national government as an instrument of the general welfare, had deserted the true faith.

The pure Jeffersonian doctrine was a witness rather than a policy, which is why Jefferson and Madison themselves abandoned it. The pure Jeffersonian idea of decentralized power receded in the course of American history because local government simply did not offer the means to attain Jeffersonian ends. In practice, pure Jeffersonianism meant a system under which the strongest local interests, whether planters, landlords, merchants, bankers, or industrialists, consolidated their control and oppressed the rest; it meant all power to the neighborhood oligarchs. Theodore Roosevelt explained at the start of the twentieth century why Hamiltonian means had become necessary to achieve Jeffersonian ends, how national authority was the only effective means of correcting injustice in a national society. "If Jefferson were living in our day," said Wilson in 1912, "he would see what we see: that the individual is caught in a great confused nexus of complicated circumstances, and that . . . without the watchful interference . . . of the government there can be no fair play." And, for the first Roosevelt and for Wilson, as for their joint heir, the second Roosevelt, national authority was embodied in the presidency.

This has not been a bad thing for the Republic. It is presidential leadership, after all, that brought the country into the twentieth century, that civilized American industry, secured the rights of labor organization, defended the livelihood of the farmer. It is presidential leadership that has protected the Bill of Rights against local vigilantism and natural resources against local greed. It is presidential leadership, spurred on by the Supreme Court, that has sought to vindicate racial justice against local bigotry. Congress would have done few of these things on its own; local government even fewer. It would be a mistake to cripple the presidency at home because of presidential excesses abroad. History has shown the presidency to be the most effective instrumentality of government for justice and progress. Even Calvin Coolidge, hardly one of the more assertive of Presidents, said, "It is because in their hours of timidity the Congress becomes subservient to the importunities of organized minorities that the President comes more and more to stand as the champion of the rights of the whole country."

The scheme of presidential subordination can easily be pressed to the point of national folly. But it is important to contend not for a strong presidency in general, but for a strong presidency within the Constitution. The presidency deserves to be defended on serious and not on stupid points. Watergate has produced flurries of near hysteria about the life expectancy of the institution. Thus Charles L. Black, Jr., Luce Professor of Jurisprudence at the Yale Law School, argues that, if Nixon turned over his White House tapes to Congress or the courts, it would mean the "danger of degrading or even destroying the Presidency" and constitute a betrayal of his "successors for all time to come." The Republic, Black says, cannot even risk diluting the "symbolism" of the office lest that disturb "in the most dangerous way the balance of the best government yet devised on earth"; and it almost seems that he would rather suppress the truth than jeopardize the symbolism.

Executive privilege is not the issue. No President cherished the presidency more than, say, Jackson or Polk, but both readily conceded to Congress the right in cases of malversation to penetrate into the most secret recesses of the executive department. Nor, in the longer run, does either Ervin's hope of presidential subordination or Black's fantasy of presidential collapse have real substance. For the presidency, though its wings can be clipped for a time, is an exceedingly tough institution. Its primacy is founded in the necessities of the American political order. It has endured many challenges and survived many vicissitudes. It is nonsense to suppose that its fate as an institution is bound up with the fate of the particular man who happens to be President at any given time. In the end, power in the American order is bound to flow back to the presidency.

Congress has a marvelous, if generally unfulfilled, capacity for oversight, for advice, for constraint, for chastening the presidency and informing the people. When it really wants to say no to a President, it has ample means of doing so; and in due course the President will have no choice but to acquiesce. But it is inherently incapable of conducting government and providing national leadership. Its fragmentation, its chronic fear of responsibility, its habitual dependence on the executive for ideas, information, and favors—this is life insurance for the presidency.

Both Nixon and Ervin are wrong in supposing that the matter can be settled by shifting the balance of power in a decisive way to one branch or the other. The answer lies rather in preserving fluidity and re-establishing comity. Indeed, for most people—here Ervin is a distinguished exception—the constitutional and institutional issues are make-believe. It is largely a matter, as Averell Harriman says, "of whose ox is getting gored: who is in or out of power, and what actions either side may want." When Nixon was in the opposition, there was no more earnest critic of presidential presumption. Each side dresses its arguments in grand constitutional and institutional terms, but their contention is like that of the two drunken men described long ago by Lincoln who got into a fight with their greatcoats on until each fought himself out of his own coat and into the coat of the other.*

VII

What is required is, in Herbert Wechsler's phrase, a set of neutral principles—principles, that is, that are not shaped in response to a particular situation but work all the time, transcending any particular result involved. The supreme neutral principle, as vital in domestic policy as in foreign policy, is that all great decisions of the government must be shared decisions. The subsidiary principle is that if the presidency tries to transform what the Constitution sees as concurrent into exclusive authority, it must be stopped; and if Congress tries to transform concurrent into exclusive authority, it must be stopped too. If either the presidency or Congress turns against the complex balance of constitutional powers that has left room over many generations for mutual accommodation, then the ensuing collision will harm both branches of government and the Republic as well. Even together, Congress and the presidency are by no means infallible; but their decisions, wise or foolish, at least meet the standards of democracy. And, taken together, the decisions are more likely to be wise than foolish.

All Presidents affect a belief in common counsel, but most after a time prefer to make other arrangements. Still, the idea is right, and the process of accountability has to begin inside the President himself. A constitutional President can do many things, but he

---

* Lincoln to H. L. Pierce *et al.,* April 6, 1859. Lincoln, *Collected Works,* ed. R. P. Basler (New Brunswick: Rutgers University Press, 1953), III, 375. Lincoln was amused by the fact that the Democrats of his day had stopped mentioning Jefferson while the Republicans constantly invoked him. "If the two leading parties of this day are really identical with the two in the days of Jefferson and Adams, they have performed about the same feat as the two drunken men."

has to believe in the discipline of consent. It is not enough that he personally thinks the country is in trouble and genuinely believes he alone knows how to save it. In all but the most extreme cases, action has to be accompanied by public explanation and tested by public acceptance. A constitutional President has to be aware of what Whitman called "the never-ending audacity of elected persons" and has to understand the legitimacy of challenges to his own judgment and authority. He has to be sensitive directly to the diversity of concern and conviction in the nation, sensitive prospectively to the verdict of history, sensitive always to the decent respect pledged in the Declaration of Independence to the opinions of mankind.

Yet Presidents chosen as open and modest men are not sure to remain so amid the intoxications of the office, and the office has grown steadily more intoxicating in recent years. A wise President, having read George Reedy and observed the fates of Johnson and Nixon, will take care to provide himself, while there still is time, with antidotes to intoxication. Presidents in the last quarter of the twentieth century might, as a beginning, plan to rehabilitate (I use the word in almost the Soviet sense) the executive branch of government. This does not mean the capitulation of the presidency to the permanent government; nor should anyone forget that it was the unresponsiveness of the permanent government that gave rise to the aggressive White House of the twentieth century. But it does mean a reduction in the size and power of the White House staff and the restoration of the access and prestige of the executive departments. The President will always need a small and alert personal staff to serve as his eyes and ears and one lobe of his brain, but he must avoid a vast and possessive staff ambitious to make all the decisions of government. Above all, he must not make himself the prisoner of a single information system. No sensible President will give one man control of all the channels of communication; any man sufficiently wise to exercise such control properly ought to be President himself.

As for the Cabinet, while no President in American history has found it a very satisfactory instrument of government, it has served Presidents best when it has contained men strong and independent in their own right, strong enough to make the permanent government responsive to presidential policy and independent enough to carry honest dissents into the Oval Office. Franklin Roosevelt, who is fashionably regarded these days as the cause of it all, is really a model of how a strong President can operate within the constitutional order. While no President wants to create the impression that his Administration is out of control, FDR showed how a masterful President could maintain the most divergent range of contacts, surround himself with the most articulate and positive colleagues, and use debate within the executive branch as a means of clarifying issues and trying out people and policies. Or perhaps FDR is in a way the cause of it all, because he alone had the vitality, flair, and cunning to be clearly on top without repressing everything underneath. In a joke that Henry Wallace, not usually a humorous man, told in my hearing in 1943, FDR could keep all the balls in the air without losing his own. Some of his successors tried to imitate his mastery without understanding the sources of his strength.

But not every President is an FDR, and FDR himself, though his better instincts generally won out in the end, was a flawed, willful, and, with time, increasingly arbitrary man. When Presidents begin to succumb to delusions of grandeur, when the checks and balances inside themselves stop operating, external checks and balances may well become necessary to save the Republic. The nature of an activist President in any case, in Samuel Lubell's phrase, is to run with the ball until he is tackled. As conditions abroad and at home have nourished the imperial presidency, tacklers have had to be more than usually sturdy and intrepid.

How to make external checks effective? Congress can tie the presidency down by a thousand small legal strings, but, like Gulliver, the President can always break loose. The effective means of controlling the presidency lie not in law but in politics. For the American President rules by influence; and the withdrawal of consent, by Congress, by the press, by public opinion, can bring any President down. The great Presidents have understood this. The President, said Andrew Jackson, must be "accountable at the bar of public opinion for every act of his Administration." "I have a very definite philosophy about the Presidency," said Theodore Roosevelt. "I think it should be a very powerful office, and I think the President should be a very strong man who uses without hesitation every power that the position yields; but because of this fact I believe that he should be sharply watched by the people [and] held to a strict accountability by them."

Holding a President to strict accountability requires, first of all, a new attitude on the part of the American people toward their Presidents, or rather a return to the more skeptical attitude of earlier times: it requires, specifically, a decline in reverence. An insistent theme in Nixon's public discourse is the necessity of maintaining due respect for the presidency. The possibility that such respect might be achieved simply by being a good President evidently does not reassure him. He is preoccupied with "respect for the office" as an entity in itself. Can one imagine Washington or Lincoln or the Roosevelts or Truman or Kennedy going on in public, as Nixon repeatedly does, about how important it is to do this or that in order to maintain "respect for the office"? But the age of the imperial presidency has produced the idea that run-of-the-mill politicians, brought by fortuity to the White House, must be treated thereafter as if they have become superior and perhaps godlike beings.

The Nixon theoreticians even try to transform reverence into an ideology, propagating the doctrine, rather novel in the United States, that institutions of authority are entitled to respect per se, whether or not they have done anything to earn respect. If authority is denied respect, the syllogism ran, the whole social order will be in danger. "Your task, then, is clear," Pat Moynihan charged his President in 1969: "To restore the authority of American institutions." But should institutions expect obedience that they do not, on their record of performance, deserve? To this question the Nixon ideologues apparently answer yes. An older American tradition would say no, incredulous that anyone would see this as a question. In that spirit I would argue that what the country needs today is a little serious disrespect for the office of the presidency; a refusal to give any more weight to a President's words than the intelligence of the utterance, if spoken by anyone else, would command; an understanding of the point made so aptly by Montaigne: "Sits he on never so high a throne, a man still sits on his bottom."

But what if men not open and modest, even at the start, but from the start ambitious of power and contemptuous of law, reach the place once occupied by Washington and Lincoln? What if neither personal character nor the play of politics nor the Constitution itself avail to hold a President to strict accountability? In the end, the way to control the presidency may have to be not in many little ways but in one large way. In the end, there remains, as Madison said, the decisive engine of impeachment.

VIII

This is, of course, the instrument provided by the Constitution. But it is an exceedingly blunt instrument. Only once has a President been impeached, and there is no great national desire to go through the experience again. Yet, for the first time in a century, Americans in the 1970s have to think hard about impeachment, which means that, because most of us flinch from the prospect, we begin to think hard about alternatives to impeachment.

One alternative is the censure of the President by the Congress. That was tried once in American history—in 1834, when the Senate censured Andrew Jackson on the ground that, in removing the government deposits from the Second Bank of the United States, he had "assumed upon himself authority and power not conferred by the Constitution and laws, but in derogation of both." Jackson's "protest" to the Senate was eloquent and conclusive. The Senate resolution, he said, charged him with having committed a "high crime." It was therefore "in substance an impeachment of the President." If Congress really meant this, Jackson said, let it be serious about it: let the House impeach him and the Senate try him. Jackson was plainly right. The slap-on-the-wrist approach to presidential delinquency makes little sense, constitutional or otherwise. There is no halfway house in censure. If a President has committed high crimes and misdemeanors, he should not stay in office. This does not mean, of course, that a fainthearted Congress may not pass a resolution of censure and claim to have done its duty. But, unless the terms of the resolution make it clear why the President is merely censurable and not impeachable, the action is a cop-out and a betrayal of Congress's constitutional responsibility.

Are there other halfway houses? Another proposal seems worth consideration: that is, the removal of an offending President by some means short of impeachment. A resolution calling on the President to resign and passed by an overwhelming vote in each house could have a powerful effect on a President who cares about the Constitution and the country. If either the President or the Vice President then resigned, the President, old or new, could, under the Twenty-fifth Amendment, nominate a new Vice President, who would take office upon confirmation by both houses of Congress. "Admirable," said Cardinal Fleury after he read the Abbé de Saint-Pierre's *Projet de Paix Perpétuelle*, "save for one omission: I find no provision for sending missionaries to convert the hearts of princes." Alas, Presidents who succeed in provoking a long-suffering Congress into a resolution calling for their resignation are not likely to be deeply moved by congressional disapproval nor inclined to cooperate in their own liquidation.

If Presidents will not resign of their own volition, can they be forced out without the personal and national ordeal of impeachment and conviction?

A proposal advanced in various forms by leading members of the House of Representatives this year contemplates giving Congress authority by constitutional amendments to call for a new presidential election when it finds that the President can no longer perform the functions of his office (Representative Bingham) or that the President has violated the Constitution (Representatives Edith Green and Morris Udall).

The possibility of dissolution and new elections at times of hopeless stalemate or blasted confidence has serious appeal. Dissolution would give a rigid electoral system flexibility and responsiveness. It would permit, in Bagehot's phrase, the timely replacement of the pilot of the calm by the pilot of the storm. It would remind intractable Congresses that they cannot block Presidents with immunity, as it would remind high-flying Presidents that there are other ways of being shot down besides impeachment. But my instinct is somehow against it. One congressman observes of the Green-Udall amendment that it "would, in effect, take one-half of the parliamentary process and not the entire parliamentary process." This is certainly the direction and logic of dissolution. The result might well be to alter the balance of the Constitution in unforeseeable and perilous ways. It might, in particular, strengthen the movement against the separation of powers and toward a plebiscitary presidency. "The republican principle," said the 71st Federalist, "demands that the deliberate sense of the community should govern the conduct of those to whom they intrust the management of their affairs; but it does not require an unqualified complaisance to every sudden breeze of passion, or to every transient impulse which the people may receive from the arts of men, who flatter their prejudices to betray their interests."

I think that the possibility of inserting dissolution into the American system is worth careful examination. But digging into the foundations of the state, as Burke said, is always a dangerous adventure.

IX

Impeachment, on the other hand, is part of the original foundation of the American state. The Founding Fathers placed the blunt instrument in the Constitution with the expectation that it would be used, and used most especially against Presidents. "No point is of more importance," George Mason told the Convention, "than that the right of impeachment should be continued. Shall any man be above Justice? Above all shall that man be above it, who [as President] can commit the most extensive injustice?" Benjamin Franklin pointed out that, if there were no provision for impeachment, the only recourse would be assassination, in which case a President would be "not only deprived of his life but of the opportunity of vindicating his character." Corruption or loss of capacity in a President, said Madison, was "within the compass of probable events. . . . Either of them might be fatal to the Republic."

The genius of impeachment lies in the fact that it can punish the man without punishing the office. For, in the presidency, as elsewhere, power is ambiguous: the power to do good means also the power to do harm, the power to serve the Republic also the power to demean and defile it. The trick is to preserve presidential power but to deter Presidents from abusing that power. Shall any man be above justice? George Mason asked. Obviously not, not even a President of the United States. But bringing Presidents to justice is not all that simple.

History has turned impeachment into a weapon of last resort—more so probably than the Founding Fathers anticipated. Still, it is possible to exaggerate its impact on the country. It took less than three months to impeach and try Andrew Johnson, and the nation —in a favorite apprehension of 1868 as well as of 1973—was not torn apart in the process. Three months of surgery might be better than three years of paralysis. Yet impeachment presents legal as well as political problems. There is broad agreement, among scholars at least, on doctrine. Impeachment is a proceeding of a political nature, by no means restricted to indictable crimes. On the other hand, it plainly is not to be applied to cases of honest disagreement over national policy or over constitutional interpretation, especially when a President refuses to obey a law that he believes strikes directly at the presidential prerogative. Impeachment is to be reserved, in Mason's phrase at the Constitutional Convention, for "great and dangerous offenses."

The Senate, in trying impeachment cases, is better equipped to be the judge of the law than of the facts. When Andrew Johnson was impeached, there had been no dispute about the fact that he had removed Stanton. When Andrew Jackson was censured, there had been no dispute about the fact that he had removed the deposits. The issue was not whether they had done something but whether what they had done constituted a transgression of the laws and the Constitution. But in the Nixon case the facts themselves remain at issue—the facts, that is, of presidential complicity—and the effort of a hundred senators to determine those facts might well lead to chaos. The record here may be one of negligence, irresponsibility, and even deception, but it is not necessarily one of knowing violation of the Constitution or of knowing involvement in the obstruction of justice. While impeachment is in the Constitution to be used, there is no point in lowering the threshold so that it will be used casually. All this argues for the determination of facts before the consideration of impeachment. There are two obvious ways to determine the facts. One is through the House of Representatives, which has the sole power to initiate impeachment. The House could, for example, instruct the Judiciary Committee to ascertain whether there were grounds for impeachment, or it could establish a select committee to conduct such an inquiry. The other road is through the courts. If the Special Prosecutor establishes incriminating facts, these can serve as the basis for impeachment.

But what if a President himself withholds evidence—for example, Nixon's tapes—deemed essential to the ascertainment of facts? If a President says, "The time has come to turn Watergate over to the courts, where the questions of guilt and innocence belong," and then denies the courts the evidence they need to decide on innocence or guilt, what recourse remains to the Republic except impeachment? Apart from the courts, President Polk said quite explicitly that the House, if it were looking into impeachment, could command testimony and papers, public and private, official or unofficial, of every agent of the government. If a President declines for whatever reason to yield material evidence in his possession, whether to the courts or to the House, this itself might provide clear grounds for impeachment.

All these things are obscure in the early autumn of 1973. It is possible that Nixon may conclude that the Watergate problems are not after all (as he told the Prime Minister of Japan) "murky, small, unimportant, vicious little things," but are, rather, evidence of a profound and grievous imbalance between the presidency and the Constitution. Perhaps he may, by an honest display of candor and contrition, regain a measure of popular confidence, re-establish constitutional comity, and recover presidential effectiveness. But full recovery seems unlikely unless the President himself recognizes why his presidency has fallen into such difficulties. Nixon's continued invocation, after Watergate, of national security as the excuse for presidential excess, his defense to the end of unreviewable executive privilege, his defiant assertion that, if he had it to do over again, he would still deceive Congress and the people about the secret air war in Cambodia—such unrepentant reactions suggest that he still has no clue as to what his trouble was, still fails to understand that the sickness of his presidency is caused not by the overzealousness of his friends or by the malice of his enemies, but by the expansion and abuse of presidential power itself.

X

For the issue is more than whether Congress and the people wish to deal with the particular iniquities of the Nixon Administration. It is whether they wish to rein in the runaway presidency. Nixon's presidency is not an aberration but a culmination. It carries to reckless extremes a compulsion toward presidential power rising out of deep-running changes in the foundations of society. In a time of the acceleration of history and the decay of traditional institutions and values, a strong presidency is both a greater necessity than ever before and a greater risk—necessary to hold a spinning and distracted society together, necessary to make the separation of powers work, risky because of the awful temptation held out to override the separation of powers and burst the bonds of the Constitution. The nation requires both a strong presidency for leadership *and* the separation of powers for liberty. It may well be that, if continuing structural compulsions are likely to propel future Presidents in the direction of government by decree, the rehabilitation of impeachment will be essential to contain the presidency and preserve the Constitution.

Watergate is potentially the best thing to have happened to the presidency in a long time. If the trails are followed to their end, many, many years will pass before another White House staff dares take the liberties with the Constitution and the laws the Nixon White House has taken. If the nation wants to work its way back to a constitutional presidency, there is only one way to begin. That is by showing Presidents that, when their closest associates place themselves above the law and the Constitution, such transgressions will be not forgiven or forgotten for the sake of the presidency, but exposed and punished for the sake of the presidency.

If the Nixon White House escapes the legal consequences of its illegal behavior, why will future Presidents and their associates not suppose themselves entitled to do what the Nixon White House has done? Only condign punishment will restore popular faith in the presidency and deter future Presidents from illegal conduct—so long, at least, as Watergate remains a vivid memory. Corruption appears to visit the White House in fifty-year cycles. This suggests that exposure and retribution inoculate the presidency against its latent criminal impulses for about half a century. Around the year 2023 the American people will be well advised to go on their alert and start nailing down everything in sight.

A constitutional presidency, as the great Presidents have shown, can be a very strong presidency indeed. But what keeps a strong President constitutional, in addition to checks and balances incorporated within his own breast, is the vigilance of the people. The Constitution cannot hold the nation to ideals it is determined to betray. The reinvigoration of the written checks in the American Constitution depends on the reinvigoration of the unwritten checks in American society. The great institutions—Congress, the courts, the executive establishment, the press, the universities, public opinion—have to reclaim their own dignity and meet their own responsibilities. As Madison said long ago, the country cannot trust to "parchment barriers" to halt the encroaching spirit of power. In the end, the Constitution will live only if it embodies the spirit of the American people.

"There is no week nor day nor hour," wrote Walt Whitman, "when tyranny may not enter upon this country, if the people lose their supreme confidence in themselves,—and lose their roughness and spirit of defiance—Tyranny may always enter—there is no charm, no bar against it—the only bar against it is a large resolute breed of men."

6. Congress

The Ralph Nader study *Who Runs Congress* raised serious questions over the status of Congress. It suggested that the seniority system, the arduous floor process, and the time-consuming demands of constituency service made Congress incapable of responding to Presidential initiative in any meaningful way. The Congressional response to Watergate leads other observers to take issue with this thesis. The Senate hearings during the summer of 1973 and Chairman Peter Rodino's skillful handling of the House Judiciary Committee impeachment proceedings have inspired new confidence in Congress.

James Hurst undertakes to analyze in some detail this legislative power of investigation, in the use of which Congress's success in Watergate has been most noted. The Watergate controversy has opened up some basic issues about the conduct of lawmaking agencies, particularly about Congressional oversight. As a rule, Congress may investigate three types of matters. Under the general appropriations power, the legislature is entitled to inquire how the executive has been spending the public's money. Secondly, Congress may conduct investigations in search of facts to amend existing legislation and to propose new legislation. Finally, Congress may use the power of investigation to inform and even generate public opinion on an issue of national importance.

The Senate Select Committee's activity fell within the third category. Both the publicly televised hearings and the carefully planned agenda of witnesses were designed to maximize the Committee's opinion-forming and opinion-gathering powers. While Committee members continually stressed the fact-gathering mission, it was clear to most, including the White House, that the drama was being played to a nation. Hurst notes that even with television's potential for abuse, the Senate Watergate Committee deserved "overall good marks for fairness." The same, however, can not be said for its efficiency.

Such investigations confront Congress with serious issues of executive-legislative and judicial-legislative relations. Executive officials appearing before Congress invoked executive privilege; Congressional subpoenas were not complied with; Watergate special prosecutor Archibald Cox was fired in defiance of Congress; Congressional investigations may prejudice trials with pretrial publicity. The White House transcripts indicated a clear disdain for Congress and the Senate Committee. Rather than cooperate with the Senate investigation, the White House opted for the "limited hangout" route.

President Nixon had never worked hard on Congressional relations. The 1972 campaign was run to achieve an ideological majority to support the mandate, not a Republican majority. Nixon took little time to consult with legislative leaders before making policy decisions; most Republicans reported it impossible to get beyond the office of H. R. Haldeman or John Ehrlichman. The Ninety-third Congress, *Congressional Quarterly* reported, backed the President on fewer than half the issues he supported. In the final days before resignation, Republican Congressmen who had opposed the President's impeachment were not consulted before evidence implicating the President was revealed to the public.

What can Congress do when faced with an active President pressing for a popular mandate that ignores Congressional prerogatives and powers? The impeachment proceedings finally forced the President's hand, ultimately producing his resignation. However, short of these drastic measures, which did eventually recoup Congressional self-respect, is Congress a responsive representative body capable of lawmaking in this era of stewardship Presidents? Watergate has produced a number of Congressional critics who cite the lack of Congressional checks on Presidential abuses of power. This, in turn, has prompted the cry for reform of the procedures and operations of Congress, not only in order to strengthen its position in opposing the executive but also to heighten its lawmaking powers. Congressional preoccupation with oversight has been at the expense of initiating legislation, the critics charge. Hugh Gallagher, however, in "Presidents, Congress, and the Legislative Functions" maintains that the Congress of the United States has been more innovative in proposing legislation than has the President. Once the myth of the "FDR Presidency" is dispelled—a model no other President can fulfill—a more realistic Congressional-Presidential relationship can be established. In fact, Gallagher stresses, Watergate demonstrates the relative weakness of a presidency that lost control over executive departments, domestic policy, and even its own house.

Watergate: Some Basic Issues

JAMES WILLARD HURST

The controversy surrounding the Presidential campaign of 1972 leads into a broad range of issues concerning the legitimacy of legal and social order in the United States. Some of those issues call for judgments on ultimate goals of public policy. This article focuses on an important but narrower cluster of problems concerning the allocation of functions among principal agencies of lawmaking. These problems involve relations between Congress and the office of the President, between the courts and the legislative and executive branches, and between the electorate and the branches of government.

The Constitution does not expressly grant either house of Congress the authority to investigate matters involving general public policy or the operations of the other branches of government. But those who framed and ratified the Constitution built on what they knew of the functions of Parliament as these had developed in English experience before 1787. The founding generation especially drew on seventeenth-century English experience of conflicts involving Parliament, the Crown, and the judges, from which emerged the main lines of the English separation of powers. A salient feature of that experience was the strong development of Parliament's authority to control taxes and public spending, and to inquire into what the executive did in making policy and in acting or failing to act to carry out public policy defined in statutes. From early years the House and the Senate by their practice asserted their inheritance of the investigatory powers of Parliament, including authority to compel testimony and production of documents by subpoena. From the first occasion on which the Supreme Court confronted a challenge to the legality of investigative activity of a house of Congress, the Court has acknowledged broad authority in

Reprinted from the January-February, 1974, issue of *The Center Magazine*, a publication of the Center for the Study of Democratic Institutions, Santa Barbara, California. James Willard Hurst is Professor of Law at the University of Wisconsin. He is the author of *The Growth of American Law: The Law Makers* and *Law of Treason in the United States*, among other books and essays.

Congress to conduct investigations of matters which Congress reasonably determines to be of public concern.

The classic use of the legislative power of investigation is to inquire about the successes or failures and the quality of executive performance. Based on its control of the public purse, the legislature has clearest warrant for asking how the executive has been spending the public money the legislature gave it to spend. Under the broad standards with which the Constitution grants "legislative powers" to Congress, Congress has the primary authority to declare the public policy of the United States; each house has commensurate authority to inquire how faithfully executive officers are implementing policies which Congress has adopted. Within these extensive boundaries the handling of particular inquiries inevitably calls on legislators to use wisdom and prudent self-restraint. But the pattern of Court decisions indicates that judges will leave to legislators the drawing of lines.

The record of legislative practice and judicial reaction shows that investigation does not lack legitimacy simply because it embarrasses the executive. Friction is an accepted cost and, to some considerable measure, a desired result of the balancing of powers to which legislative scrutiny of the executive essentially contributes. Thus it should be judged a proper objective of legislative investigation to inquire whether executive officers have obstructed enforcement of laws against crimes, or have violated the Bill of Rights in order to facilitate prosecutions, or have used federal tax enforcement to harass political opponents or those whose public-policy views the Administration abhors, or have offered inducements which might affect the conduct of judges sitting in cases which the executive is prosecuting. Likewise, it should be judged a proper objective of legislative investigation to inquire whether officers high in the executive have been grossly negligent in overseeing subordinates who have abused their authority or shown themselves incompetent at their jobs.

Either house of the legislature may investigate to learn whether what is going on in the society—including what is going on inside the government—calls for new legislation, changes in existing legislation, or no fresh legislation—which is a second legitimate function of congressional investigation. From their own experience and their contacts with constituents and interest groups legislators bring to their jobs a good deal of knowledge about the society without need of special inquiry. This fact reality is one basis for the Court's ruling that procedural due process does not require that legislators investigate before they legislate. This may explain why, though the first Congress investigated executive inefficiency (manifest in the defeat of General St. Clair on the Detroit frontier), it was not until 1827 that a congressional committee inquired to obtain facts for legislating.

In any event, rational lawmaking—including rational judgment about when not to make law—implies decisions based on knowledge. Hence, long-standing legislative practice, validated by the Supreme Court, establishes as a legitimate goal of legislative investigation the search for facts that legislators feel they need to know in order sensibly to decide to legislate or not to legislate. Here, too, there is full scope for legislative discretion, established in legislative practice and accepted by the over-all pattern of Court decisions. Thus it is proper for either house of Congress to inquire whether experience in the Presidential campaign of 1972 shows the need of new laws to regulate campaign funding, or to limit campaign tactics, or to enlarge the categories of executive officers whose appointments should require hearings and confirmation by the Senate. Legislative inquiry into such matters is proper even though Congress may ultimately decide that there should be no fresh legislation.

A third use of Congress's powers of investigation has been gaining legitimacy through some years of legislative practice. This is the use of investigation to inform, or even to generate, public opinion about matters that Congress reasonably regards as affecting general welfare. No Supreme Court decision yet validates this use of the investigative power. Some rulings and dicta suggest that here the Court might someday impose limits such as it has never put on investigations aimed at appraising executive performance or laying the fact basis for lawmaking. There may be reason for some judicial check on this public-information, opinion-generating type of legislative investigation.

Apart from what the Court may do, responsible legislators may well find special need for self-discipline in this area. Inherent in such proceedings are peculiar dangers of abuse. Such investigations tempt the ambitious legislator to enjoy personal power, to seek sensations for the publicity they bring, to ride roughshod over witnesses, and to make himself a national name, which may win him a Presidential nomination.

The purpose of informing or generating public opinion began to color legislative investigation with the rise of mass media of communication. An early instance was the Pujo Committee inquiry of 1911 into practices of great banks, investment banking houses, and other financial intermediaries. Another example—the prime one to highlight the special dangers of this style of inquiry—was the succession of congressional inquiries linked to the names of Representatives Martin Dies and Parnell Thomas and Senator Joseph McCarthy, probing alleged Communist infiltration of executive offices and some sectors of private industry. The more responsible Kefauver investigation of organized crime in the United States probably focused as much on rousing public concern as it did on producing legislation.

We may grant that special dangers of abuse attach to the opinion-informing, opinion-generating function. But the social context within which this use of the investigative power has grown warrants this as a third, legitimate goal of legislative inquiry.

The United States has become a big country. Most of its people live in an impersonal urban setting. Most of them are privatized by specialized occupations and by attractive consumer enjoyments. Most of them are baffled in will and understanding by the intricate webs of experience in which their lives are caught up. Social interdependence as well as the pressures of powerful special interests have multiplied the jobs given to government. Both in public and in private affairs technological development, the rise of more intricate patterns of organized action, and the volume and density of transactions make individuals feel smaller, more and more ignorant of the chains of cause and effect that shape their lives, and less and less inclined to believe that they can exert effective force to affect what happens to them.

This social setting breeds political apathy, if not political despair. People feel that decisions of great impact on their lives are being taken by processes they cannot surely identify, let alone influence, and by decision-makers—perceived as a mysterious, remote *Them*—whom they cannot surely identify, let alone control.

This state of affairs is more subversive of representative government than any radical conspiracy yet unearthed. In this setting, when events lead to disclosure of misdeeds of individuals in high public or private places, public response is likely to retreat into cynicism rather than grapple realistically with the control of power. There is, therefore, great functional need of able, vigorous, legislative investigation to inform public opinion and generate active concern. In this light, legislative investigation properly seeks to help people understand the processes of decision that affect their lives, and assures them that they can identify power-holders and hold them to account.

The dangers of abuse may warrant the Court in imposing some curbs of which it has so far only hinted. The Court has warned that investigation should not seek exposure simply for the sake of sensation; investigators may have to satisfy some judicially enforced requirements that an investigation be shown relevant to matters of public substance. The Court has warned against fishing expeditions; investigators may have to satisfy some judicially enforced requirement that an inquiry relate to a reasonably focused subject of public interest. In some questionable rulings the Court has narrowed the scope of legislators' constitutional protection against being questioned in any other place for any speech or debate in either house; the result may put at legal hazard those who disseminate the product of legislative hearings outside the institutional channels of the legislative house itself. But the Court has disavowed intent to curb the substance of legislators' hearing activity. In any event, all that the Court so far has said or done deals only with the borders and not with the core of the matter. Should direct challenge be made to the legality of the opinion-informing, opinion-generating function of legislative investigation, the same social context which has led Congress to develop this part of its role as the Grand Inquest of the nation will probably lead the Court to validate it.

The work of the Senate Select Committee on Presidential Campaign Activities of 1972 adds substantially to congressional precedent for the opinion-forming, opinion-generating function. Committee members repeatedly stressed the relation of their inquiry to the goals of appraising how officials had caused the laws to be executed and of considering the need for fresh legislation. But the Committee also openly pursued the third objective, even though—as has been characteristic of congressional practice in this field—it did not clearly define it. The importance of the television audience, the unfolding before that audience of matter already dealt with in executive session, the probing to elicit from witnesses lessons of political ethics and practice drawn from the matters explored, the care taken to identify the tables of organization within the executive branch and the campaign committees—all these indicate the Senate Select Committee's opinion-forming and opinion-generating intention. The public impact of the hearings, notably in the first thirty-seven days, put these opinion-related functions in a central place. Of course, public reaction probably included the superficial interest in the sensational that always attends high political drama. But to a sizable public the hearings offered education in the behind-the-scenes practice of power, and fostered a new concern over important matters ranging from worry about partisan pressure on the Internal Revenue Service and the national police and security agencies to some fresh thinking about the dangers that attach to the insulation of the President and his top advisers from effective exposure to the reactions of the Congress or the country.

The legitimate goals of legislative investigation are important to the good working of the separation of powers (including effective functioning of the legislative branch itself) and to a healthy relation of voters to government. Hence it is proper that there should be, as there has been, little curb on the subject matter of investigation other than that imposed by the self-discipline of the legislature. So far the Supreme Court has imposed no material checks on the subject matter of legislative investigation.

In this state of affairs the more importance attaches to defining and enforcing rational and decent procedures for conducting investigations. Attention to procedure is warranted because investigation always carries the threat of compulsion and often goes forward under compulsion, by subpoena; because experience shows that legislators may investigate in ways that hurt witnesses or harass public officials without serving the public interest; and because limits may be imposed on procedure without impairing the ultimate objectives of the power.

Sensitive to the legislative importance of investigative power, the Court has been wary of imposing procedural limits. The only judicially enforced constitutional limits that stand clearly in the decisions are the privilege against self-incrimination and the protection against unreasonable search and seizure. The Court has indicated that before a legislative committee there is no right to notice or a hearing, no right to counsel, no right to cross-examine, no right to invoke the rules of evidence that apply in a court trial, no right to any particular order of presentation of evidence.

However, pressed by complaints of committee abuses, especially since the years in which Senator McCarthy bludgeoned witnesses, the Supreme Court has shown some readiness to develop defenses found in limiting terms of statutes or resolutions authorizing committee activity. Thus a witness may win the court's protection against compelled testimony if he establishes that neither the legislature nor the parent house of the committee has authorized inquiry into the subject matter of investigation, or that the questions asked are not relevant to the authorized subject matter, or that the questioning committee members lack authority to proceed as a subcommittee. This kind of ruling achieves wise resolution of some difficult tensions between values. It also offers external checks against some committee abuses, while avoiding the stark showdown between legislative and judicial power that is involved when judges invoke the Constitution.

In their greatest reach, however, judicial remedies offer little relief to witnesses haled before a legislative investigating committee. For most practical purposes the committee controls setting and procedure. Such rights as the witness has, he enjoys by grace of the committee. In this aspect good marks go to the 1973 Senate Select Committee investigating the Presidential campaign of 1972. Most witnesses appeared before that Committee under compulsion of subpoena. In important instances, however, the use of the subpoena was coupled with grant of limited immunity against use in a later prosecution of testimony given to the Committee. The Committee heard its witnesses in closed session before exposing them to a public hearing, minimizing dangers of unfair surprise and of avoidable damage to reputation.

Past legislative inquiries have been known to arrange testimony less to develop an ordered presentation of evidence than to time sensations for national wire service deadlines. In contrast, the 1973 Select Committee built its presentations with so much care for groundwork and logical order as to evoke complaints because of the slowness with which it sometimes seemed to move. The Committee gave witnesses opportunity to make opening and closing statements, and it granted this privilege with a generosity which again produced complaints over the time consumed. The Committee allowed any witness to have his lawyer at his elbow and to consult with him at will. In striking contrast to the bullying tactics of some past notorious hearings, the Committee also allowed counsel to break into the proceedings to object to the relevance of questions or to claim surprise over documents not used in the closed hearings.

The over-all tone of the hearings was temperate and respectful of the personal dignity of those called before the Committee. Of course, there were sharp exchanges between the Committee or its counsel and witnesses, and occasionally between majority and minority members of the Committee. But generally these brushes were marginal and no more than what one should expect where witnesses are reluctant or recalcitrant, and political hazards high. On the whole, the 1973 Committee laid down good precedent for order and fairness. Since judges have left this domain so much to the self-discipline of the legislative branch, this is an important accomplishment of the Committee.

Two aspects of the 1973 Committee's proceedings, however, seem open to criticism on grounds of procedural looseness that was unfair to witnesses. The news media created the impression of a sizable volume of leaks from the Committee's closed sessions and deliberations. Given the drama and the stakes in this particular hearing, the difficulties of preventing leaks must have been great, indeed much greater than in most investigations. Control of leaks may have been harder because it involved not only staff discipline, but also policing of Committee members highly conscious of their senatorial prerogatives. Probably there is no solution to this problem except to create more exacting traditions of confidentiality which only the participating legislators can develop and monitor.

Another procedural point was well within the Committee's control, however. For the sake of public confidence, legislative investigation should normally involve public hearings. Most hearings arouse such limited interest that the only practical way of making them public is to open a hearing room to all comers. But where, as in the 1973 proceedings, public interest is such as to command broad, live coverage by radio and television, there seems no reason to allow a large, on-the-spot audience.

The Committee did not control reactions of its on-the-spot audience with the strictness desirable for the dignity of the occasion. At the least, the Committee should have disciplined the on-the-spot audience by excluding it after a substantial violation of good order. Indeed, as long as there was substantial live coverage of the hearings by radio and television there appears to have been no functional reason for permitting an on-the-spot audience at all; its total exclusion would have been a useful preventive measure in the interests of seemly procedure.

Over-all, the 1973 Committee earned good marks for fairness. The score is not so clear for efficiency. Of course, from some standpoints fair procedure limits efficiency. But this is a cost worth paying to promote confidence in the responsibility of government processes. However, some aspects of efficiency do not necessarily affect fairness.

The 1973 hearings spun out into too many questions and too many repetitious questions. This may be because there were too many questioners: seven senators in addition to majority and minority counsel. If there were often too many questions, there were sometimes too few. Sometimes a viewer felt that follow-through was not acute or dogged enough. Again, this may have been because there were too many questioners. A classically efficient and effective legislative investigation, such as that of the Armstrong Committee in New York in 1906 (inquiring into the financial practices of great insurance companies), has usually been so because the conduct of the inquiry was firmly centered in strong committee counsel—in that instance, under the direction of Charles Evans Hughes.

The 1973 hearings might have saved time and had still more impact and depth than they achieved, if majority and minority Committee counsel had been given practically the sole conduct of the proceedings. Such a procedure is easier recommended than adopted. It is asking much of senators to give up center-stage positions in an inquiry that attracts the public attention this one did. If it is realistic to acknowledge this, it is also realistic to acknowledge the costs of a diffused, sometimes blunted, hearing process. The Select Committee and counsel took the 1973 hearings seriously; the open question is whether they took them seriously enough. If the function of legislative investigation is ever given the priority it deserves, responsible legislators will find ways to organize proceedings to deliver the best yield.

Legislative investigation should be conducted under rules that are fair to the public interest as well as to witnesses. In this respect, the prime issue of principle in the 1973 hearings was the claim of executive privilege invoked against producing tape recordings of conversations between the President and some of his aides.

The impressive label of "executive privilege" implies a claim running back to constitutional foundations. In fact there is little sustained precedent in executive or legislative practice for asserting or recognizing a privilege in the executive to withhold information desired for a legislative inquiry. Over the years, Presidents or officers under their direction have claimed executive privilege sparingly. Typically the executive branch has responded to Congress's requests for information. Indeed, in the 1973 inquiry the President maintained this general pattern by waiving executive privilege as to much of the testimony and documents which the Senate committee sought from Presidential lieutenants.

The broadest claims of executive privilege in executive practice date from quite recent years. They were the product of President Eisenhower's understandable resentment of and desire to protect his Administration from the bullying of Senator Joseph McCarthy. At the base of current claims, then, lies relatively recent political accident rather than the respectability of constitutional history or long-sustained practice of the executive and legislative branches.

The origins of the federal Constitution look against the existence of any broad executive privilege. Those who led in framing and ratifying the Constitution were jealous of conceding prerogative powers to the office of President. They looked upon executive power as a likely source of invasion of the rights of the citizen, and—as was to be expected from heirs of the seventeenth-century English conflicts—they looked to the legislative branch as the principal maker of public policy. True, by 1789 there was a sharper distrust of abuses of legislative power than appeared in the first state constitutions. The framers showed this concern when they enumerated heads of legislative power, provided for two chambers, and gave the President a veto. Nonetheless they delegated legislative authority in terms which set broad standards for federal legislative authority. They left the organization of executive apparatus almost entirely to the Congress and committed to Congress ultimate control of the national public purse. Meeting close to the adoption of the Constitution, the first Congress asserted its right to inquire into executive operations by investigating the bungled campaign of General St. Clair. In all of this, there is little foundation on which to erect bastions of privilege against congressional efforts to find out whether the President is taking care that the laws be faithfully executed.

Judges have not had occasion to contribute much to spelling out the content of such executive privilege as may exist within our constitutional scheme. No decision matches the drama of the Burr treason trial. But the outcome there was inconclusive for doctrine. Sitting on circuit, Mr. Chief Justice Marshall ruled that the Court could not be concluded by the President's judgment whether public interest required withholding documents sought by Burr as material to his defense. Marshall issued a subpoena to the President to produce the documents or to show cause why he should not do so. Jefferson would not concede that he must obey the subpoena, but in fact made the desired evidence available.

Other cases have presented demands by defendants or private suitors for evidence withheld by public officers on claims of executive privilege. Rulings vary but acknowledge that on some matters executive privilege may properly be claimed. No decision before 1973 presented a clash between demands of legislative investigation and executive resistance. However, the decisions we do have indicate that the Court will not grant complete discretion to the President—and, of course then, not to his subordinates—to fix the bounds of executive privilege. If this point stands out from cases in which private suitors or defendants have sought the courts' aid in extracting evidence from the executive, constitutional history and principle dictate that the executive enjoy no greater prerogative against legislative inquiry. To reach this point is only to determine that contests over the scope of executive privilege may present cases or controversies within the constitutional power of courts to decide, and issues which can be deemed justifiable within the self-denying doctrine by which judges have hedged their operations.

Due care for the capacity of the executive to do its work undoubtedly warrants recognizing some areas of executive privilege. Thus it seems proper that the executive protect its plans for conducting sensitive negotiations with other nations. If the Court cannot at a stroke spell out the entire proper content of executive privilege, this, in our experience, is not an insuperable problem. The bulk of our successfully working constitutional law has been built case by case, analogous to processes of common law. The Court can mark out executive privilege in this familiar fashion. But it fits our constitutional tradition that we not leave unchecked discretion to the President to fix his authority.

Once it is decided that the President does not enjoy unchecked discretion to define executive privilege, both Congress and the judges face further problems of definition. Congress should exercise responsibility toward the President's capacity to function, and use self-restraint in what it asks for. If there is need for the courts to build law, case by case, in this difficult area, no less is there need for Congress to do the same. Moreover, Congress may find it wise to draw on its broad Article III powers to define the structure and procedures of the federal courts.

Some have spoken their concern that the office of the President may be hampered or harassed by battles over executive privilege staged in trial courts all over the country. The concern is probably exaggerated. The executive has usually supplied information sought by Congress; contests have been rare. But insofar as the concern is warranted, Congress can meet the problem by centralizing trial of this type of issue in one court in the District of Columbia, as it did for review of contests over regulations of the wartime Office of Price Administration and as it has more recently done regarding administration of the Voting Rights Act of 1965.

The courts will confront the need to devise fresh procedures of their own, but none so novel as to outreach the ingenuity judges have shown in the past. Proper regard for the merits of privilege claimed by the executive may call for preliminary consideration of desired testimony or documents in closed session, perhaps with the help of counsel for each affected interest. Contempt sanctions exist to enforce due secrecy, and if Congress deems this protection not enough it can legislate more.

Of course, no sanctions can guarantee against indiscretion or venality. But what is at stake in denying unchecked executive discretion to withhold evidence is the basic organizing principle of our system—the ideal of constitutional organization of power, that no center of power should exist which is not subject to some material accountability to power outside itself. For the sake of that organizing principle, our tradition is that we are prepared to pay costs and take risks because the alternatives are unacceptable.

There are doctrinal points which the courts probably must define as experience unfolds in reviewing claims of executive privilege. Some forecasts seem reasonable, though the event may show a given forecast to be wrong. Over the past fifty years the executive and administrative arms of government have grown to great proportions. Executive privilege could hardly be recognized as commensurate with all operations within this great apparatus without gutting the principle of constitutionalism. In that period, the office of President has itself grown to a payroll including hundreds of individuals. It would make a mockery of the functional rationale of executive privilege to treat it as covering transactions involving any members of that large establishment. Whatever the justifying principle of the privilege in any given instance, that principle will call for some close if not always direct involvement of the President himself in the matter for which privilege is sought.

Given the high stakes involved in proper claims of the Congress —or even proper claims of defendants or litigants—the President should not be allowed to take inconsistent positions regarding the same matter. Judges should recognize that the President's conduct may waive whatever privilege exists and should enforce waivers. Again, recognizing what is at stake for congressional functions and for the needs of litigants, courts will likely be impelled to recognize executive privilege only as it clearly bears on executive functions as such. Thus there is at least a debatable issue if the President claims privilege with reference to his activity not in causing the laws to be faithfully executed but in playing his—entirely proper—role as head of his party and campaigner for re-election.

These are not easy questions. But, again, they are well within the

bounds of the kinds of issues out of which the Court has successfully made a great deal of the law of our Constitution in the past,
one piece at a time. When we must deal with such sensitive issues
in achieving workable relations among the top, coordinate branches
of government, the case-by-case approach gives best assurance of
an enduring product.

State and national constitution-makers in the formative years
from 1776 to 1789 intended that all the authority to make public
policy which had historically inhered in the English Crown as royal
prerogative should vest in the legislative branch of governments
in this country. There was profound distrust of the tendencies
to abuse of executive powers. A substantial—though not unanimous—opinion viewed the executive as the branch of government
most dangerous to the liberties of individuals and to the desired
allocation of authority among the major agencies of government.

In any case, whatever the varying estimates of abuse to be feared
from one or the other branch of government—our constitutional
tradition is wary of likely abuse of any kind of official power—
the presumption from the constitution-making years favors a narrow reading of authority inherent in creation of the office of chief
executive in the states or the nation. Out of abundance of caution
the Virginia Constitution of 1776 declared what was implicit in the
prevailing temper the country over when it specified that the governor "shall not, under any pretense, exercise any power or prerogative by virtue of any law, statute, or custom of England." Thus,
for example, though the King had prerogative power to charter
corporations, practice and doctrine were plain from the outset of
our national independence that sole authority to create corporations
here lay in the legislature.

By 1789, experience had already bred enough conservative distrust
of state legislatures to produce in the federal Constitution an executive potentially much stronger than any that state constitutions thus
far had been willing to sanction. Even so, conscious of the broad
distrust of executive power, framers of the federal Constitution said
little about the affirmative powers of the President. From the decisions taken at Philadelphia the potential strength of that office most
clearly emerged as a strength of independence from the Congress
to allow the President to check Congress rather than to make him
a policy-maker in his own right. There was no readiness to put in
the President policy-making authority analogous to royal prerogative.

The Supreme Court affirmed this as binding history in 1952 when it ruled unlawful the President's executive order—issued without statutory authority—that the Secretary of Commerce take possession of most of the steel mills in the country and operate them to provide material necessary to carry on hostilities then in progress in Korea. For the Court, Mr. Justice Black spoke crisply to the point:

> [T]he seizure order [cannot] be sustained because of the several constitutional provisions that grant executive power to the President. In the framework of our Constitution, the President's power to see that the laws are faithfully executed refutes the idea that he is to be a lawmaker. The Constitution limits his functions in the lawmaking process to the recommending of laws he thinks wise and the vetoing of laws he thinks bad. And the Constitution is neither silent nor equivocal about who shall make laws which the President is to execute. . . . The founders of this nation entrusted the lawmaking power to the Congress alone in both good and bad times.

Concurring, Mr. Justice Frankfurter spoke in somewhat less sweeping terms. He read legislative history as specifically denying the authority the President sought to exercise in the steel mills seizure. But at basis Mr. Justice Frankfurter, too, emphasized that Congress is the maker of general public policy in our system. And he said we accepted this allocation of power, and all its risks, for the benefits we found in it:

> A scheme of government like ours no doubt at times feels the lack of power to act with complete, all-embracing, swiftly moving authority. No doubt a government with distributed authority, subject to be challenged in the courts of law, at least long enough to consider and adjudicate the challenge, labors under restrictions from which other governments are free. It has not been our tradition to envy such governments. . . . I know no more impressive words on this subject than those of Mr. Justice Brandeis: "The doctrine of the separation of powers was adopted by the Convention of 1787, not to promote efficiency but to preclude the exercise of arbitrary power. The purpose was not to avoid friction, but, by means of the inevitable friction incident to the distribution of the governmental powers among three departments, to save the people from autocracy."

These are strong currents of our constitutional history which deny policy-making prerogative to the executive or to administrative agencies, save as Congress delegates such authority. Yet, the over-all pattern of history is not so clear. On critical occasions "strong" Presidents have taken affirmation action of great policy impact which they deemed essential to the welfare of the nation, though they lacked statutory authority to do so. Not surprisingly it was Theodore Roosevelt who furnished the most vigorous justification for this approach to the office when he asserted in his autobiography, "Occasionally great national crises arise which call for immediate and vigorous executive action; . . . in such cases it is the duty of the President to act upon the theory that he is the steward of the people; . . . the proper attitude for him to take is that he is bound to assume that he has the legal right to do whatever the needs of the people demand unless the Constitution or the laws explicitly forbid him to do it."

This is a point of view which can carry a bold President far. How far, Roosevelt himself revealed, for he did not limit his concept of stewardship to dealing with national emergencies. In the manner of a Tudor monarch, he made no concession to Congress's authority to scrutinize the performance of the officials whose salaries it provided, under the laws it enacted:

The Jackson-Lincoln view is that a President who is fit to do good work should be able to form his own judgment as to his own subordinates, and, above all, of the subordinates standing highest and in closest and most intimate touch with him. My secretaries and their subordinates were responsible to me, and I accepted the responsibility for all their deeds. As long as they were satisfactory to me I stood by them against every critic or assailant, within or without Congress; and as for getting Congress to make up my mind for me about them, the thought would have been inconceivable to me. . . . Of course, believers in the Jackson-Lincoln theory of the Presidency would not be content with this town-meeting majority and minority method of determining by another branch of the government what it seems the especial duty of the President himself to determine for himself in dealing with his own subordinates in his own department.

The first Roosevelt pushed his assertion of Presidential prerogative farther than his own record of action or that of other Presidents supports. He was on more solid ground of fact when he defined the President's stewardship authority as one for emergencies. There is functional appeal in the idea that a faithful steward will act to preserve his master's interest in pressing exigencies to which his instructions do not clearly run, with courage to await the master's approval or disavowal after the fact. It was in this light that Jefferson viewed what may be counted the first "stewardship" action of a President, when he seized the unexpected opportunity to buy Louisiana in 1803, though he was troubled because, as he saw it:

> The Constitution has made no provision for our holding foreign territory, still less for incorporating foreign nations into our Union. The executive, in seizing the fugitive occurrence which so much advances the good of their country, have done an act beyond the Constitution. The legislature in casting behind them metaphysical subtleties, and risking themselves like faithful servants, must ratify and pay for it, and throw themselves on their country for doing for them unauthorized what we know they would have done for themselves had they been in a situation to do it. It is the case of a guardian investing the money of his ward in purchasing an important adjacent territory; and saying to him when of age, I did this for your good; I pretend to no right to bind you; you may disavow me, and I must get out of the scrape as I can; I thought it my duty to risk myself for you.

The office of President has grown in practical power as strong-willed Presidents have taken on themselves the steward's responsibility. This was the basis on which, in April, 1861, Lincoln called for seventy-five thousand volunteers and ordered a naval blockade of the Southern ports. It was the basis on which, in 1902, Theodore Roosevelt intervened to settle a national coal strike. It was the practical, though not the formal, basis on which, in 1940, Franklin D. Roosevelt concluded the exchange of American destroyers for leases of English naval bases. It was the basis on which President Truman seized the steel mills in 1951, only to be overruled by the Supreme Court. It appears to be the basis on which President Nixon instructed aides to use wiretaps and such other means of covert investigation as they might find necessary to pursue individuals divulging information which the executive wished to hold to itself. It appears to be the basis on which, asserting urgent need to combat inflation, President Nixon caused massive impoundment of funds appropriated by Congress for congressionally authorized or mandated programs.

However, Presidential power grew mainly by the options and responsibilities which Congress itself put in the Presidency. From the nineteen-thirties on, Congress mightily enlarged the federal government's roles in the domestic society. In that same time, Congress also authorized and financed a great military capacity under the direction of the President as Commander in Chief. In addition, under Presidential leadership, it committed the country to extensive economic and military aid to other nations. Compounding the burdens thus accumulating on the office was the attendant business which went with the two major constitutional responsibilities of the President—to take care that the laws be faithfully executed and to take the lead in foreign relations.

The growing load on the Presidency brought changes in apparatus and decision-making processes. Increase in burdens preoccupied departmental secretaries and attenuated whatever capacity they had ever had to function as a Cabinet. Concurrently, Presidents responded to the pressures of public business by seeking more concentrated counsel and support than either the Cabinet could give or that could readily come from contacts in Congress. The rapid course of events tended to isolate the President's decision-making, confine it within a tight inner circle of trusted counselors and aides. This developing pattern made it easier for a President to insulate himself from informative, if often abrasive, contacts with Congress, the press, and interest groups or concerned people throughout the country. Thus major policy decisions could be made and policy trends could gain imperious momentum inside a relatively tight Presidential circle before outsiders could clearly identify the course of affairs, let alone effectively intervene in it.

The personality and working habits of any given President had distinctive impact; Presidential policy-making was more open in some administrations than in others. But from the nineteen-thirties on, the net sum of events showed more concentration and insulation of decision-making in the White House.

Insofar as the 1973 hearings showed the disturbing growth in the power and insulation of the Presidency, they involved foundation issues of late-twentieth-century legal order. To say this is not to deny that the hearings dealt with other areas of great importance —notably, collection and use of campaign funds, and the use of campaign tactics to subvert the election process. But the Senate inquiry threw into sharp relief critical separation-of-powers problems concerning the Presidency.

The experience of the last forty years teaches that for an indefinite future most public business will be done through massive executive and administrative establishments. To meet politically effective demands on government for service, regulation, and protection, nothing will suffice but the specialization, continuity, and focused force, experience, and initiative which executive and administrative organizations can supply. At the highest level of power, influence, and example stands the office of the President. The same factors which forecast continued dependence on pervasive executive-administrative power take on compound force in the Presidency. For that office has its unique assets in its special command of the armed forces, its control of national police and intelligence agencies, the means it holds to channel and time public spending, its endowment with rich and tempting patronage, its possession of a unique forum from which to shape public opinion.

The practical as well as formal power that has developed in the office of President may be incompatible with real checks and balances in the federal government. Nothing in the last forty years' experience suggests that this problem will go away through any processes immanent in the legal order. We cannot will or wish the problem away. Yet there is evidence—implicit in the creation of the 1973 Senate investigation and the popular concern with it—that our politics includes a stubbornly vital demand that the constitutional ideal be implemented. Constitutionalism insists that there be no center of public or private power in the society that is not subject in material degree to external check on how power-holders define and pursue their goals. The 1973 hearings invite the country to take stock of its resources for holding accountable the great and dangerously insulated power that has come to reside in the office of the President.

Another separation-of-powers issue is the problem of achieving wise balances between centralized and decentralized direction of public policy. The size, diversity, and specialization of public business committed to executive and administrative agencies made it increasingly difficult for the Chief Executive or the legislature to exercise effective oversight and coordination of public policy. Particular programs thus became the bases for setting up bureaucratic baronies which cultivated their own influence, protected their own comfortable ways, and settled into informal truce or working alliance with the most immediately affected private interests. Interventions by the White House secretariat were ad hoc and did not respond to the needs for coordination and general accountability. To the contrary, the 1973 hearings showed that ad hoc interventions from the top were likely sources of abuse of government administration. Cases in point were pressures on the Internal Revenue Service to harass political or policy opponents of the Administration.

Since the nineteen-thirties, the development of budgeting procedures under White House direction has given the President an effective planning and control instrument within the limits of a calculus which emphasized money and government tables of organization. Of course, budget and administrative organization were key elements in productive public policy. But they did not embrace all the values to which human needs and politically effective demands required response. In creating the Council of Economic Advisers, the Employment Act of 1946 added, in aid of White House policy leadership, another instrument to broaden the considerations of top decision-makers. But these devices were specialized and did not match the sweep of public affairs affected by federal executive and administrative operations. As the 1973 hearings showed, the working response was likely to be to add to the White House secretariat one or two aides whose responsibilities were of such scope that they became, in effect, assistant Presidents. Although White House operations vary according to the temperament and working habits of particular Presidents, a big federal executive-administrative establishment needs strong contributions from the White House to direct and coordinate public policy. But the stronger the White House, the greater the need for effective outside scrutiny of Presidential performance.

As the 1973 Senate hearings began to produce evidence of illegal conduct of executive officers, some critics argued that pursuit of lawbreakers was solely the business of public prosecutors and courts. Critics said that the Senate Committee should drop such lines of investigation because lawbreaking was not a proper subject of legislative inquiry, or because legislative inquiry might be bought at the price of grants of immunity which would let lawbreakers go free of prosecution, or because adverse publicity might, in a court's judgment, so prejudice opportunity for fair trial as to require that the court dismiss an indictment.

There are institutional limits to what judges can do about public affairs that are out of joint. Occasionally a court may prevent trouble by an injunction. Rarely it may be able to take affirmative action to restructure a situation, as judges did when they themselves reapportioned, or threatened to reapportion, a malapportioned legislature. But normally when someone has done a public or private wrong, all that judges have legal or practical power to do is to punish or order monetary compensation for that part of the harm that money can offset. Where an out-of-joint situation calls for fresh force or new apparatus to implement public policy, reformers must resort to the legislature, which alone commands the public purse and the authority to create or remodel government organization and procedures beyond the few matters fixed by the Constitution.

Illegal or at least questionable conduct revealed in the 1973 hearings brought in question the adequacy of existing law and machinery to deal with campaign finance, campaign tactics, and wiretapping. It is within ordinary legislative discretion for Congress to decide whether the problems revealed make it more important to get new law for the future than to leave the field wholly free for prosecutors to act under existing law. If Congress decides that consideration of new law is important enough in the public interest to be worth the cost of letting a few wrongdoers escape the hazard of trial or jail, this is a choice well within legislative prerogative.

Moreover, other dimensions of public problems may make it sensible for courts to yield place to the legislature. A court must work within the confines of a record made by pleadings and evidence brought before it by counsel. Counsel on their part must limit the matter they bring forward to issues sharply enough focused to make a case or controversy, must hold issues to those that fix on defined litigants, and must limit evidence to what is relevant to the particular litigants and the focused issues and to what is admissible under rules of evidence that have developed with reference to functions and problems of litigation.

Such limitations—appropriate enough to judges' work in applying law to particular situations—are not well adapted to producing generalized public policy. Judge-made law has been useful where cautious, case-by-case testing sufficed or where the range of relevant policy coincided with the interests represented by particular suitors. But a private lawsuit or a public prosecution is an instrument not well adapted to examining the moral tone or the ethical sensitivity with which executive officers wield power. These may be the most important questions concerning the legitimacy of executive power, but they will likely be too general and too subtle to be captured within the record of a trial.

Again, court procedures are not sympathetic to wide-ranging exploration. "Fishing expedition" is a term of reproach in a courtroom context. Even where litigation allows discovery procedures, discovery must be sought only regarding matter brought to quite close definition. Yet, where legislators or aggrieved or suspicious citizens confront the expertness, specialized experience, and massive files of executive officers who may have their own reasons for withholding candid disclosure of their actions, the prime problem may be to know what questions to ask. A fishing expedition may be just what will serve the public interest. If so, only the flexibility of legislative investigative power may do.

It was such exploratory inquiry, incident to the 1973 hearings, which informed not only the Congress but the public of the existence of tape recordings of Presidential conferences. It was such an exploratory inquiry which pointed to executive maneuvers to cover up responsibility for illegal activity against the incumbents' loyal opposition.

Finally, there may be matters important to public trust in government and to necessary mutual trust and confidence between the legislative and executive branches which present no violation of the penal code and no subject amenable to a civil lawsuit. If executive officers lie to the Congress about matters of fact important for Congress's exercise of its purse power, or its power to declare war or to provide supplies to maintain hostilities, or important to the Senate's responsibility to advise and consent in matters of foreign policy; or if the President breaks faith with the Congress on commitments properly made to obtain confirmation of an Attorney General, how is such executive conduct to be brought to accounting within a lawsuit?

One functional limitation of judicial process is of such practical importance to separation-of-powers values as to warrant distinct emphasis. In a significant aspect courts are passive agencies; they do not go looking for trouble, but wait for appropriate parties to bring troubles before them. The executive is charged to be the aggressive agency, to ferret out wrongdoing, mistakes, or inefficiency in carrying out public policy. But if executive officers are responsible for lawbreaking or negligence or impropriety in using public power, they may block rather than help resort to the courts.

The vigor of Special Prosecutor Archibald Cox promised to produce some important resolutions of disputed aspects of the 1972 Presidential campaign. But there might not have been a special prosecutor without concern generated by the probings of the press and the threat and then reality of a Senate investigation. The President's dismissal of Mr. Cox showed how dependent court processes are on the executive's attitude toward prosecutions.

Moreover, judicial process may be balked by executive decisions in another way. If the executive refuses to make available evidence it possesses, which a defendant claims to be essential to his defense to a criminal charge, the court—if it cannot overcome the executive balk—must, as a matter of due process, dismiss the prosecution. On the other hand, as the storm aroused by the Cox dismissal showed, public opinion still trusts the courts as guardians of legal order. If there is the necessary prosecuting vigor and independence to put the judicial process in motion, judges can provide significant checks on abuse of executive power.

The importance of legislative powers of inquiry and decision is reflected in the legislature's power to take its own action against an individual who stands in contempt of proper legislative process. Both federal and state statutes make it a criminal offense to commit contempt against legislative proceedings. But the law is that a legislative chamber need not rely on the good will or cooperation of executive officers to act under such statutes. Each legislative chamber has inherent authority itself to cite, try, and convict for contempt of its process, and to commit the contemptuous individual to the custody of its own sergeant-at-arms. No more should the legislative branch be dependent on the good will of the executive, by initiating court proceedings, to pursue possible executive misconduct.

It is also true that courts are not without significant independent authority to serve public interest, despite shortcomings of the other branches. A court may protect its processes against impairment by legislative investigation. If it is willing to risk the costs of forgoing a prosecution, the legislature may cause its investigating committee to pursue inquiries which may create public opinion so harmful to an individual that he may properly claim that he cannot obtain a fair trial on charges thereafter brought against him in court. But, though the court will not order a halt to the legislative investigation, it may dismiss a prosecution because of the prejudicial climate of opinion which the investigation created.

On the other hand, once proceedings in court have been carried to the point of producing a proper order by the court on the executive, the court may on its own motion find want of compliance and judge the respondent executive officer in contempt, though there is no longer a prosecutor able or willing to press the matter. So, too, a duly convened grand jury may inquire into executive misconduct, and of its own motion seek the assistance of a court to require response to its inquiries, though there is no public prosecutor able or willing to assist it.

A private person or a class of private persons sharing a common interest may put the judicial process in motion to consider redress of alleged executive wrongdoing. And in some matters a private suitor may be recognized as in effect a private attorney general, to set judicial process in motion not for some special benefit to the complainant, but to enforce general standards or rules of law upon the executive. Of course, either type of private litigation may present issues of the standing of the suitor or the justiciability of the matter sued on; these issues loom larger as barriers to private litigating initiative in proportion as the lawsuit raises matters of diffuse impact. Altogether, however, the possibilities of judicial, as well as of legislative, means of examining executive performance are sufficiently varied to show the emphasis of our separation-of-powers tradition on keeping open options for checking abuse of official power.

Those who led in framing and ratifying the federal Constitution included a procedure of impeachment primarily as a remedy against serious abuse of power by the President. They regarded it as supplemental to other formal constitutional limitations and to informal political checks. Prime—indeed nearly exclusive—attention went to fears of overreaching by a President. Only belatedly and with little discussion did the framers broaden the impeachment clause to include all civil officers of the United States.

Impeachment is a procedure of potentially broad but not unlimited reach. It may lie for "treason, bribery, or other high crimes or misdemeanors." "Treason" has a narrow definition elsewhere in the Constitution. "Bribery" has a narrow definition by its familiar common-law meaning. "High crimes or misdemeanors" is a phrase which draws for meaning on English political history and has had some development in our own experience. The framers did not intend the phrase to confer unlimited discretion on Congress to determine allowable grounds of impeachment. They chose this language in preference to looser terms in order to bar using impeachment simply for partisan combat. To this end, notably, they rejected "maladministration" as a stated ground of removal from office.

On the other hand, they expressly protected against the worst excesses of English political battles by stipulating that conviction on impeachment should carry no sanction other than removal from office and disqualification to hold future office. This limitation leaves the Congress the more free in good conscience to follow the guidelines offered by English history.

Parliamentary precedent teaches that "other high crimes or misdemeanors" are not limited to violations of existing criminal law, but include gross negligence by the President, flagrant refusal to implement duly enacted statutes, obstruction of the regular processes of justice through the courts, and, as an underlying principle, any executive conduct which may fairly be deemed to violate the basics of the constitutional separation of powers.

Congressional precedents point the same way. The Senate did not convict Mr. Justice Chase. Various judgments, including those of partisan politics, entered into that result. But the Chase impeachment trial record does not bring into question the proposition that a high officer may be duly impeached and convicted for violating the constitutional character of his office or using his office in ways that otherwise go against the Constitution, as by violating the Bill of Rights. The acquittal of Chase was in substance a verdict of "Not Proven." The Senate failed to convict President Andrew Johnson in part because the statute he was charged with violating was unclear in interpretation and was arguably unconstitutional as itself infringing the separation of powers.

There is here nothing to deny that deliberate Presidential violation of valid statute law may not be an impeachable offense. More generally, congressional precedent establishes that grounds for impeachment are not limited to proof of commission of crimes. Federal judges have been removed by impeachment on a showing of gross impropriety in office short of criminal misbehavior.

One use of the impeachment process has had almost no test in United States experience, but has in it the potential for more flexibility as a supplemental remedy against executive abuse than lies in the possibility of impeaching a President. The outcome of the impeachment of Andrew Johnson points to the great practical difficulties likely to oppose the conviction of a President. There are such high partisan stakes in getting or holding that office and such public-interest values in keeping the office effective that acquittal is the more likely outcome than conviction. The partisan stakes are not so high, nor the public interest so weighted toward the stability of office, as to executive officers of high rank below the President, such as departmental secretaries or top Presidential aides. English precedent is ample for using impeachment against such officers; the King could do no wrong, but his ministers could, and were held to account by Parliament for doing it.

Congress has been finding it hard to exercise effective supervision over the great executive and administrative apparatus we have erected. Perhaps the time has come for Congress to test the uses of the supplemental remedy of impeachment process against officials at levels of great responsibility but below the President. At those levels the odds against constructive use of the process may not be so great, and there may be more likelihood of outcomes that will support the legitimacy of legal order.

If the House finds that it must decide whether or not to bring impeachment against a President, it will confront factors extremely difficult to weigh. If a President has acted so as to create serious questions of the legitimacy of his Administration, there may be grave damage to popular confidence in the legal order if impeachment is not used. But a prudent Congress will observe two major cautions in launching impeachment proceedings. The Chase and Johnson impeachments teach that this is a process likely to be shot through and through with savage cut-and-thrust partisan conflict. Such conflict is divisive in itself. It is likely to be so overt as to imperil the standing in general opinion of either a bill of impeachment or a finding of no bill, or of conviction or acquittal. Moreover, as adamant partisans line up on one side of the aisle or the other, the balance may turn in the outcome on a dangerously few votes of those who keep more detachment.

The other caution is one specially addressed to those who believe that a President has done such serious wrong as to warrant impeachment. From their own point of view they must soberly weigh the consequences of failure to convict, assuming that they prevail in voting a bill of impeachment. Acquittal or failure to convict may consolidate the practical power of the man they sought to oust, and all the more so if many people interpret the result as showing that the accused was persecuted or was made a martyr. Whether appraised in terms of principle or strategy, the hazards are such as to raise a strong presumption against impeaching a President.

But the imponderables raise only a presumption. The Constitution judges that this supplemental remedy against official abuse should be available. And the House cannot avoid that which may rebut the presumption—the damage that may be done to the legitimacy of legal order if the House does not invoke the procedure against a President whose conduct, in the view of a large part of the country, has put constitutional order in jeopardy.

Legal and practical constraints on judicial power and on the impeachment process point us back to the general resources of the legislative branch for examining performance and curbing abuse in the executive and administrative arms of government. The question here is one of legislative will and courage rather than of legislative power.

Where public interest calls for positive power, it is no answer to parade forth horrible prophecies of abuse. If as a practical matter the bulk of the working content of law is going to emerge from executive and administrative decision, under authority delegated by legislators, the legislators must learn how to make their effective contribution to the real separation of powers through more effective superintendence.

Presidents, Congress, and the
Legislative Functions

HUGH G. GALLAGHER

Once upon a time, there was a President who was master of all he surveyed. The people around him—the white, the black, the yellow, the halt, the lame, the poor, even the farmers—loved him. He commanded huge majorities in Congress; they hastened to do his bidding. He did battle with the Supreme Court and, in the end, always won. The press was devoted to him. He dined with Kings and heads of state. He was the master politician of the age. He was the commander in chief, the economist, the diplomat, the mediator, the legislator, the father of us all. He gave us confidence when all was despair. He led us to victory when defeat loomed large. All news, all events emanated from the White House, in fact, from the President himself.

This President was Franklin D. Roosevelt and this, unfairly summarized perhaps, was his concept of the Presidency. It was certainly not the image of the Presidency held by his predecessors. Beard said that Roosevelt, in his Administration, changed the concept of the President's role more than had all the previous Presidents lumped together. Beard was not wrong.

Roosevelt sold us all his bill of goods. As political scientist Thomas E. Cronin has pointed out, FDR's concept of his office has now come to be universally accepted. We are taught in school that the President is the most powerful man on earth—head of state, head of party, chief legislator, and so on and so forth. All Presidents since FDR are measured by this standard and are found wanting. The men who have tried hardest to imitate this Rooseveltian image have been the least successful of postwar Presidents: Kennedy, Johnson, and Nixon. Kennedy failed with Congress and learned, only under great pressure, the hazards of nuclear foreign policy.

Reprinted from *The Presidency Reappraised,* edited by Rexford G. Tugwell and Thomas E. Cronin, published for the Center for the Study of Democratic Institutions, Santa Barbara, California by Praeger Publishers, Inc. Copyright 1974 by the Fund for the Republic, Inc. Hugh G. Gallagher is the author of *Advise and Obstruct: The Role of The United States Senate in Foreign Policy Decisions* and *ETOK: A Story of Eskimo Power.* He is currently Washington Representative of British Petroleum.

Johnson, though outstanding in many areas—legislation, for one—
failed in his manic perseverance to be all things to all people in
the FDR manner. Nixon has been the saddest case of all.

The "FDR Presidency" is beyond the capability of any man to
fill, especially in this postnuclear, cybernetic, synergistic age. It was,
in fact, beyond the ability of any man in the time of FDR. Roosevelt seemed to be doing all those things, filling all those roles. But,
in fact, he was not. No man in history, perhaps, was better equipped
to fill them all, but, in fact, he did not. He was many things, one
of them being a consummate actor. He wasn't guiding the wave,
controlling its crest; he just thought he was—and he made us
think so, too.

If FDR is set aside as a separate matter—a unique case—as one
President out of thirty-six, it is possible to place the Presidency
in a more realistic perspective with Congress. If we stop looking
at the President as some sort of colossus towering over Congress
and the country and look at him, instead, as the man he is, we find
him at the head of a coequal branch of our national government.
He may propose legislation, in the State of the Union message
or otherwise. His proposals will be received by Congress, and, depending on a host of variables, Congress will give its attention to
them.

Sometimes he is more influential, sometimes less influential, with
Congress as it considers legislation. Sometimes his legislative proposals are innovative, sometimes not. Sometimes his authority is
great in one policy area but not in others. Our system of government is not a see-saw, with the President up while Congress is
down. It is a system with separation of executive and legislative
powers. In regard to his legislative powers, the President is a
constitutional monarch with hardly more authority over Congress
than Elizabeth II has over Parliament.

In the years since FDR, the executive branch has run amuck.
The various departments have grown in size and responsibility; the
executive office of the President has grown; the White House staff
itself is larger now than the whole Washington government was
under Hoover. But this growth of the executive branch of government does not mean a growth in the power of the President. Far
from it.

The President is not strong but weak: He has lost control of
the departments, of domestic policy, and, as we see in Watergate,
even his own House. He has retreated into foreign policy, but even
there he must share his authority with Congress.

So much attention has been given, in recent years, to the growth of executive power that an essential point has been overlooked. It is true the executive branch has taken upon itself extraordinary powers—war, peace, control of the economy. This does not mean, however, that the man elected by the people to the Presidency can actually wield these powers. He does not rule, he reigns—with the deplorable result that no one responsive to the people governs the country.

It is axiomatic that, sooner or later, all Presidents come to hate Congress. They have reason to do so. During the course of Presidential campaigns, the country is encouraged to hold the last President responsible for what has happened in his Administration and to expect the new President to produce on his promises in the new Administration. Clearly and repeatedly, Congress comes between the President and the expectations of the people. This leads to Presidential frustration of a high order.

After the messianic hundred days and then some, even Roosevelt's relations with the Congress settled down into the normal bad. After the great purge effort of 1938, they became worse and continued so until his death. After 1938, with the exception of declarations of war and other necessities, FDR received little congressional support for his innovative legislative and social proposals. It is true that Congress gave him the executive powers he sought in order to direct the war, but not fast enough to suit him. In a peculiar address to Congress, rather chilling in its overtone, Roosevelt said, in 1942, "in event that the Congress should fail to act adequately, I shall accept the responsibility and will act. . . I have given the most thoughtful consideration to meeting this issue without further reference to Congress . . . when the war is won the powers under which I act automatically revert to the people to whom they belong."

Many a President has threatened to horsewhip congressmen, but this is, I believe, the only time a President has stood in the halls of Congress and threatened to abolish it.

Harry Truman, originally a Senate club member if ever there was one, ended up making his living by giving hell to the Eightieth "Do Nothing Congress"—actually, a most responsible, productive session. Lyndon Johnson, after that *annus mirabilis* of 1964, during which he conducted Congress through its most productive session in history, came to despise congressional criticism. He was at length to be driven from the White House because of it. "Go ask Walter Lippmann for your appropriation," LBJ was overheard growling to a senator who had questioned his Vietnam policy.

There is very little left by which a President can reward a friend in Congress. Patronage and the Post Office are not the help they once were. An opportunity to share the Presidential publicity spotlight for a few moments at a bill-signing ceremony is nice but brief, and there are other ways to obtain publicity. A Presidential campaign swing through a member's district just before election is supposed to be of value, but anyone who has lived through such an exercise must have his doubts. The value of Presidential endorsements, always debatable, has in recent years become largely discredited.

So, although the President has little to trade, he has a desperate need for congressional cooperation. Congress can undo him at every turn. It can make his program appear successful by approving it and funding it; it can turn it into disgrace by harassment, underfunding, and overinvestigation.

No wonder Congress so often produces a Presidential rage of impotence. It is built into the System—it is the System—and we can perhaps take comfort in the thought that it is not new. When the Senate rejected not only his first but his second nomination to the Supreme Court, President Nixon lashed out, accusing the Senate of action vicious, false, and hypocritical. It is, he said, the "constitutional responsibility of the President to appoint members of the Court." The Senate's rejection of the nominations amounted to the substitution of the Senate's "own subjective judgment for that of the one person entrusted by the Constitution with the power of appointment . . . the fact remains, under the Constitution it is the duty of the President to appoint and of the Senate to advise and consent." Failure to consent, he said, placed the "traditional constitutional balance in jeopardy."

John Tyler, tenth President of the United States, would have had great sympathy with President Nixon's frustration, for certaintly John Tyler was the all-time champion of bad relations with his Congress. A fine and decent Virginian, he became President by mistake, upon the death of William Henry Harrison, who died of a chill contracted while giving a much too lengthy inaugural address. Tyler had broken with the Jacksonian Democrats to accept second place on the Whig ticket with Harrison. The Whigs thought he would bring Virginia with him. He failed to do so. He was not a Whig. He thus came to the White House with virtually no party support in Congress. There ensued three zany years in the history of the Republic.

When Harrison died, the congressional Whigs confidently expected Tyler to serve as acting President only. They soon found out how mistaken they were: "I am the President and am responsible for my Administration."

The President vetoed the Bank Bill. The Congress promptly passed another Bank Bill. The President vetoed it. The House of Representatives drew up a Bill of Indictment with intent to impeach the President. The President protested by message—a message the House refused to receive, let alone consider. The President's Cabinet resigned en masse, excepting only Webster, who had his own Presidential ambitions. The charade reached its zenith—or perhaps nadir—over Senate confirmation of Tyler's appointments. In the last session of his Administration, the Senate rejected four Cabinet nominations, four Supreme Court nominations, nominations of ministers to France and Brazil, five marshals, one attorney, fourteen deputy postmasters, thirty-one custom officials, four receivers of public money, and four registrars of land offices. These figures must of necessity be approximate. The records are confused because several of the nominations were submitted and rejected a number of times.

President Tyler was a stubborn man.

On the last night of the session, as was the custom of the day, Tyler went to the President's Room adjacent to the Senate chamber, ready for battle. That night, the Senate received and rejected three times the nomination of Caleb Cushing to be the Secretary of the Treasury. Similarly, that night Henry A. Wise was nominated three times and rejected three times as minister to France. Old Senator Benton reported that "nominations and rejections flew backwards and forwards as in a game of shuttlecock—the same nomination in several instances being rejected . . . within the same hour."

Never was a President more badly treated by a Congress.

And perhaps it can fairly be said that never was a Congress more badly treated by a President than in the actions of Abraham Lincoln. At the beginning of the Civil War, the President purposefully delayed calling Congress into session to avoid the criticisms and delays that Congress invariably produces. To save the Union, President Lincoln used powers he did not have, knowingly and repeatedly overstepping the Constitution.

In a statement, breathtaking and sweeping, to Senator Chandler, Lincoln said, "I conceive that I may, in an emergency, do things on military grounds which cannot constitutionally be done by the Congress." Roosevelt threatened to assume powers held by Congress, but, until Nixon, only Lincoln claimed powers held neither by

Congress nor by the President. No wonder Senator Wade said
the country was going to hell.

President Lincoln called up troops, drafted men, and spent un-
appropriated money. He used his own friends to carry unappropri-
ated money from the Treasury to pay arms and ammunition makers.
He interned persons of suspected loyalty and abolished habeas
corpus.

As a politician, a candidate, and a President, it was his theory
to watch and wait for the big event and to ignore the small, en-
tangling ones. Utilizing his concept of his war powers, against the
advice of his Cabinet, without consulting Congress, he issued the
Emancipation Proclamation. This action, its moral significance
aside, abolished without compensation, at one fell swoop, considerably more than a billion dollars of personal property held by
American citizens. He issued his Proclamation even as the Congress
was considering legislation of its own to provide for the freeing
of the slaves.

As war President, Lincoln dictated the terms of the peace. He
appointed military governors without congressional approval and
declared what terms and procedures must be satisfied before returning Southern states could take up their places in Congress
and the Union. He was preparing to implement his Reconstruction
program (which he had prepared without consulting Congress)
at the time of his assassination. Lincoln saved the Union, but
upset the comity between the President and Congress for a generation.

We have allowed strong Presidents like Lincoln to assume
sweeping powers in times of great crisis. After the crisis, Congress
has always moved to reassert itself, to bring the President down
to size, to redress the balance. The danger of allowing a President
like Lincoln to act without regard to constitutional restraints in
a great crisis is that lesser men may take Lincoln as precedent in
lesser causes.

In general, and from the beginning, the President and his Administration have always had to lobby Congress to obtain what
they wished. Secretary of the Treasury Alexander Hamilton thought
of himself as President Washington's Prime Minister and for five
years lobbied Congress to obtain approval of the President's program. Congress has, from the beginning, been indignant at such
interference in the legislative process.

The business of rallying support for the Administration in a
tight vote is an extraordinarily difficult thing to categorize. It involves all the things we read about in textbooks and newspapers:

patronage, judgeships, projects, grants, bargains with labor, pressure from industry, swaps of support of dubious programs, appeals to one's higher instincts—and the President can play a central role. President Cleveland was once busy dispensing patronage in exchange for votes. When told he would not win until hell froze over, he replied with some confidence, "Hell will freeze over in exactly twenty-four hours."

Woodrow Wilson is widely believed to have been the first modern President to utilize his officials to lobby Congress in any consistent, continuing manner. Albert Sydney Burleson, Wilson's Postmaster General, used the President's Room off the Senate chamber for his office as he lobbied the Wilson program through the Senate. Upon occasion, this Room has seen President's themselves pleading for their program. Harding used it during his extraordinary efforts to defeat the Soldier's Bonus Bill. President Grant lobbied in favor of his Santo Domingo Treaty from it.

Presidents have actually taken their lobbying to the floor of the Senate and occasionally to the floor of the House. There is nothing in the Senate rules that allows the President to speak. He has, however, never been denied the opportunity. President Harding spoke directly to the Senate as it was considering the Bonus Bill. In one extraordinary moment, President Hoover pleaded with an unresponsive Congress for passage of his tax bill. In the depth of the Depression and the depth of his despair, he appeared late one night, without previous notice, before the Senate to plead that "in your hands at this moment is the answer to the question whether Democracy has the capacity to act speedily enough to save itself in an emergency." In this case, the Democratic Congress cooperated. Otherwise, it was congressional politics as usual until Roosevelt took office.

The best-known case of an incumbent President appearing before a congressional committee was unexpected, unannounced. The Joint Committee on the Conduct of the War was considering, in secret session, reports of treason within President Lincoln's immediate family. Lincoln walked in, to the astonishment and dismay of the Committee, told its members there were no traitors in the White House, turned, and left. This killed the investigation.

Presidential efforts at influencing committee investigations or congressional actions are seldom that effective. Probably the basic reason for this, trite as it may be, is that the President is a short-termer, while Congress, like the Civil Service, is a career. Of the thirty-six Presidents preceding Nixon, only eleven, or fewer than one-third, have been elected to two consecutive terms. The popular conception that incumbent Presidents tend to be re-elected is just not true. It was true through the first forty-eight years of the Republic, when five of the seven Presidents were re-elected. Since then, there have been twenty-nine Presidents, and only six of these have been elected to two consecutive terms. Four were wartime leaders (Lincoln, McKinley, Wilson, and Roosevelt), and two were beloved war heroes (Grant and Eisenhower).

This is important to the balance of power between the executive and the legislative. Congressional leaders, with their years of seniority, full of "stubbornness and penicillin," as Senator Eugene McCarthy once put it, are cunning with experience. They have seen Presidents come and go, but they remain. If a new President does not get his legislative program—and, since TR, all Presidents have had a program—approved by Congress in his first two years, he won't get it approved at all. Woodrow Wilson pointed this out, and FDR used to quote Wilson on the subject, although, as his term wore on, he stretched Wilson's two years to four. In any case, by that time Congress has decided what it likes and will approve and what it will not. The President, without experience or very much influence, is seldom able to revive a program once bogged down in a recalcitrant Congress.

It is my impression that, on the whole, Congress has been more innovative and creative in proposing legislaton than has the President. Even though subject to numberless exceptions, excuses, and explanations, this statement is defendable.

The root reason for its truth is a simple one. There is, after all, a basic difference between what it is that the two branches do. To garble a Bernard Shaw quotation, the Administration looks at things the way they are and tries to improve them; Congress looks at the way things should be and tries to achieve them.

There are intelligent, able men in both branches of government. Those in the executive branch are intent to keep things from flying apart or from grinding at last to a full stop. The Administration tries to administer rather than to innovate. Its people react to events. Congress has the opportunity to act, not react; to create events. It can create new institutions; it can abolish old ones. It is not limited, like the Administration, to adjusting or perfecting the existing machinery of government.

Congress attracts intelligent men. It would not do so if it were but an empty honor. Intelligent men would not be content merely to ratify the President's ideas, appropriate him money, and go home. There are over 500 members of Congress (including the Vice-President). Not all of them may be intelligent, but all of them carry a degree of ambition. This combination of intelligence, ambition, and place provides an encouragement to creativity. The disparate many in Congress are struggling for the respect of their peers, the approval of their constituents, and national recognition. This brings about a congressional search that never ceases. Members and their staffs are ever looking for the issues that will catch on the bandwagon that is going to go, the Big One. They are anxious for an interview on *Meet the Press*, an article in *Parade*, an item on the front page of the *New York Times*.

The story of each piece of legislation is different, but all arise out of a complicated struggle of powers and ambitions, inspiration, public interest, and re-election.

An innovative proposal will come from one or two or several voices in Congress. It may be an old proposal brought to life again, like revenue sharing and the direct election of the President—ideas that date back at least to Andrew Jackson's first State of the Union message. They may be new ideas fresh from a sociology course or the mind of a congressman. The idea, once expressed, may cause discussion. If it is taken up by the press, debated by the intelligentsia, deplored by the establishment, there may come, in due course, serious congressional attention to the proposal. Hearings will be held. More discussion will be generated; radicals will support it; the establishment will continue to oppose it. At some point, it passes from heresy to dogma. It receives the Presidential imprimatur; it is mentioned in the State of the Union message and becomes part of the official Presidential legislative program.

The State of the Union message in which this program is set forth is largely an empty institution. It consists normally of harmless homilies, one or two headline-grabbing innovative proposals, and a list of legislative items that, though not new, carry reasonable prospects of passage into law. These serve to maintain a fairly respectable Presidential batting average. The message is usually universally ignored the week after it is given. There is no sadder task than reading through the messages of past years. For example: Lyndon Johnson made it an annual practice to pledge a massive clean-up of the Potomac River to make it a model for the nation's rivers. And public-health officials annually advise Washingtonians that their model river remains a cesspool, a mortal peril to upturned canoeists.

The writing and preparation of the actual bills and amendments have become a profession, and each branch of our government now has its experts in legislative preparation and interpretation.

The camaraderie that in many cases has grown up between the

professional staff of a congressional committee and the career staff of the agency over which the committee has jurisdiction is a source of uneasiness both to the White House and to members of Congress —and properly so.

Each Senate and House committee is staffed with persons of specialized knowledge in the area of the committee's competence. Each executive department and agency has its corresponding staff of legislative counsel and liaison. Over the years, they develop a working relationship that continues no matter what the election results. To check this intimacy, there is, within the executive office of the President, the Office of Management and Budget, a group of dedicated men with that "passion for anonymity" defined by Louis Brownlow. These men perform a service called "Legislative Reference." They are not political; they do not make policy. It is their duty to see that the legislative statements, testimony, and reports emanating from all the many executive agencies reflect Administration policy, are consistent, and are not contradictory. They serve as a clearing house, a court of appeal, a traffic cop. It is not their duty to question Administration policy; simply, to see that it is applied, to interpret and implement it throughout government. "Policy" itself is supposedly made across the street, in the White House, by the politicians, perhaps by the President himself. In fact, there are many times when there is *no* policy, and it is made consciously or unconsciously by the nonpolitical civil servants of Legislative Reference. These men see Presidents come and go, and they have no great respect for the ability of the White House staff, whether it be Republican or Democratic. So, in the absence of policy, they make it—in order to keep the executive end of legislation functioning. They make it one way until someone tells them to make it another.

In this strange and shifting world of legislative policy, authority is there to be used by those who take it. Legislative Reference in OMB has the advantage and wiliness that come from years of experience. Actually, they can be—and have been—overruled, by a ribbon clerk in the White House who claims to be, and occasionally may be, close to the President. Most junior White House clerks, however, do not know they can do this, and, by the time they learn, they are usually on their way back to private business or wherever they came from.

Confrontation within an Administration, of course, depends on the character of the Administration. In recent Administrations, not including the present, the secretary of any department had the right to reject the dicta of the Office of Management and Budget on legislation or, indeed, on anything else. He could appeal directly to the President. This was done, often enough, in a state of high dudgeon. The strength, importance, and utility of OMB depended on the ability of its director to get to the President *first*. A wise President supports his director, for the Office of Management and Budget offers his one last, sad hope of retaining control over that vast bureaucracy, the U.S. Government. Over the past years, there have been reports that even OMB has lost its grip and the Executive Office of the President, as wildly proliferating as any coral reef, is itself out of control.

If Watergate means anything, it is that this is indeed the case. The men around the President appeared to distrust not only their departments but their own colleagues in OMB. Our executive branch is now so large that perhaps there is no way to make it efficient and responsive to the President. Certainly, the Nixon men's attempt to create a tight little government within the government, a group of "loyal" men who could be trusted to do what the agencies and OMB could not, is only demonstration of the lack of Presidential direction and control over the executive branch.

The President himself, in search of legislative achievement, must buck Congress, the established Civil Service, the departments, and now the executive office itself. No wonder John Kennedy is reported to have said that he found "no pleasure" in the job.

Once a proposal has become part of the President's program, it gains in stature. Lobbyists and interest groups—including states, cities, and localities, federal agencies, and commissions—struggle over its terms. The professional syndicates take over—that is, the organizations, the clients, the lobbyists, the civil servants, the philanthropists, and the congressmen who are bound together by a common interest in education, mental health, SST, or whatever. The bill may become a partisan issue. Democrats and Republicans vie to develop, according to their lights, a more acceptable version of the measure. Finally, it is passed, and its sponsors and cosponsors are invited to the White House to participate in the Presidential signing ceremony. The President passes out pens to all concerned and makes a moving statement on the progress thus achieved, a statement carried by all major networks on their evening news program. And this is how the original idea of Congressman "X" becomes a major achievement in the record of the Administration of the President.

In 1946, Dr. Lawrence Chamberlain of Columbia University

published his book *The President, Congress and Legislation*. Professor Chamberlain analyzes the legislative history of ninety major pieces of legislation passed by Congress between the years 1880 and 1940. He chooses measures in the fields of business, tariff, labor, national defense, agriculture, federal credit, banking and currency, immigration, conservation, and railroads. Over the sixty years studied—including the New Deal years—Chamberlain found, "Of the entire ninety laws no less than seventy-seven traced their ancestry directly to bills which originally had been introduced without Administration sponsorship." He says, rather quietly, "These figures do not support the thesis that Congress is unimportant in the formulation of major legislation." It was Chamberlain's contention that the creative role of Congress could not be denied, even in the major pieces of Roosevelt legislation: the National Industrial Recovery Act, the Securities and Exchange Act, the Agricultural Adjustment Act, the National Labor Relations Act, the Fair Labor Standards Act, the Social Security Act.

> Most of the great mass of regulatory Legislation of the past decade, popularly dubbed 'New Deal Legislation,' had a well defined prenatal history extending back several years before it was espoused by the Roosevelt Administration. This is true not only of the more conventional fields such as banking, railroads and taxation but of the newer areas of social security, holding company regulation and security control.

Ronald C. Moe and Stephen C. Teel of San Diego College have done a valuable update of the Chamberlain study. Their results are published in the September, 1970, *Political Science Quarterly*. Their appraisal of Congress through the 1960's confirms Chamberlain's observation—Congress remains the innovator.

Judgment and selection are necessarily subjective. With this caveat, I list some bills essentially of congressional origin in recent years:

The Area Redevelopment Act of 1961 (Douglas)
The Taft-Hartley Labor Management Relations Act of 1947 (Taft-Hartley)
The Labor Management Reporting and Disclosure Act of 1959 (Landrum-Griffin)
The Interstate Highways System (Gore)
The Federal Merchant Marine Program (Magnuson-Bartlett)
The Atomic Energy Act of 1946 (McMahon)

The National Aeronautics and Space Act of 1958 (Anderson-
Johnson)
Civil Rights Legislation (Kefauver *et al.*)
The Cold War GI Bill of Rights (Yarborough)
Consumer Legislation (Magnuson)
The National Environmental Policy Act (Muskie-Jackson)
Antipollution Legislation (Muskie)
The War on Hunger (McGovern)
The Anti-ABM Movement (Symington)
The Anti-SST Movement (Proxmire)
The Atomic Test Ban Treaty (Humphrey)
The Disarmament Agency (Humphrey)
The Peace Corps (Neuberger-Reuss)
Health Care (Hill)
Education (Morse)

And of course the areas of taxes, import duties, and immigration
have always been Congress's.

Moe and Teel also take note of what I consider a most interesting
and significant development. The President has found it increasingly
difficult to exert leadership over the executive branch and its policies,
let alone compete with or lead Congress as chief legislator. It
appears that the President increasingly tends to retreat into foreign
policy and world affairs—areas over which he has clear constitutional
and historical dominion. Because of the exigencies of great power
and H-bomb missile technology, perhaps this is unavoidable, but
every President since 1940 has devoted more time to foreign affairs
than he has to domestic matters.

After the recent debacle in Vietnam, the cries became general
that Congress has relinquished its "traditional and constitutional"
responsibility to share foreign policy–making with the President.
This is said as though the President had deliberately and impudently
seized powers in the field hitherto held by Congress. Such is just
not the case.

Cecil Crabb, Jr., summarized what has been happening since
World War II. "A striking phenomenon associated with the control
of foreign relations in recent American history is the expanded role
of Congress in virtually all phases of external affairs." Moe and
Teel quote Crabb and list the areas of dominance—economic-aid
policy, military assistance, agricultural-surplus disposal, location of
facilities, immigration and tariff policies. To this list I would add
several other specific items—the Nuclear Test Ban Treaty; the
approval and withdrawal of the Gulf of Tonkin Resolution; the

Lebanese and Quemoy and Matsu Resolutions; the Fulbright Vietnam hearings, televised nationwide; the Pearl Harbor hearings after World War II; the hearings on the Dominican Republic invasion; and the congressional investigation into the Pentagon Papers.

In spite of President Nixon's brilliant innovations in foreign policy, Congress continues to have its way. The Senate insists on amendment to the SALT treaty; it blocks the Russian trade *détente*. Congress forces the President to cease Cambodian bombing. Such things demonstrate to the world, as did Woodrow Wilson's Senate, that the President *alone* cannot commit the United States to a foreign policy.

Even with regard to Vietnam, Congress condoned the President's policy by appropriation and resolution. When it withdrew its support, America's active involvement came to a halt. This simply demonstrates that Congress plays a substantial role in American foreign policy-making, a role larger than that of confirming ambassadors and ratifying treaties. The President may have more power to act on his own initiative in this area, but, even here, he is a limited constitutional monarch, with no more control over Congress than over his own departments.

The President of the United States has many titles. Chief legislator is one of them. It is a paper title.

Congress legislates, and, except in rare instances, the President has little to say about it. The origins of most of the innovative legislation in the last ten years, or the last century, can be found in Congress.

Presidents, like Kings, provide a handy chronology. They are easy to remember. The personality of a King is more memorable than the multitudes of a Parliament. To identify a measure as part of the Kennedy New Frontier program is to fix it in times as a silver spoon is fixed as Georgian. In most cases, upon examination the Kennedy Administration had about as much to do with the initiation of the proposal as the Georges had to do with the design and craftsmanship of the spoon.

Congress is a small and diverse body. It is a career. It is run by old men at the top, with the young men at the bottom. The old have the experience of age; the young have the ideas of youth. These ideas are sifted by experience, and what results is usually timely and responsive.

Congress is close enough to the people to determine when change is necesasry and, unlike the executive bureaucracy, small enough to provide it.

Do not worry too much about Congress. It is doing its job. If anyone is in trouble, it is the President, who is more in danger of losing control over his own executive branch than he is in a position to seize control over the legislative branch of our federal government. As the size and responsibilities of the federal government grow, the President's lack of control grows apace.

The Presidency is a weak office. It always has been. Only very few men have transcended its weakness.

In 1838, James Fenimore Cooper wrote, "As a rule, there is far more danger that the President of the United States will render the office less efficient than was intended, than that he will exercise an authority dangerous to the liberties of the country."

This is still the case.

7. Bureaucracy

The bureaucracy has been the center of concern during much of the Watergate controversy. The CIA's role, from supplying E. Howard Hunt's famous red wig to outfitting the "plumbers," violated statutory law; the acting director of the FBI destroyed documents upon instruction from the White House; the Internal Revenue Service was asked to harass political enemies. In all this it became evident to many that the scope of Presidential power included political control over the bureaucracy.

The bureaucracy, in fact, consists of two groups of people. There are the career civil servants whose jobs continue despite Presidential elections. These more than 2.5 million people make up the federal structure headed by the Cabinet. The other group comprises Presidential advisers, special assistants, counsels to the President and people with assorted other titles, who, Thomas Cronin notes, have together burgeoned into the "Presidential Establishment." These men serve at the pleasure of the President, do not require Senate confirmation, and are accountable only to the President.

From this Presidential Establishment Watergate emanated. The White House staff was most intimately implicated in the Watergate cover-up, and its blind devotion to the President led it to misunderstand and misrepresent the public interest. As Cronin notes, the growth of the White House has made traditional views of the executive nearly obsolete and has potentially alarming consequences. This proliferation of Presidential staff and advisers, accelerated by the Nixon Administration, has been at the expense of the bureaucracy and traditional sources of executive power; the White House became an isolated inner sanctum, unavailable to party leaders, Cabinet members, or, for that matter, subordinate staff members. Furthermore, the White House office was staffed with people with a public-relations or legal background; in either case, they had little experience in politics. With disregard for political and Constitutional constraints, these brash, powerful young men felt free to intrude in departmental political affairs. It seems one of Richard Neustadt's 1959 teachings on Presidential power was ignored: "The Presidency is no place for amateurs."

As for the permanent bureaucracy, much debate in the 1960's centered on bureaucratic autonomy versus political accountability. J. Edgar Hoover—irascible, seemingly permanent Director of the FBI—ran his Bureau as he saw fit, unresponsive to Presidential requests. The 1960's also saw alarm over the operations of the CIA. No one knew what the supersleuths were doing, to whom were they accountable, how they could be made responsible. Watergate changed all this. We have seen what a politically responsive bureaucracy can effect. Under directives from the President, the White House staff worked to contain the FBI investigation of Watergate. The Justice Department's chief Watergate prosecutor, Henry Peterson, reported Department findings directly to the President. Richard Kleindienst pleaded guilty for failing to testify fully on the ITT antitrust case before the Senate Judiciary Committee during his confirmation hearings.

Peter Woll and Rochelle Jones maintain, however, that the efforts to undermine the bureaucracy and use it for political purposes were largely unsuccessful. To the bureaucracy's credit, it resisted and managed to thwart the administration's directives. The FBI resisted efforts to activate the Huston Plan. The CIA, though tainted by Watergate, did maintain its independence from the cover-up, and FBI leaks were instrumental in unraveling that cover-up. Woll and Jones argue that, in the Nixon Administration, the permanent bureaucracy was a little-noticed safeguard of the democratic system.

The Swelling of the Presidency

THOMAS E. CRONIN

The advent of Richard Nixon's second term in the White House is marked by an uncommon amount of concern, in Congress and elsewhere, about the expansion of presidential power and manpower. Even the President himself is ostensibly among those who are troubled. Soon after his re-election, Mr. Nixon announced that he was planning to pare back the presidential staff. And in recent days, the President has said he is taking action to cut the presidential workforce in half and to "substantially" reduce the number of organizations that now come under the White House. Mr. Nixon's announcements have no doubt been prompted in part by a desire to add drama and an aura of change to the commencement of his second term. But he also seems genuinely worried that the presidency may have grown so large and top-heavy that it now weakens rather than strengthens his ability to manage the federal government. His fears are justified.

The presidency has, in fact, grown a full 20 per cent in the last four years alone in terms of the number of people who are employed directly under the President. It has swelled to the point where it is now only a little short of the State Department's sprawling domestic bureaucracy in size.

This burgeoning growth of the presidency has, in the process, made the traditional civics textbook picture of the executive branch of our government nearly obsolete. According to this view, the executive branch is more or less neatly divided into Cabinet departments and their secretaries, agencies and their heads, and the President. A more contemporary view takes note of a few prominent presidential aides and refers to them as the "White House staff." But neither view adequately recognizes the large and growing coterie that surrounds the President and is made up of dozens of assistants, hundreds of presidential advisers, and thousands of mem-

Reprinted from the *Saturday Review* by permission of Thomas E. Cronin. Copyright © 1973. Thomas E. Cronin is a Scholar in Residence at the Aspen Institute for Humanistic Studies. Among his books are *The Presidency Advisory System, The State of the Presidency,* and *The Presidency Reappraised,* edited with Rexford G. Tugwell.

bers of an institutional amalgam called the Executive Office of the President. While the men and women in these categories all fall directly under the President in the organizational charts, there is no generally used term for their common terrain. But it has swelled so much in size and scope in recent years, and has become such an important part of the federal government, that it deserves its own designation. Most apt perhaps is the Presidential Establishment.

The Presidential Establishment today embraces more than twenty support staffs (the White House Office, National Security Council, and Office of Management and Budget, etc.) and advisory offices (Council of Economic Advisers, Office of Science and Technology, and Office of Telecommunications Policy, etc.). It has spawned a vast proliferation of ranks and titles to go with its proliferation of functions (Counsel to the President, Assistant to the President, Special Counselor, Special Assistant, Special Consultant, Director, Staff Director, etc.). "The White House now has enough people with fancy titles to populate a Gilbert and Sullivan comic opera," Congressman Morris Udall has reasonably enough observed.

There are no official figures on the size of the Presidential Establishment, and standard body counts vary widely, depending on who is and who is not included in the count, but by one frequently used reckoning, between five and six thousand people work for the President of the United States. Payroll and maintenance costs for this staff run between $100 million and $150 million a year. (These figures include the Office of Economic Opportunity [OEO], which is an Executive Office agency and employs two thousand people, but not the roughly fifteen thousand–man Central Intelligence Agency, although that, too, is directly responsible to the Chief Executive.) These "White House" workers have long since outgrown the White House itself and now occupy not only two wings of the executive mansion but three nearby high-rise office buildings as well.

The expansion of the Presidential Establishment, it should be emphasized, is by no means only a phenomenon of the Nixon years. The number of employees under the President has been growing steadily since the early 1900s when only a few dozen people served in the White House entourage, at a cost of less than a few hundred thousand dollars annually. Congress's research arm, the Congressional Research Service, has compiled a count that underlines in particular the accelerated increase in the last two decades. This compilation shows that between 1954 and 1971 the number of presidential advisers has grown from 25 to 45, the White

House staff from 266 to 600, and the Executive Office staff from 1,175 to 5,395.

But if the growth of the Presidential Establishment antedates the current administration, it is curious at least that one of the largest expansions ever, in both relative and absolute terms, has taken place during the first term of a conservative, management-minded President who has often voiced his objection to any expansion of the federal government and its bureaucracy.

Under President Nixon, in fact, there has been an almost systematic bureaucratization of the Presidential Establishment, in which more new councils and offices have been established, more specialization and division of labor and layers of staffing have been added, than at any time except during World War II. Among the major Nixonian additions are the Council on Environmental Quality, Council on International Economic Policy, Domestic Council, and Office of Consumer Affairs.

The numbers in the White House entourage may have decreased somewhat since November when the President announced his intention to make certain staff cuts. They may shrink still more if, as expected, the OEO is shifted from White House supervision to Cabinet control, mainly under the Department of Health, Education, and Welfare. Also, in the months ahead, the President will probably offer specific legislative proposals, as he has done before, to reprogram or repackage the upper reaches of the executive.

Even so, any diminution of the Presidential Establishment has so far been more apparent than real, or more incidental than substantial. Some aides, such as former presidential counselor Robert Finch, who have wanted to leave anyway, have done so. Others, serving as scapegoats on the altar of Watergate, are also departing.

In addition, the President has officially removed a number of trusted domestic-policy staff assistants from the White House rolls and dispersed them to key sub-Cabinet posts across the span of government. But this dispersal can be viewed as not so much reducing as creating yet another expansion—a virtual setting up of White House outposts (or little White Houses?) throughout the Cabinet departments. The aides that are being sent forth are notable for their intimacy with the President, and they will surely maintain direct links to the White House, even though these links do not appear on the official organizational charts.

Then, too, one of the most important of the President's recent shifts of executive branch members involves an unequivocal addition to the Presidential Establishment. This is the formal setting up of a second office—with space and a staff in the White House—for Treasury Secretary George Shultz as chairman of yet another new presidential body, the Council on Economic Policy. This move makes Shultz a member of a White House inner cabinet. He will now be over-secretary of economic affairs alongside Henry Kissinger, over-secretary for national security affairs, and John Ehrlichman, over-secretary for domestic affairs.

In other words, however the names and numbers have changed recently or may be shifted about in the near future, the Presidential Establishment does not seem to be declining in terms of function, power, or prerogative; in fact, it may be continuing to grow as rapidly as ever.

Does it matter? A number of political analysts have argued recently that it does, and I agree with them. Perhaps the most disturbing aspect of the expansion of the Presidential Establishment is that it has become a powerful inner sanctum of government, isolated from traditional, constitutional checks and balances. It is common practice today for anonymous, unelected, and unratified aides to negotiate sensitive international commitments by means of executive agreements that are free from congressional oversight. Other aides in the Presidential Establishment wield fiscal authority over billions of dollars in funds that Congress has appropriated, yet the President refuses to spend, or that Congress has assigned to one purpose and the administration routinely redirects to another —all with no semblance of public scrutiny. Such exercises of power pose an important, perhaps vital, question of governmental philosophy: Should a political system that has made a virtue of periodic electoral accountability accord an ever-increasing policy-making role to White House counselors who neither are confirmed by the U.S. Senate nor, because of the doctrine of "executive privilege," are subject to questioning by Congress?

Another disquieting aspect of the growth of the Presidential Establishment is that the increase of its powers has been largely at the expense of the traditional sources of executive power and policy-making—the Cabinet members and their departments. When I asked a former Kennedy-Johnson Cabinet member a while ago what he would like to do if he ever returned to government, he said he would rather be a presidential assistant than a Cabinet member. And this is an increasingly familiar assessment of the relative influence of the two levels of the executive branch. The Presidential Establishment has become, in effect, a whole layer of government between the President and the Cabinet, and it often stands above the Cabinet in terms of influence with the President. In spite of the exalted position that Cabinet members hold in textbooks and protocol, a number of Cabinet members in recent administrations have complained that they could not even get the President's ear except through an assistant. In his book *Who Owns America?*, former Secretary of the Interior Walter Hickel recounts his combat with a dozen different presidential functionaries and tells how he needed clearance from them before he could get to talk to the President, or how he frequently had to deal with the assistants themselves because the President was "too busy." During an earlier administration, President Eisenhower's chief assistant, Sherman Adams, was said to have told two Cabinet members who could not resolve a matter of mutual concern: "Either make up your mind or else tell me and I will do it. We must not bother the President with this. He is trying to keep the world from war." Several of President Kennedy's Cabinet members regularly battled with White House aides who blocked them from seeing the President. And McGeorge Bundy, as Kennedy's chief assistant for national security affairs, simply sidestepped the State Department in one major area of department communications. He had all important incoming State Department cables transmitted simultaneously to his office in the White House, part of an absorption of traditional State Department functions that visibly continues to this day with presidential assistant Henry Kissinger. Indeed we recently witnessed the bizarre and telling spectacle of Secretary of State William Rogers insisting that he *did* have a role in making foreign policy.

In a speech in 1971, Senator Ernest Hollings of South Carolina plaintively noted the lowering of Cabinet status. "It used to be," he said, "that if I had a problem with food stamps, I went to see the Secretary of Agriculture, whose department had jurisdiction over that problem. Not anymore. Now, if I want to learn the policy, I must go to the White House to consult John Price [a special assistant]. If I want the latest on textiles, I won't get it from the Secretary of Commerce, who has the authority and responsibility. No, I am forced to go to the White House and see Mr. Peter Flanigan. I shouldn't feel too badly. Secretary Stans [Maurice Stans, then Secretary of Commerce] has to do the same thing."

If Cabinet members individually have been downgraded in influence, the Cabinet itself as a council of government has become somewhat of a relic, replaced by more specialized comminglings that as often as not are presided over by White House staffers. The Cabinet's decline has taken place over several administrations. John Kennedy started out his term declaring his intentions of using the Cabinet as a major policy-making body, but his change of mind was swift, as his Postmaster General, J. Edward Day, has noted. "After the first two or three meetings," Day has written, "one had the distinct impression that the President felt that decisions on major matters were not made—or even influenced—at Cabinet sessions, and that discussion there was a waste of time. . . . When members spoke up to suggest or to discuss major administration policy, the President would listen with thinly disguised impatience and then postpone or otherwise bypass the question."

Lyndon Johnson was equally disenchanted with the Cabinet as a body and characteristically held Cabinet sessions only when articles appeared in the press talking about how the Cabinet was withering away. Under Nixon, the Cabinet is almost never convened at all.

Not only has the Presidential Establishment taken over many policy-making functions from the Cabinet and its members, it has also absorbed some of the operational functions. White House aides often feel they should handle any matters that they regard as ineptly administered, and they tend to intervene in internal departmental operations at lower and lower levels. They often feel underemployed, too, and so are inclined to reach out into the departments to find work and exercise authority for themselves.

The result is a continuous undercutting of Cabinet departments —and the cost is heavy. These intrusions can cripple the capacity of Cabinet officials to present policy alternatives, and they diminish self-confidence, morale, and initiative within the departments. George Ball, a former undersecretary of state, noted the effects on the State Department: "Able men, with proper pride in their professional skills, will not long tolerate such votes of no-confidence, so it should be no surprise that they are leaving the career service, and making way for mediocrity with the result that, as time goes on, it may be hopelessly difficult to restore the Department."

The irony of this accretion of numbers and functions to the Presidential Establishment is that the presidency is finding itself increasingly afflicted with the very ills of the traditional departments that the expansions were often intended to remedy. The presidency has become a large, complex bureaucracy itself, rapidly acquiring many dubious characteristics of large bureaucracies in the process: layering, overspecialization, communication gaps, interoffice rivalries, inadequate coordination, and an impulse to become consumed with short-term, urgent operational concerns at the expense of thinking systematically about the consequences of varying sets of policies and priorities and about important long-range problems. It takes so much of the President's time to deal with the members of his own bureaucracy that it is little wonder he has little time to hear counsel from Cabinet officials.

Another toll of the burgeoning Presidential Establishment is that White House aides, in assuming more and more responsibility for the management of government programs, inevitably lose the detachment and objectivity that is so essential for evaluating new ideas. Can a lieutenant vigorously engaged in implementing the presidential will admit the possibility that what the President wants is wrong or not working? Yet a President is increasingly dependent on the judgment of these same staff members, since he seldom sees his Cabinet members.

Why has the presidency grown bigger and bigger? There is no single villain or systematically organized conspiracy promoting this expansion. A variety of factors is at work. The most significant is the expansion of the role of the presidency itself—an expansion that for the most part has taken place during national emergencies. The reason for this is that the public and Congress in recent decades have both tended to look to the President for the decisive responses that were needed in those emergencies. The Great Depression and World War II in particular brought sizable increases in presidential staffs. And once in place, many stayed on, even after the emergencies that brought them had faded. Smaller national crises have occasioned expansion in the White House entourage, too. After the Russians successfully orbited *Sputnik* in 1957, President Eisenhower added several science advisers. After the Bay of Pigs, President Kennedy enlarged his national security staff.

Considerable growth in the Presidential Establishment, especially in the post-World War II years, stems directly from the belief that critical societal problems require that wise men be assigned to the White House to alert the President to appropriate solutions and to serve as the agents for implementing these solutions. Congress has frequently acted on the basis of this belief, legislating the creation of the National Security Council, the Council of Economic Advisers, and the Council on Environmental Quality, among others. Congress has also increased the chores of the presidency by making it a statutory responsibility for the President to prepare more and more reports associated with what are regarded as critical social areas—annual economic and manpower reports, a biennial report on national growth, etc.

Most recently, President Nixon responded to a number of troublesome problems that defy easy relegation to any one department —problems like international trade and drug abuse—by setting up special offices in the Executive Office with sweeping authority and sizable staffs. Once established, these units rarely get dislodged. And an era of permanent crisis ensures a continuing accumulation of such bodies.

Another reason for the growth of the Presidential Establishment is that occupants of the White House frequently distrust members of the permanent government. Nixon aides, for example, have viewed most civil servants not only as Democratic but as wholly unsympathetic to such objectives of the Nixon administration as decentralization, revenue sharing, and the curtailment of several Great Society programs. Departmental bureaucracies are viewed from the White House as independent, unresponsive, unfamiliar, and inaccessible. They are suspected again and again of placing their own, congressional, or special-interest priorities ahead of those communicated to them from the White House. Even the President's own Cabinet members soon become viewed in the same light; one of the strengths of Cabinet members, namely their capacity to make a compelling case for their programs, has proved to be their chief liability with Presidents.

Presidents may want this type of advocacy initially, but they soon grow weary and wary of it. Not long ago, one White House aide accused a former Labor Secretary of trying to "out-Meany Meany." Efforts by former Interior Secretary Hickel to advance certain environmental programs and by departing Housing and Urban Development Secretary George Romney to promote innovative housing construction methods not only were unwelcome but after a while were viewed with considerable displeasure and suspicion at the White House.

Hickel writes poignantly of coming to this recognition during his final meeting with President Nixon, in the course of which the President frequently referred to him as an "adversary." "Initially," writes Hickel, "I considered that a compliment because, to me, an adversary is a valuable asset. It was only after the President had used the term many times and with a disapproving inflection that I realized he considered an adversary an enemy. I could not understand why he would consider me an enemy."

Not only have recent Presidents been suspicious about the depth of the loyalty of those in their Cabinets, but they also invariably become concerned about the possibility that sensitive administration secrets may leak out through the departmental bureaucracies, and this is another reason why Presidents have come to rely more on their own personal groups, such as task forces and advisory commissions.

Still another reason that more and more portfolios have been given

to the presidency is that new federal programs frequently concern
more than one federal agency, and it seems reasonable that someone
at a higher level is required to fashion a consistent policy and to
reconcile conflicts. Attempts by Cabinet members themselves to solve
sensitive jurisdictional questions frequently result in bitter squab-
bling. At times, too, Cabinet members themselves have recommended that these multidepartmental issues be settled at the White
House. Sometimes new presidential appointees insist that new offices for program coordination be assigned directly under the President. Ironically, such was the plea of George McGovern, for
example, when President Kennedy offered him the post of director
of the Food for Peace program in 1961. McGovern attacked the
buildup of the Presidential Establishment in his campaign against
Nixon, but back in 1961 he wanted visibility (and no doubt celebrity
status) and he successfully argued against his being located outside
the White House—either in the State or Agriculture Department.
President Kennedy and his then campaign manager, Robert Kennedy, felt indebted to McGovern because of his efforts in assisting
the Kennedy presidential campaign in South Dakota. Accordingly,
McGovern was granted not only a berth in the Executive Office of
the President but also the much coveted title of special assistant
to the President.

The Presidential Establishment has also been enlarged by the
representation of interest groups within its fold. Even a partial listing of staff specializations that have been grafted onto the White
House in recent years reveals how interest-group brokerage has
become added to the more traditional staff activities of counseling
and administration. These specializations form a veritable index of
American society:

Budget and management, national security, economics, congressional matters, science and technology, drug abuse prevention,
telecommunications, consumers, national goals, intergovernmental
relations, environment, domestic policy, international economics,
military affairs, civil rights, disarmament, labor relations, District
of Columbia, cultural affairs, education, foreign trade and tariffs,
past Presidents, the aged, health and nutrition, physical fitness,
volunteerism, intellectuals, blacks, youth, women, "the Jewish community," Wall Street, governors, mayors, "ethnics," regulatory agencies and related industry, state party chairmen, Mexican-Americans.

It is as if interest groups and professions no longer settle for
lobbying Congress, or having one of their number appointed to a
departmental advisory board or sub-Cabinet position. It now appears
essential to "have your own man right there in the White House."

Once this foothold is established, of course, interest groups can play upon the potential political backlash that could arise should their representation be discontinued.

One of the more disturbing elements in the growth of the Presidential Establishment is the development, particularly under the current administration, of a huge public-relations apparatus. More than 100 presidential aides are now engaged in various forms of press-agentry or public relations, busily selling and reselling the President. This activity is devoted to the particular occupant of the White House, but inevitably it affects the presidency itself, by projecting or reinforcing images of the presidency that are almost imperial in their suggestions of omnipotence and omniscience. Thus the public-relations apparatus not only has directly enlarged the presidential workforce but has expanded public expectations about the presidency at the same time.

Last, but by no means least, Congress, which has grown increasingly critical of the burgeoning power of the presidency, must take some blame itself for the expansion of the White House. Divided within itself and ill-equipped, or simply disinclined to make some of the nation's toughest political decisions in recent decades, Congress has abdicated more and more authority to the presidency. The fact that the recent massive bombing of North Vietnam was ordered by the President without even a pretense of consultation with Congress buried what little was left of the semblance of that body's war-making power. Another recent instance of Congress's tendency to surrender authority to the presidency, an extraordinary instance, was the passage by the House (though not the Senate) of a grant to the President that would give him the right to determine which programs are to be cut whenever the budget goes beyond a $250 billion ceiling—a bill which, in effect, would hand over to the President some of Congress's long-cherished "power of the purse."

What can be done to bring the Presidential Establishment back down to size? What can be done to bring it to a size that both lightens the heavy accumulation of functions that it has absorbed and allows the Presidential Establishment to perform its most important functions more effectively and wisely?

First, Congress should curb its own impulse to establish new presidential agencies and to ask for yet additional reports and studies from the President. In the past Congress has been a too willing partner in the enlargement of the presidency. If Congress genuinely wants a leaner presidency, it should ask more of itself. For instance, it could well make better use of its own General Accounting Office and Congressional Research Service for chores that are now often assigned to the President.

Congress should also establish in each of its houses special committees on Executive Office operations. Most congressional committees are organized to deal with areas such as labor, agriculture, armed services, or education, paralleling the organization of the Cabinet. What we need now are committees designed explicitly to oversee the White House. No longer can the task of overseeing presidential operations be dispersed among dozens of committees and subcommittees, each of which can look at only small segments of the Presidential Establishment.

Some will complain that adding yet another committee to the already overburdened congressional system is just like adding another council to the overstuffed Presidential Establishment. But the central importance of what the presidency does (and does not do) must rank among the most critical [concerns] of the contemporary Congress. As things are organized now, the presidency escapes with grievously inadequate scrutiny. Equally important, Congress needs these committees to help protect itself from its own tendency to relinquish to the presidency its diminishing resources and prerogatives. Since Truman, Presidents have had staffs to oversee Congress; it is time Congress reciprocated.

Similar efforts to let the salutary light of public attention shine more brightly on the presidency should be inaugurated by the serious journals and newspapers of the nation. For too long, publishers and editors have believed that covering the presidency means assigning a reporter to the White House press corps. Unfortunately, however, those who follow the President around on his travels are rarely in a position to do investigative reporting on what is going on inside the Presidential Establishment. Covering the Executive Office of the President requires more than a President watcher; it needs a specialist who understands the arcane language and highly complex practices that have grown up in the Presidential Establishment.

Finally, it is time to reverse the downgrading of the Cabinet. President Nixon ostensibly moved in this direction with his designation several days ago of three Cabinet heads—HEW's Caspar W. Weinberger, Agriculture's Earl L. Butz, and HUD's James T. Lynn —as, in effect, super-secretaries of "human resources," "natural resources," and "community development," respectively. The move was expressly made in the name of Cabinet consolidation, plans for which Mr. Nixon put forward in 1971 but which Congress has so far spurned.

The three men will hold on to their Cabinet posts, but they have been given White House offices as well—as presidential counselors—and so it may be that the most direct effect of the appointments is a further expansion of the Presidential Establishment, rather than a counterbolstering of the Cabinet. But if the move does, in fact, lead to Cabinet consolidation under broader divisions, it will be a step in the right direction.

Reducing the present number of departments would strengthen the hand of Cabinet members vis-à-vis special interests, and might enable them to serve as advisers, as well as advocates, to the President. Cabinet consolidation would also have another very desirable effect: it would be a move toward reducing the accumulation of power within the Presidential Establishment. For much of the power of budget directors and other senior White House aides comes from their roles as penultimate referees of interdepartmental jurisdictional disputes. Under consolidated departments, a small number of strengthened Cabinet officers with closer ties to the President would resolve these conflicts instead. With fewer but broader Cabinet departments, there would be less need for many of the interest-group brokers and special councils that now constitute so much of the excessive baggage in the overburdened presidency.

Meantime, the presidency remains sorely overburdened—with both functions and functionaries—and needs very much to be cut back in both. Certainly, the number of presidential workers can and should be reduced. Harry Truman put it best, perhaps, when he said with characteristic succinctness: "I do not like this present trend toward a huge White House staff. . . . Mostly these aides get in each other's way." But while the number of functionaries is the most tangible and dramatic measure of the White House's expansion, its increasing absorption of governmental functions is more profoundly disturbing. The current White House occupant may regard cutting down (or transferring) a number of his staff members as a way of mollifying critics who charge that the American presidency has grown too big and bloated, but it is yet another thing to reduce the President's authority or his accumulated prerogatives. As the nation's number-one critic of the swelling of government, President Nixon will, it is hoped, move—or will continue to move if he has truly already started—to substantially deflate this swelling in one of the areas where it most needs to be deflated—at home, in the White House.

Bureaucratic Defense in Depth

PETER WOLL AND ROCHELLE JONES

The Watergate hearings have intensified the debate over the growth—and proper limits—of Presidential power. Among many concerned people in and out of government the feeling is that Richard Nixon was making an unprecedented attempt to concentrate political power in the White House. For evidence the critics point to Nixon's attempt to dismantle the Office of Economic Opportunity, an office created by Congress, his impoundment of funds appropriated by Congress for water pollution, highways, and other programs, and his repeated disregard of Congressional resolutions on the war in Southeast Asia. Only after he was pushed to the wall by Congressional action that threatened to cut off funds for the entire federal government if he did not stop the bombing of Cambodia, did he agree to an August 15 deadline for a bombing halt. In a recent series of articles in the *New York Times* Henry Steele Commager said that the United States is closer to one-man rule than at any time in its history.

While there is no doubt that Nixon frequently thwarts the will and intent of Congress, it does not necessarily mean we are on the verge of one-man rule. Nixon apparently would like to retitle the federal government "U.S. Government, Inc.; President: Richard M. Nixon," but the federal bureaucracy, composed of the Cabinet, independent regulatory commissions, and administrative agencies, puts important limits on the power of the President. Under the Nixon Administration the bureaucracy is turning into a vital although little noticed safeguard of the democratic system.

The bureaucracy, sometimes with Congress but often by itself, has frequently been able to resist and ignore Presidential commands. Whether the President is FDR or Richard M. Nixon, bureaucratic frustration of White House policies is a fact of life. Furthermore, the bureaucracy often carries out its own policies which are at times the exact opposite of White House directives. A classic case occurred

Reprinted by permission of *The Nation* and Peter Woll and Rochelle Jones. Copyright © 1973. Peter Woll teaches Political Science at Brandeis University and is the author of *American Bureaucracy*. Rochelle Jones is a reporter for the Palm Beach *Post* and is the author of *The Other Generation*.

during the India-Pakistan war in 1971 when the State Department supported India while the White House backed Pakistan. The State Department's behind-the-scenes maneuvering in support of India prompted Henry Kissinger's famous enraged order "to tilt" toward Pakistan.

In a system marked by a weak Congress and a Supreme Court that is increasingly taking its direction from Nixon appointees, the bureaucracy is turning into a crucial check on Presidential power. Under the Constitution Nixon is chief executive, but this does not mean he has legal authority or political power to control the bureaucracy. On the contrary, the bureaucracy has become a fourth branch of government, separate and independent of the President, Congress, and the courts. There are limits to bureaucratic discretion, but these are set as much by Congress and the courts as by the President. Decisions of independent regulatory commissions may be overturned under certain circumstances by the courts. And while the administrative agencies created by Congress are delegated considerable discretionary authority, this authority must be exercised within broad guidelines that are set by the legislature. It is precisely this accountability of the bureaucracy to the courts and Congress that helps it to be a powerful constraint on Presidential power. For example, in *State Highway Commission of Missouri* v. *Volpe* (1973) the Eighth Circuit Court of Appeals ruled that the Secretary of Transportation could not legally follow Nixon's directives and impound highway funds. The court held that Congress had clearly specified in the Federal Highway Act that appropriated funds were to be apportioned among the states. In effect, the court was saying that the Department of Transportation, a Cabinet department presumably under Presidential control, must comply with the intent of Congress, as it is interpreted by the court, instead of following the orders of the President.

Ultimately the bureaucracy curbs the President because it has independent sources of political power. Nixon's attempt to cut back governmental programs and reduce spending conflicts with the vested interests of powerful groups in and out of government. Like Congress and the President, administrative agencies and regulatory commissions have constituencies that are relied on for political support. The Defense Department needs the armaments industry, Agriculture the farmers, Labor the AFL-CIO, the ICC the railroads and truckers, and the Food and Drug Administration the giant pharmaceutical companies.

Because the bureaucracy depends on the political support of these allies for its continued existence, and because this alliance survives the four or eight years a President is in office, the bureaucracy is apt to prefer its interests over the wishes of the President. This is not new. On numerous occasions, for instance, the independent regulatory agencies have adopted policies that directly opposed the programs of the President. In the early 1960s both the Interstate Commerce Commission and Civil Aeronautics Board ignored White House directives in approving railroad and airline mergers that reduced competition.

Outside political support enables agencies to act independently. The regulatory agencies have been able to resist, for the most part, attempts by Presidents from Franklin D. Roosevelt to Richard Nixon to organize and bring them under Presidential supervision. A number of Presidents on a number of occasions have tried to transfer the regulatory functions of the Interstate Commerce Commission to a Cabinet department like the Department of Transportation, which is more capable of being controlled by the White House. But the railroads' support for the ICC has been felt in and reflected by Congress, and the ICC has retained its separate identity. With the help of equally strong support from their allies, other agencies have defeated attempts, most recently by Nixon, to reorganize them. In 1971 Nixon proposed a major reorganization of the executive branch that would have meant a major shift of authority. The Department of Agriculture, for example, would have lost control over a variety of programs to a proposed super Department of Natural Resources. But the Department of Agriculture rallied its constituency behind it, and the reorganization plan languished in Congress.

Agencies that lack independent political support in Congress and are not supported by private pressure groups are apt to be swayed by the President. There is a big difference between the Department of Transportation and the Department of State. The former is supported by a wide range of groups, from proponents of federal airport subsidies to groups connected with aviation safety, urban transit, highway safety, and the Coast Guard. The latter is without Congressional and interest group backing. When Nixon tried to create a "super-Cabinet" at the start of his second term, Secretary of Transportation Claude S. Brinegar announced loudly and repeatedly that he was not going to be subordinate to the super-Cabinet Secretary James Lynn, Secretary of the Department of Housing and Urban Development, who had been named his superior by Nixon. But Secretary of State William Rogers was up-staged from the very start of the Nixon Administration by Henry Kissinger. Kissinger has usurped the major foreign policy-making responsibilities of the State Department while serving as an un-official ambassador at large and roving emissary to foreign govern-ments, a pleasant duty that is traditionally the prerogative of the Secretary of State. Secretary of State John Foster Dulles played such a role in the Eisenhower Administration. But this is possible only if the Secretary of State enjoys the confidence of the President as Dulles did. If he doesn't, the Secretary of State will be a mere figurehead in the foreign policy field because the State Department is exceedingly vulnerable to domination by the White House. Its lack of domestic allies enables it to win very little support from Congress. When Senator Joseph McCarthy [R., Wis.] launched his witch hunt after subversives in government, he wisely tackled the State Department first. As long as he was battling the State Department, he was safe. When he turned on the Department of the Army, with its close links to a powerful domestic constituency and hence to key Congressional committees, his downfall was im-minent.

In addition to its political support the bureaucracy contains the President in other ways. The President has minimal influence within the bureaucracy because of its size, complexity, wide-ranging re-sponsibilities, and continuity. More than one-half of the 3 million civilian employees of the federal government work for the Defense Department, for one good example. Tens of thousands of them are in key policy-making positions. All recent Secretaries of Defense, with the possible exception of McNamara, have had difficulty keep-ing up with day-to-day shifts in policy that are the result of decisions made by subordinates. Obviously Nixon cannot keep up with the operations of this mammoth department. And this is true in every large department of government. The President must delegate au-thority, and by doing so tends to lose control. Admittedly Nixon has made a strong attempt to change this. Before Watergate height-ened the debate over the limits of Presidential power, Washington civil servants were operating in an atmosphere that was permeated with fear. Since the Watergate hearings started, however, bureau-crats have resumed their traditional independent stance.

Moreover, since Nixon can't know what is going on in every nook of the federal bureaucracy, he must rely on the information that is provided by it for his decision making. By carefully controlling the information that reaches the President, the bureaucracy can control his decision making. This is not necessarily Machiavellian. Very often administrators, even subordinate administrators, are the only ones who possess the background and arcane knowledge to fill in the details of vague Congressional legislation. The strength of the bureaucracy is magnified when the President and Congress must come to it for the necessary information and technical skills to formulate and implement public policy. In a highly technical and increasingly specialized society the power of bureaucracy grows because the bureaucracy is the domain of the specialist, while the Congress and President are necessarily generalists.

The use of bureaucratic expertise in Congressional policy making will be facilitated through the Office of Technological Assessment (OTA), being formed under the sponsorship of Senator Edward Kennedy (D., Mass.). The OTA, created by legislation in 1972, is a way of challenging the present power of the Office of Management and Budget [OMB] to prevent agencies from going directly to Congress with policy-making proposals. Such administrative inputs to the legislative process must first be cleared by the OMB. But the OTA is authorized to use the technical resources of the bureaucracy to draft policies that reflect the priorities of Congress. With these outside sources of information Congress will be able to challenge the President in a way previously impossible. Because Congress will be relying on information that comes from the bureaucracy, the bureaucracy will have vastly increased influence in the policy-making process. And since agency personnel assigned to the OTA will be working for Congress, not the President, they can give substantial help in developing programs that may directly contradict the programs of the President. A new bureaucratic check on the President is emerging.

Presidents come and go; the bureaucracy stays. Even if the President's only concern were the control of the bureaucracy, he would find this extremely difficult to accomplish in eight years. Obviously the President has many other pressing concerns besides the bureaucracy. At the beginning of his first term he is concerned with making a good impression. With the election mandate behind him and the Congressional honeymoon ahead of him, the President wants to charge ahead, to do great things which, if they don't win him a place in the history books, may at least win him a second term in office. But such great plans can be abruptly halted by the bureaucracy. The newly elected President can find that many top bureaucrats who were appointed by the previous President are entrenched in power, protected by civil service regulations or terms of office that are set by statutes. The President is reduced to watching helplessly as the bureaucracy stymies his key programs. By the start of his second term the President may decide to make a determined effort to control the bureaucracy in a final, valiant attempt to push through his program.

And in fact, Nixon tried exactly that, finding that it is easy to try to curb the bureaucracy but exceedingly difficult to succeed. Nixon created a super-Cabinet last January in an attempt to centralize power in the White House; it was a dismal failure. It never functioned as it was supposed to. Agencies ignored it and did as they pleased or bypassed it and went directly to the President. Nixon finally junked the super-Cabinet four months after it was established.

In opposing Presidential programs, the bureaucracy relies heavily on informal contacts with Congress. The White House may, and often does, try to muzzle administrators, but the bureaucracy has ways of getting necessary information to key Congressmen. Information flows back and forth among bureaucrats and Congressmen over the phone, at casual meetings and cocktail parties. Pressure groups also channel information from the agencies to Congressional committees.

For example, the President can order the Department of Agriculture to eliminate or reduce various agricultural programs, but these orders are likely to fail eventually because of the strong support for the department in Congress and among various agricultural interest groups. The department might have to go along with the President temporarily, but it would not have to wait long for Congressional support to back up its policy favoring maintenance of such programs. This happened in 1972 when the Department of Agriculture abolished several key programs at the request of Nixon. An angry Congress overwhelmingly voted to restore the programs.

Many agencies are closer to Congress than to the President. The Securities and Exchange Commission (SEC) is a good example of an agency that has stronger ties to the House and Senate than to the White House. Representative John Moss (D., Calif.), chairman of the House Subcommittee on Commerce and Finance, and Senator Harrison Williams (D., N.J.), chairman of the Securities Subcommittee of the Senate Banking Committee, deal directly with the SEC on a continuous basis. The SEC supplies these legislators with information, and they, in turn, prod the agency to implement the policy positions that they favor. With the help of a strong professional staff, these men are directly involved in the regulation of the securities industry. Of course, the White House can wield a certain amount of power, as it did when it influenced the SEC staff to withhold important information on the financial dealings of financier Robert Vesco because the information might embarrass the Committee for the Re-election of the President [CREEP]. But this influence is sporadic and limited to specific issues, while Congress deals with the SEC and other agencies on an almost daily basis.

Nixon can exert some control over the bureaucracy through his power of appointment. The President directly controls the appointment of more than 2,000 top-level bureaucrats. These positions were filled during Nixon's first term with people considered "reliable." After the 1972 election all of these appointees were required to submit their resignations. Many have been fired, producing great disillusionment throughout the ranks. As a result of the insensitive behavior of Nixon's staff, the White House faced enormous difficulty in recruiting new people, and many positions remain vacant in the top echelons of departments and agencies.

Nixon has been appointing former White House aides and CREEP employees as an elite corps of "agents," numbering more than 100, to departments, independent regulatory commissions, and agencies to find out what is going on and to carry out the Nixon philosophy. Such agents have been installed at the under secretary level in Treasury, Interior, Transportation, and HEW. At lower levels agents were placed in Commerce (25), Interior (13), Agriculture (17), Treasury (11), the Environmental Protection Agency (20), Veterans Administration (11), FAA (5), and FTC (9). Nixon has filled twenty-eight of the thirty-eight positions on six major regulatory commissions and named the chairmen of all six. White House clearance has been required of many staff appointments. This attempt to control the independent regulatory commissions prompted the House Interstate and Foreign Commerce Committee to begin an investigation of what its chairman, Harley O. Staggers (D., W. Va.), considers inappropriate White House pressure.

For a short time Nixon's appointees can undoubtedly influence administrative policy making. But Nixon has failed more often than he has succeeded in changing the direction of the bureaucracy through the appointment process. He has created anxiety, frustration, and disillusionment, and impeded independent policy making by the bureaucrats in the limited number of agencies where he has placed his agents.

In the case of the independent regulatory commissions the President may be able to stack them in his favor, but this is only a temporary impediment to the commissions' inherent ability to limit Presidential power. Nixon's appointees will constitute a major limitation on the next President. From the standpoint of the Presidency, the influence of one President on regulatory agencies through appointments can lay the groundwork for future agency resistance to a new President. Similarly, the expansion of the bureaucracy in line with the philosophy of a President who believes in an activist government, such as FDR, limits future Presidents who believe in a concept of limited governmental intervention. Thus the appointment process is a two-edged sword, working against Presidential power in the long run while giving short-term advantage.

Many of Nixon's appointees, even in his elite corps, were given jobs as a political payoff for their loyalty to him and their work in his campaigns. These strictly political types have been put in showcase jobs in many cases, often as assistants to top-echelon people, [as] consultants, and in public affairs jobs. Even "deputy administrators" . . . often [have] phony jobs with an impressive title but little clout. Moreover, most political types know little or nothing about the agencies they are appointed to. They cannot rival the top-grade permanent civil servants in policy making. And while the political appointees often have short stays in their jobs, the civil servants tend to be permanent employees. In the final analysis the expertise, continuity, and political ties of the permanent civil service severely limit the ability of any President to alter bureaucratic practices through his appointments.

The courts can help the bureaucracy in imposing limits on the President. In recent years, an active judiciary has forced administrative agencies to adhere closely to Congressional intent, as defined by the courts, reinforcing the ability of the bureaucracy to resist Presidential control. Within the last few months the courts declared *ultra vires* Nixon's actions to impound funds that would be appropriated to administrative agencies under normal circumstances. The courts also preserved, at least temporarily, the Office of Economic Opportunity, which was in the process of being dismantled under orders from Nixon.

The Watergate affair clearly reveals the value of a semi-autonomous bureaucracy. A President who could direct the activities of all administrative agencies would threaten our constitutional system. If the White House had been able to use the FBI and CIA as it had planned, a far-flung political intelligence operation would now be operating in a way that would undermine basic guarantees of our constitutional system, such as the Fourth Amendment guarantees against unreasonable searches and seizures. It was because J. Edgar Hoover and the FBI resisted that the efforts of the White House to set up a secret police operation with the approval of Nixon were stymied. Assistant Attorney-General Henry Petersen, a career attorney, refused to go along with Ehrlichman's improper requests. Richard Helms and General Walters of the CIA likewise maintained their independence under pressure by Haldeman and Ehrlichman. And it seems evident that a number of career professionals at the FBI leaked information to the press in order to frustrate what they saw as a move to corrupt the bureau.

At the same time, however, bureaucrats need to be imbued with the values of our constitutional democracy because, for the most part, the limits on them are those they impose upon themselves. It is ironic that the independence of the FBI and J. Edgar Hoover, so often criticized as a potential threat to responsible government, turned out under the Nixon Administration to be a bulwark of freedom. Perhaps, in the final analysis, we are saved from tyranny by the pluralism of our system and even its inefficiency. The pluralistic and independent bureaucracy, although often inefficient and yielding to special-interest group pressure, helps to preserve the balance of powers among the branches of government that is necessary for the preservation of our system of constitutional democracy.

8. Constitutional Issues

When will Watergate be over? The drama that began with Frank Wills's discovery of the break-in at the Democratic National Headquarters eventually revealed the "White House horrors." The drama that unfolded as Donald Sanders asked Alexander Butterfield about the existence of taped conversations in the White House concluded with the "smoking gun" and Richard Nixon's resignation. However, the Constitutional issues of executive privilege and impeachment that emerged out of Watergate will affect the future conduct of American politics.

The lower courts have already ruled several times on Presidential impoundment of Congressionally authorized funds,* though we wait for a definitive statement on the issue from the Supreme Court. The charges of conspiracy and obstruction of justice emerging out of the cover-up led to the historic confrontation before the Supreme Court over the power of a President to control information and testimony from within the executive branch. The precedent of the House Judiciary Committee's impeachment proceedings remains unclear, shortened as the impeachment proceedings were by the resignation of the President. There still remains controversy over whether the Constitutional criteria "high crimes and misdemeanors" have been defined.

In his article on impeachment, Professor Raoul Berger examines the meaning of the impeachment clause. According to Berger, the framers' intention when they wrote "high crimes and misdemeanors" into the Constitution is clear. Consistent with the old English formula, impeachment was designed as an instrument of redress for crimes against the state—political crimes. Berger's conclusion is that an impeachable offense need not be an indictable offense. Although most Constitutional scholars agree that impeachment is not criminal

---

* *Office of Economic Opportunity Employees Union* v. *Phillips, Berends* v. *Butz,* and *State Highway Commission of Mo.* v. *Volpe.*

prosecution, that impeachable offenses need not be indictable, controversy remains over the nature of the political crimes required to warrant impeachment: Is impeachment a prescribed procedural course of action, or is the "hundred-ton gun" reserved for a last resort?

The debate in the House Judiciary Committee, in nationally televised sessions, centered on the question of specificity. Could the acts charged in the articles of impeachment be directly linked to the President? The extent of subordinate responsibility is of grave concern. In voting three articles of impeachment—obstruction of justice in the Watergate cover-up, abuse of power in the misuse of government agencies and violation of the oath of office, and contempt of Congress in willfully disobeying Congressional subpoenas—the Committee put to the test the meaning of high crimes and misdemeanors.

Equally challenging to scholars is the status of executive privilege. In common use in the Truman and Eisenhower administrations, executive privilege dates back to Presidents Washington and Jefferson. In his book *Executive Privilege,* Raoul Berger challenges the mythology on the subject. The Supreme Court, however, in *United States* v. *Richard Nixon,* recognized the doctrine of executive privilege, and, in unanimous verdict, the court ruled that the needs of confidentiality and separation of powers sustain the principle. However, Nixon had asserted an absolute, unqualified right of executive privilege, and this claim the Court would not sustain. Instead it ordered Nixon to turn over to the special prosecutor the taped conversations—evidence that would bring the Nixon Administration to an end.

The impeachment proceedings and the Court's ruling on executive privilege remind us that the Constitution remains a "living document," reaffirming that government should proceed within the authority of prescribed law. Even Presidential resignation is an orderly, Constitutional process. The Constitution has risen to the need of free men to solve their problems with the aid of due processes of law; ours remains a government of law, not men.

The final issue facing the Constitutional process was prosecution of former President Nixon for his role in Watergate. But on September 8, 1974, President Ford granted his predecessor a full and unconditional pardon for all federal crimes he may have committed while in office. The Watergate grand jury had listed Nixon as an "unindicted co-conspirator" because of his role in the Watergate cover-up. In the wake of impeachment proceedings and resignation, Special Prosecutor Jaworski had been confronted by the question of whether to prosecute the former President. However, President Ford exercised his Constitutional prerogative by granting a "full, free, and absolute pardon unto Richard Nixon for all offenses against the United States." Calling Watergate's effect on Nixon an American tragedy, President Ford moved to write the end to the dramas of Watergate.

Impeachment:
An Instrument of Regeneration

RAOUL BERGER

Impeachment, to most Americans today, seems to represent a dread mystery, an almost parricidal act, to be contemplated, if at all, with awe and alarm. It was not always so. Impeachment, said the House of Commons in 1679, was "the chief institution for the preservation of the government"; and chief among the impeachable offenses was "subversion of the Constitution." In 1641, the House of Commons charged that the Earl of Strafford had subverted the fundamental law and introduced an arbitrary and tyrannical government. By his trial, which merged into a bill of attainder and resulted in his execution, and by a series of other seventeenth-century impeachments, Parliament made the ministers accountable to it rather than to the King and stemmed a tide of absolutism that swept the rest of Europe. Thereafter, impeachment fell into relative disuse during the eighteenth century because a ministry could now be toppled by the House of Commons on a vote of no confidence.

Our impeachment, modeled on that of England, proceeds as follows: a committee of the House of Representatives may be instructed to investigate rumors or charges of executive misconduct. If the committee reports that it found impeachable offenses, it is directed by the House to prepare articles of impeachment, which are the analogue of the accusations contained in the several counts of an indictment by a grand jury. Strictly speaking, it is the articles that constitute the impeachment. The articles, if approved by a majority of the House, are then filed with the Senate.

At that point, the articles are served by the Senate on the accused, who is given time within which to file an answer to the charges. At an appointed time, the Senate convenes as a court. If it is the President who is being tried, the Chief Justice of the Supreme Court acts as the presiding officer. Evidence is subject to the

Copyright 1973 by *Harper's Magazine*. Reprinted from 1973 issue by special permission. Raoul Berger is Charles Warren Senior Fellow in American Legal History at Harvard Law School. He is the author of several books, including *Executive Privilege: A Constitutional Myth*.

exclusionary rules applied by a court, and the accused is permitted by his counsel to cross-examine witnesses and to make arguments for acquittal. A vote of two-thirds of the Senators present is required for conviction.

When the Framers came to draft our Constitution, they might well have regarded impeachment as an outworn, clumsy institution, not particularly well-suited to a tripartite scheme of government protected by the separation of powers. Why, then, did they adopt it?

The reason lies in the fact that the Founders vividly remembered the seventeenth-century experience of the mother country. They remembered the absolutist pretensions of the Stuarts; they were haunted by the greedy expansiveness of power; they dreaded usurpation and tyranny. And so they adopted impeachment as a means of displacing a usurper—a President who exceeded the bounds of the executive's authority.

The colonists, after all, regarded the executive, in the words of Thomas Corwin, as "the natural enemy, the legislative assembly the natural friend of liberty." Throughout the colonial period, they had elected their own assemblies and trusted them as their own representatives. The governors, on the other hand, were often upper-class Englishmen with little understanding of American aspirations, who had been foisted on the colonists by the Crown. Hence, Congress was given the power to remove the President. This power, it must be emphasized, constitutes a deliberate breach in the doctrine of separation of powers, so that no arguments drawn from that doctrine (such as executive privilege) may apply to the preliminary inquiry by the House or the subsequent trial by the Senate.

The constitution adopts the old English formula: impeachment for and conviction of "treason, bribery, or other high crimes and misdemeanors." Because "crimes" and "misdemeanors" are familiar terms of criminal law, it is tempting to conclude that "high crimes and misdemeanors" is simply a grandiloquent version of ordinary "crimes and misdemeanors." Not so. As the terms "treason" and "bribery" suggest, these were offenses against the state, political crimes as distinguished from crimes against the person, such as murder. The association of "treason, bribery" with "other high crimes and misdemeanors" indicates that the latter also refer to offenses of a "political" nature. They were punishable by Parliament, whereas courts punished "misdemeanors," that is, lesser *private* wrongs. In short, "high crimes and misdemeanors" appears to be a phrase confined to impeachments, without roots in the ordinary English crim-

inal law and which, so far as I could discover, had no relation to
whether a criminal indictment would lie in the particular circumstances.* Certain political crimes—treason and bribery, for example
—were also indictable crimes, but English impeachments did not
require an indictable crime. Nonetheless, the English impeachment
was criminal because conviction was punishable by death or imprisonment.

In fact, under English practice there were a number of impeachable offenses that might not even be crimes under American criminal law. First and foremost was subversion of the Constitution:
for example, the usurpation of power to which Parliament laid
claim. Other impeachable offenses were abuse of power, neglect of
duty, corrupt practices that fell short of crimes, even the giving of
"bad advice" to the King by his ministers. Broadly speaking, these
categories outline the boundaries of "high crimes and misdemeanors" at the time the Constitution was adopted.

Let us now turn to Philadelphia in 1787. Article II, Section 4 of
the Constitution provides that "the President, Vice-President and all
civil Officers of the United States, shall be removed from Office on
Impeachment for, and Conviction of, Treason, Bribery, or other
high Crimes and Misdemeanors."

There is good reason to conclude that the Framers consciously
divorced impeachment from the necessity of proving an indictable
criminal offense. This is because Article I, Section 3(7) provides
that "judgment in Cases of Impeachment shall not extend further
than to removal from Office, and disqualification to hold and enjoy
any Office . . . but the Party convicted shall nevertheless be liable
and subject to Indictment, Trial, Judgment and Punishment, according to Law." Thus the Framers sharply separated removal from
office from criminal punishment by indictment and conviction, in
contrast to the English practice, which joined criminal punishment

---

* The phrase "high crimes and misdemeanors" is first met not in an ordinary criminal proceeding but in the impeachment of the Earl of Suffolk in
1386. At that time there was no such crime as a misdemeanor. Lesser crimes
were prosecuted as "trespasses" well into the sixteenth century, and only then
were trespasses supplanted by "misdemeanors." As "trespass" itself suggests,
"misdemeanors" derived from private wrongs, what lawyers call torts. Fitz-
james Stephen stated that prosecutions for misdemeanors are to the Crown
what actions for wrongs are to private persons."
Although "misdemeanors" entered into ordinary criminal law, they did
not become the criterion of the parliamentary "high" misdemeanors. Nor
did "high misdemeanors" find their way into the general criminal law. As
late as 1757, Blackstone could say that the "first and principal [high mis-
demeanor] is the *maladministration* of such high officers, as are in the public
trust and employment."

and removal in one proceeding. From the text of the Constitution there emerges a leading purpose: partisan passions should not sweep an officer to the gallows.

The starting point, therefore, to borrow from Justice Story, is that impeachment "is not so much designed to punish as to secure the state against gross official misdemeanors." It is prophylactic, designed to remove an unfit officer from office, rather than punitive. Two important considerations persuade us to understand American impeachment in noncriminal terms, though it may, of course, include offenses such as bribery and obstruction of justice, which are indictable "political" crimes. First, since Article I contemplates both indictment and impeachment, the issue of double jeopardy would be raised if impeachment were deemed criminal in nature. The Fifth Amendment, which embodies a centuries-old guarantee, provides that no person "shall be subject for the same offence to be twice put in jeopardy." This means that if a person were indicted and convicted he could not be impeached, or if he were impeached he could not be indicted. By providing that impeachment would not bar indictment, the Framers plainly indicated that impeachment was not criminal in nature. Therefore, criminal punishment may precede *or* follow impeachment.

A second consideration is the Sixth Amendment provision that "in all criminal prosecutions, the accused shall enjoy the right to a speedy and public trial by an impartial jury." If impeachment be deemed a "criminal prosecution," it is difficult to escape the requirement of trial by jury. Earlier, Article III, Section 2(3) had expressly exempted impeachment from the jury "trial of all crimes"; and with that exemption before them, the draftsmen of the Sixth Amendment extended trial by jury to "*all* criminal prosecutions" without exception, thereby exhibiting an intention to withdraw the former exemption. We must conclude either that the Founders felt no need to exempt impeachment from the Sixth Amendment because they did not consider it a "criminal prosecution," or that a jury trial is required if impeachment is in fact a "criminal proceeding."

Elsewhere * I have discussed the problems that arise from the Framers' employment of criminal terminology. I would only reiterate that if impeachment is indeed criminal in nature, it must comprehend the offenses considered grounds for impeachment at the adoption of the Constitution. On this score, the Senate, which

* *Impeachment: The Constitutional Problems* (Cambridge, Mass.: Harvard University Press, 1973).

tries impeachments, has on a number of occasions found officers guilty of nonindictable offenses, and to the Senate, at least initially, is left the construction of "high crimes and misdemeanors."

It does not follow that Representative Gerald Ford was correct when he declared that an impeachable offense is whatever the House and Senate jointly "consider [it] to be." Still less can it be, as Mr. Nixon's then Attorney General Richard Kleindienst told the Senate, that "you don't need facts, you don't need evidence" to impeach the President, "all you need is votes." That would flout all requirements of due process, which must protect the President no less than the lowliest felon. The records of the Convention make quite plain that the Framers, far from proposing to confer illimitable power to impeach, intended only to confer a *limited* power.

When an early version of impeachment for "treason, bribery" came up for discussion, George Mason moved to add "maladministration," explaining that "treason as defined in the Constitution will not reach many great and dangerous offenses. . . . Attempts to subvert the Constitution may not be Treason as above defined." Mark that Mason was bent on reaching "attempts to subvert the Constitution." But Madison demurred because "so vague a term [as maladministration] will be equivalent to a tenure during the pleasure of the Senate." In brief, Madison refused to leave the President at the mercy of the Senate. Thereupon, Mason suggested "high crimes and misdemeanors," which was adopted without objection.

Shortly before, the Convention had rejected "high misdemeanors" in another context because it "had a technical meaning too limited," so that adoption of "high crimes and misdemeanors" exhibits an intent to embrace the "limited," "technical meaning" of the words for purposes of impeachment. If "high crimes and misdemeanors" had an ascertainable content at the time the Constitution was adopted, that content marks the boundaries of the power. It is no more open to Congress to ignore those boundaries than it is to include "robbery" under the "bribery" offense, for "robbery" had a quite different common-law connotation.

Recent events are of surpassing interest, and it behooves us to weigh them in traditional common-law terms. It will be recalled that the first and foremost impeachable offense was subversion of the Constitution, of the fundamental law. Had Mr. Nixon persisted in his position that he could not be compelled by the courts to furnish the tapes of his conversations, that would have been a subversion of the Constitution. That issue may not yet be dead. In the wake of Mr. Nixon's dismissal of Special Prosecutor Archibald Cox, and the resignations of Attorney General Elliot Richardson and Deputy Attorney General William Ruckelshaus, the "fire storm," as a White House aide called it, that blew up across the country impelled President Nixon, by White House counsel, to advise Judge John Sirica, "This President does not defy the law. . . . he will comply in full with the orders of the court." Let the sober appraisal by the *Wall Street Journal* sum up the inferences we must draw from this event:

> In obeying the appeals court order requiring that the tapes be submitted to Judge Sirica, the President has indeed ceded, without a final Supreme Court test, some of the privilege to withhold information that he previously claimed for the Chief Executive. A precedent is being established whereby judges can demand White House evidence. . . . The President tried to protect a presidential claim and lost. The claim may not have been entirely valid, but the loss is for real.

Nevertheless, during his press conference on the evening of October 26, 1973, Mr. Nixon stated, "We will not provide Presidential documents to a special prosecutor . . . if it is a document involving a conversation with the President. I would have to stand on the principle of confidentiality." Thus he renews the claim, lost before the Court of Appeals, to which he apparently yielded when he advised Judge Sirica that he would comply with the court's order. "Confidentiality," in short, still remains at issue. Were an independent prosecutor set up by Congressional enactment, and were he to insist on production of White House tapes and documents, a confrontation between the President and the courts would be replayed.

If Mr. Nixon were again to refuse to comply with a court order to produce tapes or documents, that would constitute subversion of the Constitution. Ours is a government of enumerated and limited powers, designed, in the words of the Founders, to "fence" the Congress and the executive about. To police these limits the courts were given the power of judicial review. On more than one occasion they have declared Acts of Congress, though signed by the President, unconstitutional. Although the House of Representatives was made the sole judge of the qualifications of its members, the Supreme Court held that in excluding Adam Clayton Powell for misappropriation of government funds, the House had exceeded its power, the sole qualifications for membership being age, residence, and citizenship. In short, it is the function of the courts finally to interpret the Constitution and to determine the scope of the powers conferred on either President or Congress. By what reasoning the President claims to be exempted from this judicial authority passes my comprehension. In disobeying a court order, the President would undermine a central pillar of the Constitution, and take a long step toward assertion of dictatorial power. Benign or otherwise, dictatorial power is utterly incompatible with our democratic system. Disobedience of a court order, I submit, would be subversion of the Constitution, the cardinal impeachable offense.

A second article of impeachment based on subversion of the Constitution could rest on the President's impoundment of appropriated funds. The Constitution gives Congress the sole power to provide for the general welfare; in so doing, it is entitled to select priorities. Nowhere in the Constitution is power given to the President to substitute his own priorities. Some twenty courts have held his impoundments to be unconstitutional, that is, in excess of his powers and an encroachment on the prerogatives of Congress.

The secret bombing of Cambodia in 1969–70 may also be viewed as a subversion of the Constitution. It is widely agreed among eminent historians that so far as the "original intention" of the Founders is concerned, the power to make war was exclusively vested by the Constitution in Congress. They intended, in the words of James Wilson, second only to Madison as an architect of the Constitution, to put it beyond the power of a "single man" to "hurry" us into war. The argument for a President powerful enough singlehandedly to embroil the nation in war rests on comparatively recent Presidential assertions of power.

No President or succession of Presidents can by their own unilateral fiat rewrite the Constitution and reallocate to themselves powers purposely withheld from them and conferred on the Congress alone. On this reasoning, the Cambodian bombing, being a usurpation of Congressional power, constitutes a subversion of the Constitution, and is a clearly impeachable offense.

Although some twenty courts have gone against the President on the issue of impoundment, the Supreme Court has yet to speak. So too, although Presidential usurpation in the secret Cambodian bombing seems quite clear to me, the President has yet to have his day in court. Little as I attach to Presidential assertions of power plainly withheld from him by the Constitution, I am reluctant to have the Senate decide an issue of constitutional law, disputed by the President, in its own favor. That issue, the trial of Andrew Johnson teaches, is better left to the courts, removed from any suspicion of partisan bias, unclouded by conflict with the tradition that one should not sit in judgment on his own case.

There may well be other grounds of impeachment which the House Judiciary Committee will in due course consider. For example, thus far the implications of the Watergate cover-up have been considered in terms of criminal complicity, but a statement by James Madison in the First Congress indicates that it may be viewed in wider perspective. Recall that Madison was the chief architect of the Constitution, and had a hand in the introduction of "high crimes and misdemeanors" in the impeachment provisions. Who would better know what scope the Founders intended to give those terms? Arguing for an exclusive Presidential power to remove his subordinates, Madison stated that this "will make him in a peculiar manner responsible for their conduct, and subject him to impeachment himself, if he . . . neglects to superintend their conduct, so as to check their excesses."

On March 22, 1973, Mr. Nixon stated, "It is clear that unethical as well as illegal activities took place in the course of [the re-election] campaign . . . to the extent that I failed to prevent them, I should have been more vigilant." This is little short of a confession of neglect, and that neglect is no less clear with respect to the ensuing cover-up launched by his subordinates, an obstruction of justice. Mr. Nixon stated, "I must and do assume responsibility for such [re-election] actions." Responsibility carries with it accountability, not, it is true, criminal responsibility, for no principle is responsible for the crimes of his agent. But he is civilly responsible for the wrongs he enabled them to commit, and impeachment, you will recall, is prophylactic, not criminal. President Nixon can be impeached, in Madison's words, for neglect "to superintend [his subordinates'] conduct, so as to check their excesses."

The Founders feared an excess of power in executive hands; they had just thrown off the shackles of one tyrant, George III, and were not minded to submit to another. Hence, they provided impeachment as an essential restraint against arbitrary one-man rule. The wisdom of the Founders has been abundantly confirmed by recent events. The time has come to regard impeachment not as a clumsy, outworn apparatus but rather as an instrument of regeneration for protection of our liberties and our constitutional system.

United States v. Richard M. Nixon

The case of *United States* v. *Richard M. Nixon* grew from the special prosecutor's request to the U.S. District Court to subpoena *duces tecum* (that is, to produce, for use at the pending trial) sixty-four taped Presidential conversations. President Nixon moved to quash the subpoena on the grounds of executive privilege. The District Court denied the motion, and the President appealed to the U.S. Court of Appeals.

In a rare move, the U.S. Supreme Court issued a writ of certiorari, bypassing the Court of Appeals because of the public importance of the issue, and undertook consideration of the case.

In deciding the case, a unanimous Court affirmed the order of the District Court. First dealing with the question of jurisidiction, it held that the mere assertion of an "inter-agency dispute" within the executive branch does not defeat federal jurisdiction. The Court then determined that Federal Criminal Procedure Rule 17(c), governing the issuance of subpoenas *duces tecum*, had been satisfied. Finally, in the section of the decision reprinted here, the Supreme Court turned to the substantive issue of executive privilege. Chief Justice Warren Burger wrote the opinion of the Court.

THE CLAIM OF PRIVILEGE

Having determined that the requirements of Rule 17(c) were satisfied, we turn to the claim that the subpoena should be quashed because it demands "confidential conversations between a President and his close advisors that it would be inconsistent with the public interest to produce." App 48a. The first contention is a broad claim that the separation of powers doctrine precludes judicial review of a President's claim of privilege. The second contention is that if he does not prevail on the claim of absolute privilege, the court should

Warren Burger is Chief Justice of the United States Supreme Court. He served as judge of the U.S. Court of Appeals from 1956 to 1969 prior to his appointment to the Supreme Court.

hold as a matter of constitutional law that the privilege prevails over the subpoena duces tecum.

In the performance of assigned constitutional duties each branch of the Government must initially interpret the Constitution, and the interpretation of its powers by any branch is due great respect from the others. The President's counsel, as we have noted, reads the Constitution as providing an absolute privilege of confidentiality for all presidential communications. Many decisions of this Court, however, have unequivocally reaffirmed the holding of Marbury v Madison, 1 Cranch 137, 2 L Ed 60 (1803), that "it is emphatically the province and duty of the judicial department to say what the law is." Id., at 177, 2 L Ed 60.

No holding of the Court has defined the scope of judicial power specifically relating to the enforcement of a subpoena for confidential presidential communications for use in a criminal prosecution, but other exercises of powers by the Executive Branch and the Legislative Branch have been found invalid as in conflict with the Constitution. Powell v McCormack, supra; Youngstown, supra. In a series of cases, the Court interpreted the explicit immunity conferred by express provisions of the Constitution on Members of the House and Senate by the Speech or Debate Clause, US Const Art I, § 6. Doe v McMillan, 412 US 306, 36 L Ed 2d 912, 93 S Ct 2018 (1973); Gravel v United States, 408 US 606, 33 L Ed 2d 583, 92 S Ct 2614 (1972); United States v. Brewster, 408 US 501, 33 L Ed 2d 507, 92 S Ct 2531 (1972); United States v Johnson, 383 US 169, 15 L Ed 2d 681, 86 S Ct 749 (1966). Since this Court has consistently exercised the power to construe and delineate claims arising under express powers, it must follow that the Court has authority to interpret claims with respect to powers alleged to derive from enumerated powers.

Our system of government "requires that federal courts on occasion interpet the Constitution in a manner at variance with the construction given the document by another branch." Powell v McCormack, supra, 549, 23 L Ed 2d 491. And in Baker v Carr, 369 US, at 211, 7 L Ed 2d 663, the Court stated:

Deciding whether a matter has in any measure been committed by the Constitution to another branch of government, or whether the action of that branch exceeds whatever authority has been committed, is itself a delicate exercise in constitutional interpretation, and is a responsibility of this Court as ultimate interpreter of the Constitution.

Notwithstanding the deference each branch must accord the others, the "judicial power of the United States" vested in the federal courts by Art III, § 1 of the Constitution can no more be shared with the Executive Branch than the Chief Executive, for example, can share with the Judiciary the veto power, or the Congress share with the Judiciary the power to override a presidential veto. Any other conclusion would be contrary to the basic concept of separation of powers and the checks and balances that flow from the scheme of a tripartite government. The Federalist, No. 47, p 313 (C. F. Mittel ed 1938). We therefore reaffirm that it is "emphatically the province and the duty" of this Court "to say what the law is" with respect to the claim of privilege presented in this case. Marbury v Madison, supra, at 177, 2 L Ed 60.

In support of his claim of absolute privilege, the President's counsel urges two grounds one of which is common to all governments and one of which is peculiar to our system of separation of powers. The first ground is the valid need for protection of communications between high government officials and those who advise and assist them in the performance of their manifold duties; the importance of this confidentiality is too plain to require further discussion. Human experience teaches that those who expect public dissemination of their remarks may well temper candor with a concern for appearances and for their own interests to the detriment of the decision-making process.[1] Whatever the nature of the privilege of confidentiality of presidential communications in the exercise of Art II powers the privilege can be said to derive from the supremacy of each branch within its own assigned area of constitutional duties. Certain powers and privileges flow from the nature of enumerated powers;[2] the protection of the confidentiality of

---

[1] There is nothing novel about governmental confidentiality. The meetings of the Constitutional Convention in 1787 were conducted in complete privacy. 1 Farrand, The Records of the Federal Convention of 1787, xi–xxv (1911). Moreover, all records of those meetings were sealed for more than 30 years after the Convention. See 3 US Stat At Large, 15th Cong 1st Sess, Res 8 (1818). Most of the Framers acknowledged that without secrecy no constitution of the kind that was developed could have been written. Warren, The Making of the Constitution, 134–139 (1937).

[2] The Special Prosecutor argues that there is no provision in the Constitution for a presidential privilege as to the President's communications corresponding to the privilege of Members of Congress under the Speech or Debate Clause. But the silence of the Constitution on this score is not dispositive. "The rule of constitutional interpretation announced in McCulloch v Maryland, 4 Wheat 316, 4 L Ed 579, that that which was reasonably appropriate and relevant to the exercise of a granted power was considered as

presidential communications has similar constitutional underpinnings.

The second ground asserted by the President's counsel in support of the claim of absolute privilege rests on the doctrine of separation of powers. Here it is argued that the independence of the Executive Branch within its own sphere, Humphrey's Executor v United States, 295 US 602, 629–630, 79 L Ed 1611, 55 S Ct 869; Kilbourn v Thompson, 103 US 168, 190–191, 26 L Ed 377 (1880), insulates a president from a judicial subpoena in an ongoing criminal prosecution, and thereby protects confidential presidential communications.

However, neither the doctrine of separation of powers, nor the need for confidentiality of high level communications, without more, can sustain an absolute, unqualified presidential privilege of immunity from judicial process under all circumstances. The President's need for complete candor and objectivity from advisers calls for great deference from the courts. However, when the privilege depends solely on the broad, undifferentiated claim of public interest in the confidentiality of such conversations, a comfrontation with other values arises. Absent a claim of need to protect military, diplomatic or sensitive national security secrets, we find it difficult to accept the argument that even the very important interest in confidentiality of presidential communications is significantly diminished by production of such material for in camera inspection with all the protection that a district court will be obliged to provide.

The impediment that an absolute, unqualified privilege would place in the way of the primary constitutional duty of the Judicial Branch to do justice in criminal prosecutions would plainly conflict with the function of the courts under Art III. In designing the structure of our Government and dividing and allocating the sovereign power among three coequal branches, the Framers of the Constitution sought to provide a comprehensive system, but the separate powers were not intended to operate with absolute independence.

While the Constitution diffuses power the better to secure liberty, it also contemplates that practice will integrate the dispersed powers into a workable government. It enjoins upon its branches separateness but interdependence, autonomy but

accompanying the grant, has been so universally applied that it suffices merely to state it." Marshall v Gordon, 243 US 521, 537, 61 L Ed 881, 37 S Ct 448 (1917).

reciprocity. [Youngstown Sheet & Tube Co. v Sawyer, 343 US 579, 635, 96 L Ed 1153, 72 S Ct 863, 26 ALR2d 1378 (1952) (Jackson, J., concurring).]

To read the Art II powers of the President as providing an absolute privilege as against a subpoena essential to enforcement of criminal statutes on no more than a generalized claim of the public interest in confidentiality of nonmilitary and nondiplomatic discussions would upset the constitutional balance of "a workable government" and gravely impair the role of the courts under Art III.

Since we conclude that the legitimate needs of the judicial process may outweigh presidential privilege, it is necessary to resolve those competing interests in a manner that preserves the essential functions of each branch. The right and indeed the duty to resolve that question does not free the judiciary from according high respect to the representations made on behalf of the President. United States v Burr, 25 Fed Cas 187, 190, 191–192 (No. 14,694) (1807).

The expectation of a President to the confidentiality of his conversations and correspondence, like the claim of confidentiality of judicial deliberations, for example, has all the value to which we accord deference for the privacy of all citizens and added to those values the necessity for protection of the public interest in candid, objective, and even blunt or harsh opinions in presidential decision making. A President and those who assist him must be free to explore alternatives in the process of shaping policies and making decisions and to do so in a way many would be unwilling to express except privately. These are the considerations justifying a presumptive privilege for presidential communications. The privilege is fundamental to the operation of government and inextricably rooted in the separation of powers under the Constitution.[3] In Nixon v Sirica, —— US App DC ——, 487 F2d 700 (1973), the Court of Appeals held that such presidential communications are "presumptively privileged," id., at 717, and this position is accepted

[3] Freedom of communication vital to fulfillment of wholesome relationships is obtained only by removing the specter of compelled disclosure . . . [G]overnment . . . needs open but protected channels for the kind of plain talk that is essential to the quality of its functioning." Carl Zeiss Stiftung v V. E. B. Carl Zeiss, Jena, 40 FRD 318, 325 (DC 1966). See Nixon v Sirica, —— US App DC——, ——, 487 F2d 700, 713 (1973); Kaiser Aluminum & Chem. Corp. v United States, 157 F Supp 939 (Ct Cl 1958) (per Reed, J.); The Federalist No. 64 (S. F. Mittel ed 1938).

by both parties in the present litigation. We agree with Mr. Chief Justice Marshall's observation, therefore, that "in no case of this kind would a court be required to proceed against the President as against an ordinary individual." United States v Burr, 25 Fed Cas 187, 191 (No. 14,694) (CCD Va 1807).

But this presumptive privilege must be considered in light of our historic commitment to the rule of law. This is nowhere more profoundly manifest than in our view that "the twofold aim [of criminal justice] is that guilt shall not escape or innocence suffer." Berger v United States, 295 US 78, 88, 79 L Ed 1314, 55 S Ct 629 (1935). We have elected to employ an adversary system of criminal justice in which the parties contest all issues before a court of law. The need to develop all relevant facts in the adversary system is both fundamental and comprehensive. The ends of criminal justice would be defeated if judgments were to be founded on a partial or speculative presentation of the facts. The very integrity of the judicial system and public confidence in the system depend on full disclosure of all the facts, within the framework of the rules of evidence. To ensure that justice is done, it is imperative to the function of courts that compulsory process be available for the production of evidence needed either by the prosecution or by the defense.

Only recently the Court restated the ancient proposition of law, albeit in the context of a grand jury inquiry rather than a trial,

"that the public . . . has a right to every man's evidence" except for those persons protected by a constitutional, common law, or statutory privilege, United States v Bryan, 339 US, at 331, [94 L Ed 884] (1949); Blackmer v United States, 284 US 421, 438, [76 L Ed 375, 52 S Ct 252]; Branzburg v United States, 408 US 665, 688, [33 L Ed 2d 626, 92 S Ct 2646] (1972).

The privileges referred to by the Court are designed to protect weighty and legitimate competing interests. Thus, the Fifth Amendment to the Constitution provides that no man "shall be compelled in any criminal case to be a witness against himself." And, generally, an attorney or a priest may not be required to disclose what has been revealed in professional confidence. These and other interests are recognized in law by privileges against forced disclosure, established in the Constitution, by statute, or at common law. Whatever their origins, these exceptions to the demand for every man's evidence are not lightly created nor expansively construed, for they are in derogation of the search for truth.[4]

In this case the President challenges a subpoena served on him as a third party requiring the production of materials for use in a criminal prosecution on the claim that he has a privilege against disclosure of confidential communications. He does not place his claim of privilege on the ground they are military or diplomatic secrets. As to these areas of Art II duties the courts have traditionally shown the utmost deference to presidential responsibilities. In C. & S. Air Lines v Waterman Steamship Corp., 333 US 103, 111, 92 L Ed 568, 68 S Ct 431 (1948), dealing with presidential authority involving foreign policy considerations, the Court said:

> The President, both as Commander-in-Chief and as the Nation's organ for foreign affairs, has available intelligence services whose reports are not and ought not to be published to the world. It would be intolerable that courts, without the relevant information, should review and perhaps nullify actions of the Executive taken on information properly held secret. [Id., at 111, 92 L Ed 568.]

In United States v Reynolds, 345 US 1, 97 L Ed 727, 73 S Ct 528, 32 ALR 2d 382 (1953), dealing with a claimant's demand for evidence in a damage case against the Government the Court said:

> It may be possible to satisfy the court, from all the circumstances of the case, that there is a reasonable danger that compulsion of the evidence will expose military matters which, in the interest of national security, should not be divulged. When this is the case, the occasion for the privilege is appropriate, and the court should not jeopardize the security which the privilege is meant to protect by insisting upon an examination of the evidence, even by the judge alone, in chambers.

No case of the Court, however, has extended this high degree of deference to a President's generalized interest in confidentiality.

---

[4] Because of the key role of the testimony of witnesses in the judicial process, courts have historically been cautious about privileges. Justice Frankfurter, dissenting in Elkins v United States, 364 US 206, 234, 4 L Ed 2d 1669, 80 S Ct 1437 (1960), said of this: "Limitations are properly placed upon the operation of this general principle only to the very limited extent that permitting a refusal to testify or excluding relevant evidence has a public good transcending the normally predominant principle of utilizing all rational means for ascertaining truth."

Nowhere in the Constitution, as we have noted earlier, is there any explicit reference to a privilege of confidentiality, yet to the extent this interest relates to the effective discharge of a President's powers, it is constitutionally based.

The right to the production of all evidence at a criminal trial similarly has constitutional dimensions. The Sixth Amendment explicitly confers upon every defendant in a criminal trial the right "to be confronted with the witnesses against him" and "to have compulsory process for obtaining witnesses in his favor." Moreover, the Fifth Amendment also guarantees that no person shall be deprived of liberty without due process of law. It is the manifest duty of the courts to vindicate those guarantees and to accomplish that it is essential that all relevant and admissible evidence be produced.

In this case we must weigh the importance of the general privilege of confidentiality of presidential communications in performance of his responsibilities against the inroads of such a privilege on the fair administration of criminal justice.[5] The interest in preserving confidentiality is weighty indeed and entitled to great respect. However we cannot conclude that advisers will be moved to temper the candor of their remarks by the infrequent occasions of disclosure because of the possibility that such conversations will be called for in the context of criminal prosecution.[6]

On the other hand, the allowance of the privilege to withhold

[5] We are not here concerned with the balance between the President's generalized interest in confidentiality and the need for relevant evidence in civil litigation, nor with that between the confidentiality interest and congressional demands for information, nor with the President's interest in preserving state secrets. We address only the conflict between the President's assertion of a generalized privilege of confidentiality against the constitutional need for relevant evidence in criminal trials.

[6] Mr. Justice Cardozo made this point in an analogous context. Speaking for a unanimous Court in Clark v United States, 289 US 1, 77 L Ed 993, 53 S Ct 465 1933), he emphasized the importance of maintaining the secrecy of the deliberations of a petit jury in a criminal case. "Freedom of debate might be stifled and independence of thought checked if jurors were made to feel that their arguments and ballots were to be freely published in the world." Id., at 13, 77 L Ed 993. Nonetheless, the Court also recognized that isolated inroads on confidentiality designed to serve the paramount need of the criminal law would not vitiate the interests served by secrecy:

"A juror of integrity and reasonable firmness will not fear to speak his mind if the confidences of debate bar [*sic*] barred to the ears of mere impertinence or malice. He will not expect to be shielded against the disclosure of his conduct in the event that there is evidence reflecting upon his honor. The chance that now and then there may be found some timid soul who will take counsel of his fears and give way to their repressive power is too remote and shadowy to shape the course of justice." Id., at 16, 77 L Ed. 993.

evidence that is demonstrably relevant in a criminal trial would cut deeply into the guarantee of due process of law and gravely impair the basic function of the courts. A President's acknowledged need for confidentiality in the communications of his office is general in nature, whereas the constitutional need for production of relevant evidence in a criminal proceeding is specific and central to the fair adjudication of a particular criminal case in the administration of justice. Without access to specific facts a criminal prosecution may be totally frustrated. The President's broad interest in confidentiality of communications will not be vitiated by disclosure of a limited number of conversations preliminarily shown to have some bearing on the pending criminal cases.

We conclude that when the ground for asserting privilege as to subpoenaed materials sought for use in a criminal trial is based only on the generalized interest in confidentiality, it cannot prevail over the fundamental demands of due process of law in the fair administration of criminal justice. The generalized assertion of privilege must yield to the demonstrated, specific need for evidence in a pending criminal trial.

We have earlier determined that the District Court did not err in authorizing the issuance of the subpoena. If a President concludes that compliance with a subpoena would be injurious to the public interest he may properly, as was done here, invoke a claim of privilege on the return of the subpoena. Upon receiving a claim of privilege from the Chief Executive, it became the further duty of the District Court to treat the subpoenaed material as presumptively privileged and to require the Special Prosecutor to demonstrate that the presidential material was "essential to the justice of the [pending criminal] case." United States v Burr, supra, at 192. Here the District Court treated the material as presumptively privileged, proceeded to find that the Special Prosecutor had made a sufficent showing to rebut the presumption and ordered an in camera examination of the subpoenaed material. On the basis of our examination of the record we are unable to conclude that the District Court erred in ordering the inspection. Accordingly we affirm the order of the District Court that subpoenaed materials be transmitted to that court. We now turn to the important question of the District Court's responsibilities in conducting the in camera examination of presidential materials or communications delivered under the compulsion of the subpoena duces tecum.

Enforcement of the subpoena duces tecum was stayed pending this Court's resolution of the issues raised by the petitions for certiorari. Those issues now having been disposed of, the matter of implementation will rest with the District Court. "[T]he guard, furnished to [the President] to protect him from being harassed by vexatious and unnecessary subpoenas, is to be looked for in the conduct of the [district] court after the subpoenas have issued; not in any circumstances which is [*sic*] to precede their being issued." United States v. Burr, supra, at 34. Statements that meet the test of admissibility and relevance must be isolated; all other material must be excised. At this stage the District Court is not limited to representations of the Special Prosecutor as to the evidence sought by the subpoena; the material will be available to the District Court. It is elementary that in camera inspection of evidence is always a procedure calling for scrupulous protection against any release or publication of material not found by the court, at that stage, probably admissible in evidence and relevant to the issues of the trial for which it is sought. That being true of an ordinary situation, it is obvious that the District Court has a very heavy responsibility to see to it that presidential conversations, which are either not relevant or not admissible, are accorded that high degree of respect due the President of the United States. Mr. Chief Justice Marshall sitting as a trial judge in the Burr case, supra, was extraordinarily careful to point out that: "[I]n no case of this kind would a Court be required to proceed against the President as against an ordinary individual." United States v Burr, 25 Fed Cases 187, 191 (No. 14,694). Marshall's statement cannot be read to mean in any sense that a President is above the law, but relates to the singularly unique role under Art II of a President's communications and activities, related to the performance of duties under that Article. Moreover, a President's communications and activities encompass a vastly wider range of sensitive material than would be true of any "ordinary individual." It is therefore necessary [7] in the public interest to afford presidential confidentiality the greatest protection consistent with the fair administration of justice. The need for confidentiality even as to idle conversations with associates in which

[7] When the subpoenaed material is delivered to the District Judge in camera questions may arise as to the excising of parts and it lies within the discretion of that court to seek the aid of the Special Prosecutor and the President's counsel for in camera consideration of the validity of particular excisions, whether the basis of excision is relevancy or admissibility or under such cases as Reynolds, supra, or Waterman Steamship, supra.

casual reference might be made concerning political leaders within the country or foreign statesmen is too obvious to call for further treatment. We have no doubt that the District Judge will at all times accord to presidential records that high degree of deference suggested in United States v Burr, supra, and will discharge his responsibility to see to it that until released to the Special Prosecutor no in camera material is revealed to anyone. This burden applies with even greater force to excised material; once the decision is made to excise, the material is restored to its privileged status and should be returned under seal to its lawful custodian.

Since this matter came before the Court during the pendency of a criminal prosecution, and on representations that time is of the essence, the mandate shall issue forthwith.

Affirmed.

Mr. Justice **Rehnquist** took no part in the consideration or decision of these cases.